Packed full of practical and essential information, this pilgrimage guidebook covers more than seventy of Christianity's most celebrated shrines and sanctuaries in eleven Central and Eastern European countries. In these pages you can visit famous holy sites such as those found in Prague, Częstochowa, Ephesus, Budapest, Kraków, Vienna, and the Greek Islands, while also learning all about miraculous images, Marian apparitions, renowned biblical sites, cathedrals, abbeys, eucharistic miracles, relics, and more.

Inside you'll find authoritative information such as

- Histories of each of the shrines and holy places
- Addresses and phone numbers for the shrines and tourist offices
- Information about religious lodgings and pilgrim housing
- Directions for traveling by car, bus, and train
- Custom-designed maps
- Photographs of the shrines
- Travel resources on the Internet

You'll also find helpful travel tips and hints from the author, an experienced traveler who has backpacked through eighteen European countries and guided pilgrimages to many of these shrines himself.

Poland: Kantor = exchange
sklep = shop

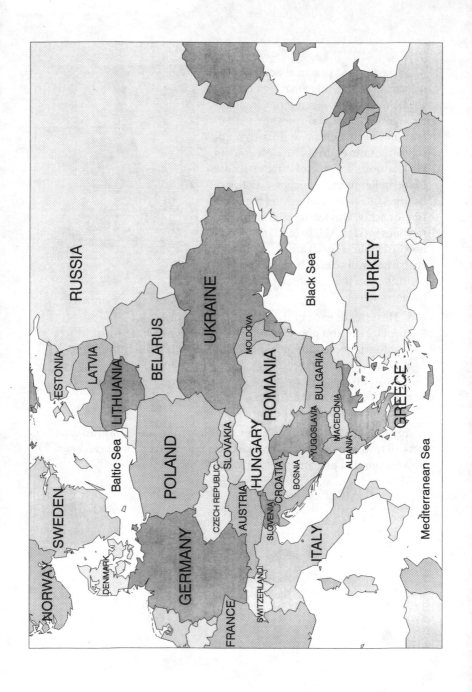

Catholic
Shrines
OF
Central and
Eastern
Europe

Catholic
Shrines
OF
Central and
Eastern
Europe

◆ A Pilgrim's Travel Guide ◆

Kevin J. Wright

Liguori
LIGUORI, MISSOURI

Published by Liguori Publications
Liguori, Missouri
http://www.liguori.org

Library of Congress Cataloging-in-Publication Data

Wright, Kevin J.
    Catholic shrines of Central and Eastern Europe : a pilgrim's travel guide / Kevin J. Wright—1st ed.
      p.   cm.
    Includes bibliographical references and index.
    ISBN 0-7648-0334-4 (pbk.)
    1. Christian shrines—Europe, Central—Guidebooks. 2. Christian pilgrims and pilgrimagaes—Europe, Central—Guidebooks. 3. Christian shrines—Europe, Eastern—Guidebooks. 4. Christian pilgrims and pilgrimages—Europe, Central—Guidebooks. I. Title.
BX2320.5.C36W75 1999
263'.04243—dc21   99–10316

Printed in the United States of America
03 02 01 00 99   5 4 3 2 1
First Edition

*To all my friends in life
who have shown me
the way to God.*

CONTENTS

Acknowledgments

IN PUTTING TOGETHER a book of this magnitude, I find myself needing to thank so many people. Among those to whom I extend my sincere appreciation and gratefulness are the following:

My good friends Kathleen Kelly, Valerie Kelly, and Mary Walsh. I will be forever thankful to God for bringing you three young ladies into my life for the pilgrimage summer of 1998. I will never forget our many fond memories, great blessings, and good times we shared during our travels through Central and Eastern Europe.

I also extend my warmest appreciation and thanks to every single person who provided me with important information from the various shrines, sanctuaries, churches, convents, monasteries, guesthouses, hotels, and tourist offices in Central and Eastern Europe.

Throughout my travels, I also met many saintly people who went completely out of their way to help me collect information for my book, including Dick Schwartzes (Cologne), Birgit Kirchherr-Adamo (Travel Escort), Tatyanna (Salzburg), Br. Albert Wiesław O.F.M. (Kalwaria Zebrzydowska), Michael Śliperski (Gneizno), Kristina Sireikaite (Lithuania tourist office), Eleanor Kelly (Hungarian shrines), Sandra Ranner (Vienna), Robert and Vesna (Marija Bistrica), Fr. Marco Chiolerio O.C.D. (Infant Child of Prague Shrine), Sr. Salvatricze (Kraków—Divine Mercy Shrine), Dr. Galavits József (Győr), Gabby and Margaret (Częstochowa tourist office), Mariusz Sąciński S.J. (Święta Lipka), Sezgin Family (Ephesus), Fr. A. Silhar (Šaštin), and the entire staff at Our Lady of Gietrzwałd Shrine.

I would like to also acknowledge the kindness and generosity of those who provided translations of foreign prayers, including Małgorzata Gajda (Polish), Jolanta Idzik (Polish), Ildiko (Hungarian), Fr. Kestutis Trimakas (Lithuanian), and Gabriella Metzger (German).

Another person who deserves outstanding recognition for his contributions, superior work, and steadfast dedication to this book is my editor from Liguori Publications, Anthony Chiffolo.

Above all, I would especially like to thank my family, and in particular my parents, for their incredible support and enthusiasm throughout this entire project.

Finally, I can never thank the Good Lord and Our Blessed Mother enough for the incredible opportunity they provided me of traveling to many of these grace-filled shrines. Specifically, I thank Our Lady of Częstochowa and the Infant Child of Prague, for I had placed the entire book under their guidance and protection from the beginning.

Introduction: Pilgrimages— No Better Way to Travel!

AFTER BACKPACKING THROUGH eighteen European countries, I have come to one conclusion: There is no better way to travel than on pilgrimage! Not only are trips of this nature the most exciting, they are the most rewarding. Pilgrimages offer people a chance to see the world under God's transforming influence. No travel company can offer a better package than that.

Today, one of the most fascinating areas of the world to visit on pilgrimage is Central and Eastern Europe. With the recent fall of Communism, the shrines in this part of the world are once again thriving. Many of the celebrated pilgrimage centers are already receiving more than several million pilgrims each year. Coupled with the recent travel boom in Central and Eastern Europe, there's never been a better time or opportunity to make a sacred journey here.

Among the many famous sites, pilgrims can pray at the Infant Child of Prague shrine in the Czech Republic or kneel inside the Cave of the Apocalypse on Patmos Island, the place where Saint John the Evangelist wrote the Book of Revelation. The faithful can also drink from the healing waters at Our Lady of Gietrzwałd in Poland or explore the inside of an abbey in Austria. In Turkey visitors can light a candle in the House of the Virgin Mary, while in Lithuania they can plant a cross at the renowned Hill of Crosses. The opportunities are endless.

Pilgrimages are exciting because they are for everyone. Whether young or old, devout or not-so-devout, Catholic or not, there is a place for you at the shrines. Countless are the stories of people affected by graces received with only one visit to a holy site.

However, as not every pilgrim will visit all the shrines described here, this book is much more than a travel guide. It is a brief history of God's constant interaction with people through the ages. For this reason the book serves not only as an excellent resource but as a delightful collection of spiritual narratives to be read by the pilgrim at home.

The shrine stories are usually based on one of three things—historical testimony, tradition, or legend. Those that are of historical testimony are based on facts and written records. Stories from tradition are transmitted through the ages by oral or written communication, and usually substantiate a historical event, but are mixed with fiction. Legends are those anecdotes that have some basis of truth but have been primarily enshrouded in fiction.

Whether a shrine's origin is based on tradition or legend, the place is made holy by the holiness of the lives of those who struggle to reach it. Częstochowa is remarkable because the Virgin Mary has been very active there. It is equally remarkable today for the millions of people who come from around the world, often with great personal sacrifice, to express their faith in God and in the promises made to them by God's Son, Jesus.

With this book I have three hopes. First, that *Catholic Shrines of Central and Eastern Europe* will help facilitate people's plans to make a pilgrimage to this part of the world. Second, that it will inspire others to promote Catholic/Christian travel through the mass media, thus informing the public of the value of pilgrimage. Third, that it will encourage young adults to embark on these remarkable journeys to the sites of the Christian faith.

This book is your ticket to begin thinking about making a pilgrimage trip to the shrines of Central and Eastern Europe. With the tourist industry rushing to this new market, the opportunity is ripe for journeying there. With God as your travel agent, there's no better way to see this fascinating part of the world.

Part 1

Traveling in the
Footsteps of God

History of Christian Pilgrimages

A PILGRIMAGE is a "journey to a holy place with a purpose." It is a form of travel a person undertakes to further enrich one's own spiritual life. It always begins with a call from God and ends with an acceptance by an individual to undertake such a journey. Our Christian ancestry is filled with stories of people making pilgrimages.

Abraham, our father in faith, was one of the first in early biblical times called by God to embark on such a journey. Picking up his belongings, Abraham left for Canaan with his wife and brother's son Lot (Genesis 12:1–6). Later, Jacob also received a call from God to go on pilgrimage (Genesis 35:1–10). Following God's directives, he immediately left home and traveled by faith to a foreign land. After the Jews' exodus from Egypt, they too experienced a pilgrimage as they traveled in the desert for forty years searching for the Promised Land.

After Solomon built the temple for the Ark of the Covenant in Jerusalem, Israelites began making the required pilgrimage to the sanctuary at least once each year. Fulfilling the Law, the Holy Family also traveled to the sacred site. In fact, during one of their annual pilgrimages to Jerusalem, Mary and Joseph discovered Jesus missing. They found him three days later in the Temple, teaching (Luke 2:41–27).

Pilgrimages played a large part in the life of Jesus. Almost the entire Gospel of John is centered on Jesus' pilgrimages to Jerusalem. These pilgrimages included the Passover (John 2:13–24), another Jewish feast at the pool of Bethsaida (John 5), the second Passover (John 6:4), the Jewish Feast of Booths (John 7), the Feast of the Dedication (John 10:22), and finally the third Passover (John 11:55–19:42).

Soon after the death of Jesus, the era of Christian pilgrimages began. However, it didn't really blossom until Constantine accepted Christianity in 314. Prior to this time, Christians would travel long distances to gather in secret at the sites of martyrs' tombs. The turning point occurred when Helen, the mother of Emperor Constantine, traveled on pilgrimage to Jerusalem early in the fourth century. While there she discovered a number of Christian relics, including the cross upon which Christ had been crucified. Upon Helen's return to Europe (with the sacred objects), Constantine began erecting churches and basilicas throughout all of Christendom, including those at Bethlehem, the Mount of Olives, Tabor, and Vatican Hill. Pilgrims living in the West traveled to the tombs of Peter and Paul in Rome, while those in the East visited biblical sites, the tombs of martyrs and saints, and the dwelling places of well-known monks. One of the earliest records of a person embarking on such a journey comes from a man often called the Bordeaux Pilgrim. Traveling to Palestine in 333, he left behind a full travelogue of his journey.

In the Middle Ages, when the Christian faith permeated all of society, the great pilgrim highways were constructed. Hospices and accommodations lined the well-trodden paths from one shrine to another. Countless pilgrims visited the holy sites of Santiago de Compostela, Częstochowa, Walsingham, Rome, Fulda, Aachen, Mariazell, and Monte Sant'Angelo. Europe gradually became a great gathering of human highways converging on places of pilgrimage. The popularity of pilgrimaging lasted throughout the Middle Ages until the Renaissance.

In the sixteenth century Protestant reformers fought the idea of pilgrimage. Many became sarcastic toward these "childish and useless works," as the Augsburg Confession wrote. Along with many other devotions, the reformers threw pilgrimages out as vain works violating the concept of "faith alone."

During the Counter Reformation, however, the Catholic Church affirmed the significance and merit of pilgrimages. Pope Paul III, during his pontificate of 1534–1549, recognized the spiritual value that pilgrimages brought to the faithful. Slowly, Europe began to see more pilgrimages to the various shrines. The number of pilgrimages made during the seventeenth and eighteenth centuries never equaled those of the Middle Ages. In the aftermath of the Reformation, stigma was still attached to pilgrimaging.

A turning point occurred, however, in the nineteenth century when the Blessed Virgin Mary began appearing in Europe and called for a return to the gospel. In 1830 she appeared at Rue de Bac, in 1846 at La Salette, in 1858 at Lourdes, in 1871 at Pontmain, and in 1877 at Gietrzwałd (Poland). Thousands of people began to journey to the shrines after her appearances.

The early twentieth century continued to see an increase in pilgrimages. After the apparitions at Fátima, thousands traveled there. The Blessed Virgin also appeared in Belgium at Banneux and Beauraing in 1932 and 1933. Within the first few years of these apparitions, several hundred thousand pilgrims journeyed to these locations also. The Second Vatican Council's *Call to Holiness* in the mid sixties inspired millions to go on pilgrimage as well. After the Council, the number of pilgrims visiting Lourdes tripled.

However, conditions were not so good at the time in Central and Eastern Europe where atheist Communist governments reigned. Unfortunately, the regime discouraged pilgrimage travel in the region, with the result that famous holy sites such as Máriapócs (Hungary), Svatá Hora (Czech Republic), Šaštín (Slovakia), Kalwaria Zebrzydowska (Poland), and the Hill of Crosses (Lithuania) received far fewer visitors during much of the twentieth century.

However, when Communism fell in 1989, pilgrimages resumed almost immediately. Today, many of the shrines are once again flourishing and receiving record numbers of pilgrims, including Częstochowa, which already ranks as one of the most visited places of Christian pilgrimage in the world. Medjugorje itself, where the Virgin Mary has allegedly been appearing to six children since 1981, has already become a world-renowned pilgrimage destination, receiving more than twenty million pilgrims in the past two decades. With tourism now booming in Central and Eastern Europe, pilgrimage travel is set to follow in its footsteps and make its presence known as well.

WHY GO ON A PILGRIMAGE?

ALMOST EVERYONE has a personal reason for going on pilgrimage. Some hope to receive special spiritual graces, others a bodily cure; some have petitions to present, while others simply wish to thank God for a prayer answered. No matter what the personal reason, everyone is drawn in some

Pilgrimages are an invitation from God to rediscover your goals, enrich your life of faith, and strengthen your love and friendship with others. They are an offer to be replenished, so that you may again experience that sweetness of life that only God can provide. *(Author)*

way by the search for faith. As each pilgrimage begins with a call from God, it is always a personal invitation to grow deeper in your relationship with him.

With the new millennium, we are living in one of the most exciting times in the history of pilgrimage travel. In the year 2000 the Church will be celebrating the two-thousandth anniversary of the Incarnation of Jesus Christ at shrines around the world. Millions will be traveling to these holy sites to join in the many festivities and events. In the following years, shrines are expecting to receive crowds unlike that ever experienced before in the Christian era.

The Holy Father himself, Pope John Paul II, has contributed much to the growing popularity of pilgrimages in the past twenty years. Known as the "Pilgrim Pope," he has traveled to almost every country of the world, visiting the major shrines. His greatest contribution to pilgrimages has probably been World Youth Day, an event held every two years in a different part of the world to celebrate the gospel of Christ. Hundreds of thousands of young people come from every continent to see the Holy Father and join in the celebrations. In 1993 he held the event in Denver, U.S.A.; in 1995, Manila, Philippines; in 1997, Paris, France; and in 2000, Rome, Italy. Young people love the thought of pilgrimaging, camping out under the stars, walking long distances, and living under more austere conditions than normal.

A native of Poland, the Holy Father has also brought great recognition to the shrines of Central and Eastern Europe through his many travels there. With a great love for visiting pilgrimage sites, Pope John Paul has spoken about shrines being like "oases in the desert, formed to provide water and shade."

Today, many people are embarking on pilgrimages because of the tremendous benefits they provide both spiritually and physically. This type of travel allows us to be regenerated, refreshed, and renewed. It inspires us to rediscover our goals, enrich our life of faith, strengthen our love and friendship with others, and dream new dreams.

Pilgrimages are an invitation from God. They are an open letter to come and journey to a sacred place under the providential hand of the Lord. They are an offer to be replenished, so that you may again experience that sweetness of life that only God can provide. Who could offer anything better?

TO TRAVEL INDEPENDENTLY OR IN A GROUP?

AFTER MAKING the decision to go on pilgrimage, the next consideration is whether to travel independently or with an organized tour group. Naturally, the pilgrim must consider a number of factors, and both ways of pilgrimaging have their pros and cons.

Traveling "independently" means making all the arrangements yourself and traveling alone, with a friend, or in a small group. You design your own schedule and find your own transportation, lodging, and meals. This type of travel provides the most flexibility, challenge, and sometimes excitement.

Traveling with a tour group means traveling with a pilgrimage organization on a fixed itinerary. Besides keeping you on a tight schedule so that you see everything as planned, the organization arranges all transportation and lodging, and often meals, making for a superb trip with no worries.

The best way to determine which type of pilgrimage travel might be best for you is to consider the following points:

- How many people will be going?
- What is the health of the pilgrims?
- Do you prefer to design your own itinerary?
- Do you prefer to have everything arranged for you?
- What are the ages of the people in your group?
  Is anyone very young or old?
- How much time do you have for the trip?
- What type of accommodations do you prefer?
- Does anyone have any foreign-language skills?
- Do you prefer your freedom and independence?
- Do you mind adhering to a tour group's fixed schedule?
- Do you mind traveling alone in a foreign country?
- Does anyone have familiarity with the shrines?
- Has anyone traveled to the shrines before?
- Does anyone have experience traveling abroad?
- What is the expense of independent travel versus tour travel?
- Is traveling with a priest a priority?

Having traveled extensively throughout Europe myself, I believe pilgrims must address five crucial points.

The first is the health of the travelers. If anyone needs special care or attention, an organized tour group would be a much better option than traveling independently in a foreign country.

Second is the rigidity of fixed schedules versus the flexibility of customized schedules. Someone hoping to visit a number of small or lesser-known shrines and monasteries would do well to consider traveling independently, whereas someone who wants just to visit the major sites might be happy on an organized tour.

Third is the foreign-language skills of those traveling. If no one in your group speaks a word of Polish, an independent pilgrimage to the shrines of Poland might be too much of a challenge. Also, you can miss out on lots of excellent information at a shrine if you do not speak the local language. A tour-group leader or guide who speaks the native language can provide you with all the information you may need or want. Of course, if you speak Polish fluently, you might find more opportunities to enjoy the culture on an independent pilgrimage to the Polish shrines than on an organized tour.

A fourth point to consider is the "peace of mind" you receive from having everything taken care of ahead of time. On an organized tour, usually the only thing a person has to worry about is what picture to take next. In contrast, traveling independently can be a real "workout" at times, especially when you do not speak the local language. Everything becomes a trial—buying groceries, reserving a hotel room, getting on the right train, figuring out the times of a shrine's activities, and the like.

The final point to consider is whether you mind traveling independently in a foreign country. Everything is different—the language, food, weather, and local customs. For some this is a great adventure; for others, a nightmare.

Probably the biggest advantage to traveling with an organized tour group is that everything is taken care of for you. Basically, all you need to do is write out a check, pack your clothes, and show up. You'll have few worries, you'll always have someone there to help you, and you'll receive excellent information about the shrines throughout the trip.

The single greatest advantage to traveling independently is the freedom to do what you want, when you want. If you visit a particular shrine and love it, you have the freedom to stay there as long as you wish. If you hope to visit several shrines not found on any single itinerary, you have the freedom to visit them all on one trip. If you have lots of time, you can visit shrines all summer long if you wish, rather than being constricted to a ten-day or two-week trip.

If you decide to travel independently, the excitement begins when you start designing your own itinerary. If you're going on pilgrimage with friends or family, everyone can have fun planning it together. (See "Organizing Your Own Pilgrimage" for more information.)

If you decide to travel with an organization, the fun begins when you start looking through the different tour options. The best thing to do first is to contact all major Catholic pilgrimage organizations and ask for their free brochures. When they arrive, look through all the different itineraries. Usually, you can find one that matches your tastes perfectly.

No matter how you decide to go, the experience will be unforgettable. Pilgrimages are life-changing experiences. Whether you travel independently or with an organized tour group, the graces last forever.

ORGANIZING YOUR OWN PILGRIMAGE

ORGANIZING YOUR own pilgrimage can be one of the most exciting parts of your journey. The possibilities are limitless as you coordinate your own trip and choose the shrines you'll be visiting.

When designing an itinerary, many people like to build their pilgrimages around "themes." For example, those with a special Marian devotion might like to visit shrines associated with the Blessed Virgin, such as Mariazell,

Częstochowa, Ephesus, Maria Taferl, Kevelaer, Máriapócs, and Marija Bistrica. Or you might like to build a theme around early biblical sites such as those in Turkey and Greece, or visit shrines in a particular country. Others may prefer to spend time at the places featuring their favorite personal devotions, such as the Infant Child of Prague or the Divine Mercy. And there are those who might like to focus on shrines found in their own native homelands and countries' heritage. The possibilities are endless.

If you are thinking about organizing a pilgrimage, keep in mind that one of the best-kept secrets in the pilgrimage industry is that you can travel for free. Many pilgrimage tour agencies offer free trips or large discounts for people who orga-

Pilgrimages are the most exciting form of travel. Here, a group of Americans are embarking on a three-day, seventy-mile walk from Notre Dame Cathedral in Paris to Chartres with fifteen thousand other pilgrims for the Feast of Pentecost. *(Author)*

nize pilgrimages. Of course, the nature of "organizing" varies from agency to agency, so it is best to contact the travel organizations personally for more information and details.

Here are some of the major points to cover when organizing a pilgrimage. (Some will be more applicable to groups than to individuals, and vice versa.)

Making the decision to go on a pilgrimage:
- Deciding whether you will travel alone, with family, or in a group.
- Deciding whether you would like to organize a small-group pilgrimage.

Initial phase of planning and organizing a pilgrimage, for group or individual:
- Contacting a (Catholic) travel agency or pilgrimage organization for an initial consultation.
- Researching the shrines.
- Designing an itinerary and theme (for example, a Marian pilgrimage).
- Deciding when to go: spring, summer, fall, or winter.

- Choosing places to stay, such as convents, monasteries, pilgrim housing, youth hostels, or secular hotels.
- Choosing a means of travel in Europe: train, bus, car rental, or a mixture of all three.
- Budgeting the cost of travel.
- Through the travel agent or pilgrimage organization: booking plane, train, and bus tickets, car-rental reservations, lodging, and other possible necessities such as travel insurance or international driver's license.
- For young adults and students under twenty-six: inquiring about certain discounts for plane and train tickets (such as the Eurail Pass).
- Spreading word around about the pilgrimage. Putting up flyers at the local church, passing them out at organization meetings, advertising in the local Catholic newspaper, putting announcements in the church's bulletin, contacting friends and family, and the like.
- Finding a priest who may like to accompany the group.
- Informing shrines of your planned dates of arrival.
- Obtaining travel documents, such as passports, visas (if applicable), driver's licenses, student and youth ID cards, traveler's checks, and credit cards.
- Reviewing health insurance and coverage—does it cover you for overseas travel?
- Reconfirming all travel information.
- Reconfirming all the people who will be traveling on your pilgrimage trip.

And here are a few extra points to remember as you plan and prepare your pilgrimage:

To telephone or fax Europe directly, follow these instructions:

- Dial the code number to exit your country.
- Dial the code number of the country you are calling.
- Dial the city code of the place you are calling.
- Dial the local phone number of the place you are calling.
- Keep in mind that to dial a number from outside a particular country, you may need to drop the first number (it is usually a zero) of the particular city code. These numbers are used if dialing only from within the country or area.

- An example of dialing internationally is the following:
  Our Lady of Gietrzwałd Shrine
  Fax (089) 512-34-06
  To fax this shrine directly from the U.S.A., you would dial:
  011-48-89-512-34-06
- Keep in mind also that as Central and Eastern Europe is currently undergoing a rapid development in their communication technologies, many of their city codes and phone numbers are changing quickly. If you experience any problems in dialing, contact your local operator for international dialing assistance. With an address in hand, and the name of the place you are attempting to call, an international operator can usually track down the newest city codes and phone numbers.
- And when writing a letter, remember always to include the country in the mailing address.

If you are organizing a pilgrimage on your own, keep in mind that many of the accommodations in this book are usually some form of Catholic or pilgrim housing. These accommodations are often reasonably priced and are known for their simplicity and cleanliness. You may wish to consult other European travel information sources, such as Rick Steve's series of European guidebooks or the Michelin Europe travel guides, for other types of lodgings. Such guides also provide detailed information about places to eat as well as other secular sites of interest that might be near your pilgrimage destinations.

If you plan on traveling independently, I strongly recommend and advise obtaining detailed Michelin maps of each country you will be visiting. As many of the shrines are located in very small villages and towns, oftentimes they do not appear on general maps. However, the Michelin maps, which are very detailed, do list the areas, and they even have symbols (a Christian cross) signifying the location of a shrine on the map.

Another recommendation is to contact both the shrine and tourist offices of a particular city when writing for information. Oftentimes, one or the other is more efficient and effective in providing information.

In general, however, the best advice I can give to anyone organizing a pilgrimage to the Catholic shrines of Central and Eastern Europe is to work closely with an experienced (Catholic) travel agent or an established pilgrimage tour agency.

TRAVELING IN CENTRAL AND EASTERN EUROPE

AS MOST PEOPLE have not traveled in Central and Eastern Europe before, I have provided below a rather general description about each of the countries in this book and what you can expect in your journeys there. First, however, let's take a general look at Central and Eastern Europe as a whole.

With the fall of the Communist regime in 1989, many of the countries are eager to embrace the new boom in tourism. The good news is that the people tend to be very hospitable and generous; the bad news is that many of the facilities are not quite up to Western standards yet. One very good aspect about currently traveling in this part of the world is that things tend to be rather inexpensive. For example, someone can have a several-course dinner in Budapest for about half the cost you would pay in America. A difficulty you can expect, however, unlike in Western Europe, is the limited number of people who speak English (and it only gets worse the further east you go). There are several ways to cope. First, pick up several good phrase books covering Central and Eastern Europe, and plan to use them extensively during your travels. Second, keep in mind that no matter where you are, English is widely spoken in most tourist offices and upscale hotels. And third, when you are in desperate need of someone to speak English, always ask the younger people. Most of them have at least some knowledge of the language, as English is the most widely taught foreign language in their schools.

One of the most fascinating places in the world to visit on pilgrimage today is Central and Eastern Europe. Here, the author with other pilgrims is standing at the site of the world-famous Hill of Crosses in northern Lithuania. *(Author)*

In regards to the individual countries, Austria serves as one of Europe's most popular destinations because of its almost unrivaled natural beauty, history, and musical legacy. A westernized country, Austria features first-class everything: hotels, transportation services, restaurants, bathrooms, and the like. The downside, however, is that everything is also very expensive. Train and bus service is excellent, with the train service being the main form of public transportation. English is widely spoken, making it a very easy country to travel in

(German is the official language). Austria is considered a fairly religious nation, and about three-fourths of the population is Roman Catholic.

Blessed with beautiful countryside and one of the world's most stunning coastlines, Croatia is currently one of the best-kept secrets for visiting. Despite the country's association with the war from the early 1990s, Croatia is today experiencing a burgeoning of new tourists from abroad. (However, as with any type of international traveling, it is best to check the current political situation of a country before visiting.) In touristy areas, the country is quite westernized, and the facilities are great. Bus service is excellent, and the train service is good too, just less convenient. For most forms of travel, the bus is the best way to get around—it's fast, frequent, and inexpensive. English is widely spoken in tourist areas, at transportation facilities, and by the young people. Catholicism is the predominant religion, and as it was suppressed under Communism, it is currently undergoing a strong resurgence in Croatia.

The Czech Republic offers a picturesque scenery with a number of hills, mountains, lakes, and valleys, all of which are dotted by hundreds of castles, medieval towns, and beautiful churches. Each year more than eighty million visitors descend on the Czech Republic and Prague, making it one of the most popular tourist destinations in the world. The country is more westernized than most of Eastern Europe but not as much as Germany or Austria. Besides Prague, much of the Czech Republic is rather surprisingly uncommercialized. Interestingly, it is estimated that about ten thousand Americans (a mix of entrepreneurs, business consultants, and English-language teachers) are already living in Prague. The train and bus service is fairly good in the Czech Republic. English is widely spoken within Prague but not elsewhere in the country (Czech is the official language). Most travelers to the Czech Republic come to visit Prague and seldom visit any other cities. Catholicism is the principal religion in the country.

Featuring world-class cathedrals, museums, and scenery, Germany has long been a favorite European destination. With first-class hotels, transportation systems, restaurants, tourist offices, and the like, this is one of the easiest places to travel in all of Europe. English is extremely widely spoken, making it even easier to travel around. Although many Germans no longer practice their inherited faiths of Catholicism and Protestantism, the southern region of Germany (Bavaria), which is predominantly Catholic, stills remains rather strong in their faith and practice.

Few places in the world can rival Greece for its incredible beauty (especially the islands) and ancient legacies. Today, the majority of today's visitors are drawn by Greece's beaches and sunshine and its festive environment. Very good, but sometimes very frustrating, ferry and hydrofoil services operate between the islands. On the mainland, bus service is often the best option, although the train service does come in handy sometimes for long-distance travel. English is widely spoken, and just about everyone living on the islands speaks it fluently. Almost 98 percent of the residents belong to the Greek Orthodox Church.

Among the Eastern European countries, Hungary is one of the most westernized. Tourists feel right at home here, especially in Budapest—despite the fact that not everyone speaks English. Train and bus service in Hungary is good, both having their respective advantages. For most long-distance travel, however, the train is the best option. More than half of the country is Catholic, and many of them relish their rich heritage of the faith.

Although Lithuania has much to offer the visitor in the way of scenery and places to visit, the country still suffers from second-rate facilities inherited from its past. Once a part of the former U.S.S.R., Lithuania declared its independence in 1991. In regards to public transportation, the country has a well-developed bus network and system though not every bus is exactly plush, and travelers should be prepared for crowded buses. Train travel is recommended for travel between long-distance cities, but still check the availability and times of the buses. English is not widely spoken except in Vilnius, tourist offices, and upscale hotels and definitely not at train or bus stations. Lithuania is a very Catholic country.

Poland is an exciting place to visit, especially for its cosmopolitan town of Kraków, the Zakopane mountains to the south, and the beautiful lakes and forests to the north. As a whole, Poland's larger cities possess the proper facilities and personnel to accommodate the needs of tourists. Kraków itself is one of the most enjoyable places to visit in Eastern Europe, and since English is widely spoken there, that helps too. The countryside of Poland can be stunningly beautiful and is worth visiting, although many fewer people speak English (although it seems as if there is at least one person who usually does—and as you can imagine, he or she is of tremendous help). Although the rail and bus service is rather extensive and very inexpensive, it is not always frequent. As the trains are notorious for being somewhat slow, the bus service can often be the best option for traveling between cities. Poland is predominately Catholic, and the people are faithful and fervent in their practice of it.

Despite Romania's possessing one of the most fascinating and richest cultures of Eastern Europe, the country still suffers heavily from the recently departed Soviet influence. As political stability has been slow to arrive, Romania no doubt makes for hard work for the independent traveler. If you plan to visit the country, it is important to brief yourself beforehand on the current political and economic climate. Train travel is by far the best way to get around the country. The Romanians are religious people on the whole, with most of them practicing Orthodox Christianity.

Although Slovakia is one of the least commercialized and visited countries of Central and Eastern Europe, it offers some of the best scenery in Europe and is a place filled with rich folk culture and beautiful traditions. The train and bus network is fairly good (the bus service reaches almost all corners of the country). English is not widely spoken, except in tourist offices and nice hotels. Catholicism is the principal religion in the country, and the Slovaks are fervent in their practice and beliefs.

Turkey is simply one of the most fascinating and incredible places to visit. A democratic and rapidly modernizing country, it is a Western-oriented nation with excellent facilities in its tourist areas. Buses and the *dolmus* (minibus) are the most widespread and popular means of transportation—they are frequent and go just about anywhere. Train travel is available but is only a good option on select routes. In tourist areas, particularly along the coastline of western and central Turkey, you will find English widely spoken. In the more remote areas, or less touristy spots, this is not always the case. The Turkish population is 99 percent Muslim.

MAKING THE BEST OF ONE'S PILGRIMAGE TRAVELS

To make the best of your pilgrimage travels, you should always remember the four essential elements:

1. Good Planning
2. Good Research
3. Good Attitude
4. Trust in Divine Providence

With proper planning, research, a good attitude, and trust in divine Providence, you can not only make the best of your pilgrimage travels but can also be assured of a "mountaintop experience."
(Author)

Without a doubt, a fruitful trip always begins with good planning. This includes everything from designing an exciting itinerary to obtaining the necessary travel documents to buying the right walking shoes several months in advance. A good thing to keep in mind when mapping out a trip is never to oblige yourself to see everything. The best advice I have ever heard on this subject is this: just visit as much as you can, and plan on coming back on another trip to do the rest.

Another vital component of making a great trip is performing the necessary research. Especially if you are embarking on travels to Central and Eastern Europe, it will be to your advantage to learn as much as possible about the countries to be visited. Using this book and other travel guides as resources before your departure can also help in providing important travel information. And, of course, the Internet can be of invaluable service. To help with this part of the research, I have provided in the Appendix a listing of travel resource Internet websites.

A good attitude is also a key ingredient for a successful and enjoyable trip and can even overcome incomplete planning and research. Although traveling can provide some of the most treasured moments of a person's lifetime, it can also provide some of the most frustrating. During one of my most recent travels, my friends and I experienced a few disappointing incidents, such as missed trains, bad restaurant meals, and overpriced taxis. Rather than sulking in our misfortune, however, we simply made the best of it. We would treat ourselves to ice cream until the next train arrived, make our own delicious sandwiches from the market instead, and set a price with the next taxi driver beforehand, and then have fun bargaining him down even more.

The most important element of any pilgrimage trip, however, is handing over the reigns to God and trusting in divine Providence. Although this is sometimes the most difficult part of the journey, it is always the most rewarding. As I often tell others, God is the real tour guide and travel agent of any pilgrimage. By abandoning yourself to divine Providence, a person opens up to the unknown but exciting plans of God. It is through divine Providence that I have seen many apparent travel "mishaps" turn into the most incredible blessings. Personally, I once had such an experience on one trip when I was only several minutes late for joining a tour of the Vatican gardens. I rescheduled for the next day, and it was during that visit that I met one of my closest and most treasured friends. Trusting in God's divine Providence in our travels is not always easy, but it does allow us to stretch in our faith, and that is the point of a pilgrimage.

Part 2

✠

Catholic Shrines of
Central and Eastern Europe

Austria

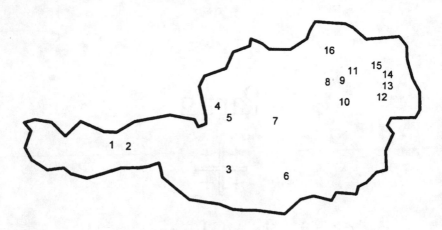

1. Eucharistic Miracle of Seefeld
2. Our Lady of Absam
3. Church of the Holy Blood
4. Our Lady of Maria Plain
5. Christ Child of Loreto
6. Cathedral of Gurk & St. Hemma
7. Church of St. Wolfgang
8. Our Lady of Maria Taferl
9. Melk Abbey ✓
10. Our Lady of Mariazell ✓
11. Göttweig Abbey
12. Heiligenkreuz Abbey
13. Cathedral of St. Stephen ✓
14. Our Lady of the Bowed Head
15. Klosterneuburg Abbey
16. Zwettl Abbey

✠

Our Lady of Absam

Austria's Beloved Lady

Surrounded by meadows, fields, and breathtaking mountains, the small village of Absam near Innsbruck is the site of a miraculous event from the eighteenth century. Here, on the night of January 17, 1797, occurred an event that forever changed the life of the local townspeople.

The incident occurred on a snowy day while an eighteen-year-old girl, Rosina Buecher, was sitting by her window, quietly sewing under a dim light. In the midst of her busy activity, a sudden sense of terror went running through her body. Thinking of her father and having a premonition that he had had an accident, the girl stretched her neck to look out the window for him. What she saw was something far different than expected—an image of a beautiful young woman's face had appeared in the windowpane.

In the small village of Absam, just outside Innsbruck, an image of the Virgin Mary appeared on a windowpane in 1797. After an exhaustive investigation by the Church, the bishop declared the event miraculous, and the glass was subsequently enshrined in the parish church. *(Wallfahrtskirche Maria Absam)*

After taking a close look at the image, her heart began to beat furiously as she quickly called out to her mother. When she came, together they gazed upon the face of the lady. Both knew immediately whom the beautiful woman resembled. Wasting no time, Rosina and her mother contacted the parish priest and informed their neighbors about the mysterious event. All agreed that it was the face of the Virgin Mary.

After visiting the family and viewing the image, the parish priest asked that the glass be removed so that experts in the field of painting and glasswork could study it more closely. During the following examination it was discovered that the image disappeared when the glass was submerged in water, but that the likeness of the Virgin reappeared as soon as the pane was dried. When analyzed chemically, the process by which the image had been applied to the glass was declared indeterminable. After an exhaustive investigation, the experts concluded that the image was created in a miraculous fashion.

The next question to be answered was why did Mary's image appear on the windowpane? As most people had their own personal opinions, Rosina's mother thought it was a sign of impending troubles. The daughter believed it to be a sign from heaven that her father and brother would return home safely—which they did, after having narrowly escaped injury in a salt-mine accident. Though lacking any explanation for the appearance, both the parish priest and the bishop declared it to be a miraculous event.

After the scientific investigations ended, the family received the glass image back. However, as the picture had quickly become an object of devotion among the villagers, the family donated the image to the church. Word of the apparition soon spread, and before long countless pilgrims began making the journey to Absam to pray before the holy image.

Miracles of healing soon began to occur. In thanksgiving for heavenly favors received, the pilgrims began contributing ex-votos to the church in the form of small paintings. Some of these depicted the sick lying in their beds or the petitioner kneeling in prayer. Sometimes both the sick and a praying figure are shown in the painting. The word *ex-voto* and the date are usually given, and in all cases a miniature reproduction of the miraculous image is added. These signs of thanksgiving are still kept in the Chapel of Ex-votos.

Today, the miraculous image of the Virgin Mary is enshrined on a side altar in the parish church of Absam. Measuring seven inches long and five inches wide, the small glass pane is surmounted by a golden crown and surrounded by golden rays that are embellished with golden flowers and precious jewels. The expression of the Virgin is one of humility, tenderness, and love. With great affection, the Germans and Austrians often refer to her as "Our Beloved Lady."

PRAYER TO OUR LADY OF ABSAM

Oh most blessed Virgin, Mother of God, you who appeared here in Absam, I pray that your image will be imprinted on my heart, and may it fill me with true repentance of my sins today, and with trust and confidence at the hour of my death. Amen.

Our Lady of Absam, pray for us.

ABOUT THE SHRINE

Located near Innsbruck, the shrine of Our Lady of Absam is open daily throughout the year. Two feast days are commemorated: January 17, the day of her appearance; and June 24, the installment of the Virgin's picture in the parish church. Celebrations take place on the 17th of each month at the shrine in commemoration of the Virgin Mary's appearance. Many other festivities also take place throughout the rest of the year, and the church is a favorite scene for special occasions such as weddings and baptisms. A typical visit to the shrine can include praying before the miraculous image of Our Lady, spending time at the spectacular Chapel of Ex-votos, and buying souvenirs at the gift shops. As Absam is a very popular summer resort and winter playground, the shrine is open year-round and receives visitors and pilgrims continuously. While there be sure to visit

• Absam parish church • Miraculous image of the Virgin Mary
• Processions and celebrations at the shrine • Surrounding countryside and mountains • Chapel of Ex-votos (located outside, near the church) • Gift shops

SHRINE INFORMATION

Absam Kirche
Pfarre Absam
W. Schindlstr. 20
6067 Absam (Tirol)

TOURIST OFFICE

Tourismusverband Absam
DörferstraBe 37
6067 Absam (Tirol)
Tel/Fax: (05223) 53-1-90

Innsbruck Tourist Information Office
Burggraben 3
6020 Innsbruck
Tel: (0512) 53-56, (0512) 59-850
Fax: (0512) 59-850-7
Website: www.tiscover.com

PLACES TO STAY

As Innsbruck is a short twenty-minute bus ride from Absam, most visitors spend the night in Innsbruck. However, Absam does offer several hotels, guesthouses, and private rooms to choose from. Contact the Absam tourist office for a full listing of these accommodations. In Innsbruck, there are several Catholic guesthouses:

Haus Marillac
Rennweg 40
6020 Innsbruck
Tel: (0512) 572-313
Fax: (0512) 572-313-10

Barmherzige Schwestern
Schwester Pia Maria
Rennweg 40
6020 Innsbruck
Tel: (0512) 587-176-15

Haus Der Begegnung
Tschurtschentaler Strasse 2a
6020 Innsbruck
Tel: (0512) 587-869
Fax: (0512) 587-869-11

HOW TO ARRIVE AT ABSAM

Absam is about six miles east of Innsbruck (just outside the city limits).

ROAD

From Innsbruck, head northeast, following the signs to Absam via Thaur.

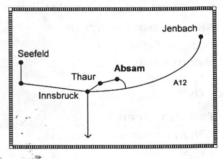

TRAIN

The nearest major railway station is in Innsbruck. However, there is a smaller railway station in Hall (within walking distance of Absam). From Innsbruck or Hall, take a bus or taxi to Absam.

BUS

Absam is most easily accessible by bus from Innsbruck and nearby small towns. From the Innsbruck train station (Hauptbahnhof), take either Bus #D or #E to Absam—the bus drops you off at the shrine (Absam Kirche).

TIPS AND HINTS

The two most important feast days at the shrine are January 17 (day of her appearance) and June 24 (installment of the Virgin's picture in the parish church).

At Christmastime, the pilgrimage church is home to one of the area's loveliest nativity scenes.

For more information about another nearby shrine, see *Eucharistic Miracle of Seefeld.*

DID YOU KNOW?
The Holy Shroud of Turin is another sacred object of devotion in the Catholic faith that has no natural explanation for the image that has been left on it.

Göttweig Abbey

"On towards Christ, the Lord."
ABBOT'S MOTTO

Over the centuries the great monasteries of Austria have developed a worldwide reputation for their achievements and contributions in the areas of culture, religion, arts, and architecture. Among these distinguished abbeys is that of Göttweig Abbey, a Benedictine

Dating from 1065, Göttweig Abbey has long served as a place of pilgrimage. With the motto "On towards Christ, the Lord," the monastery strives to be a focal point of faith, culture, and hospitality for all its guests and visitors. *(Benediktinerstift Göttweig)*

priory in the northeastern section of the country that has long served as a popular place of pilgrimage for the faithful.

The foundation of the monastery dates from 1065, when the bishop of the local diocese set out for a renewal of faith and a reform of the clergy and priories. Among his first actions, he consecrated a church and built an inn on Göttweig Mountain in 1072. Several years later, when the prelate was forced to move from Passau, he took up residence at Göttweig. While on the mountain, the bishop gathered together like-minded clergymen and set into motion a monastic community following the rules of Saint Augustine.

On September 9, 1083, Bishop Altmann consecrated his newly built monastery church to the Mother of God. In response to a beautiful Byzantine icon the prelate had received shortly before, the bishop adopted the Virgin Mary as patron of the community. Along with taking on the regular duties of maintaining a monastery, the bishop acquired a number of parishes, which he placed under the responsibility of the abbey.

After Bishop Altmann's death in 1091, the monastery took a slightly new direction by adopting the Rule of Saint Benedict. In the following years, the priory produced a number of holy abbots, including a few who were later canonized. During the next few centuries, the abbey continued to experience great success as it established two new monasteries and helped in the spiritual renewal of others.

Between the twelfth and eighteenth centuries the monastery experienced both prosperity and hard times. One great highlight occurred in 1401 when Pope Boniface IX placed the abbey directly under the Holy See. That meant that the monastery was directly responsible to the pope, not to a bishop.

In the nineteenth century the abbey brought its finances back into order, music reached its peak, as did membership, with eighty-one monks. The beginning of the twentieth century and the two world wars, however, brought many difficulties to the monastery. On May 8, 1945, Russian officers celebrated their victory over Hitler's Germany in the monastery's courtyard. The abbey had been serving as a barracks for three thousand Russian soldiers.

On August 15, 1945, the first monks were able to return to Göttweig. In the ensuing years, although everything often appeared bleak at times, the monks were able to restore the monastery to a full-functioning order, both spiritually and physically. Today, the abbey has taken on new responsibilities, and the number of its members has doubled since 1975. With the abbot's motto "On towards Christ, the Lord," the monastery continues to strive to be a focal point of faith, culture, and hospitality for all its guests and visitors.

ABOUT THE SHRINE

Perched above a hill with breathtaking views of the world-famous Danube Valley and surrounding countryside below, the Monastery of Göttweig welcomes visitors and pilgrims from around the world. With daily guided tours of the abbey, cloister, crypt, museum, art collections, and exhibitions from Easter through October, the visiting pilgrim has much to explore. All are welcome at the monks' vesper services and Mass. The monastery also operates a restaurant with specialties from the regional cuisine. While there be sure to visit

- Göttweig Abbey • Abbey Church • Museum • Vesper Service
- Abbey restaurant • Guided tours

SHRINE INFORMATION

Benediktinerstift Göttweig
Tourismus und Kultur
3511 Furth bei Göttweig
Tel: (02732) 85-581, (02732) 85-581-0, (02732) 85-581-233,
(02732) 85-231
Fax: (02732) 85-581-244, (02732) 85-581-266
E-mail: koloman@via.at
Website: http://www.stiftgoettweig.or.at/stiftgoettweig/

TOURIST OFFICE

Gästeinformation Marktgemeinde
Untere Landstraße 17
3511 Furth bei Göttweig

PLACES TO STAY

For more information on places to stay, contact the tourist office or abbey.

HOW TO ARRIVE AT GÖTTWEIG

Stift Göttweig is about two miles from Furth bei Göttweig and about thirty-five miles west of Vienna.

ROAD

From Vienna, take A1 west, then head north (in the direction of Krems), following the signs to Stift Göttweig. Another option from Vienna is to take Expressway 3 northwest to Krems, then exit and head south to Stift Göttweig.

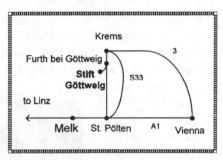

From Salzburg, head east to St. Pölten, then exit and head north to Stift Göttweig, following the signs.

TRAIN

Furth bei Göttweig is accessible by train. From Vienna there is daily service. From Furth bei Göttweig there are bus and taxi services to the abbey (Stift Göttweig).

BUS

Furth bei Göttweig is accessible by bus from many nearby cities, including Vienna and St. Pölten. Taxi and local bus services are available to the abbey (Stift Göttweig).

TIPS AND HINTS

The House of Spiritual Exercises—St. Altmann is also available for those who would like to have a retreat in a monastery. Contact the abbey for more information.

Be sure to visit the abbey's website at http://www.stiftgoettweig.or.at/stiftgoettweig/

DID YOU KNOW?

Göttweig is a Celtic word meaning "mountain blessed by God."

Cathedral of Gurk and St. Hemma

An Angelic Austrian Woman

Rising up out the green valleys of southern Austria is the renowned Cathedral of Gurk. A dominating structure, the shrine features the crypt containing the tomb altar of the beloved Saint Hemma. Home to beautiful architecture and artworks, the cathedral welcomes thousands of pilgrims annually from Austria and the rest of the world.

Although there is no extensive documentation of the life of Saint Hemma, historians have been able to compose a short biography of the angelic Austrian woman. Born of nobility in the eleventh century, Hemma is said to have been a very energetic and deeply religious wo-

Attracting pilgrims from throughout Europe and abroad, the beautiful Cathedral of Gurk in southern Austria features the tomb altar of the beloved Saint Hemma. *(Salvatorianer Kolleg)*

man. A relative of the emperor Saint Henry II, she had the great fortune of being raised at his court by Saint Cunegund.

According to sources, Hemma later married Count William of Sanngan. Together they raised two children. Disaster struck the family early on, however, as Hemma's husband died while returning home from a pilgrimage to Rome. (Another tragedy took place about twenty years later when one of her sons was killed in battle.)

From that moment on, Hemma decided to devote her life completely to God. With her large wealth and inheritance, she began distributing her goods even more generously to the poor and founded several religious houses around 1015. In Gurk she built a church to the Virgin Mary and a convent that she gave to the Benedictine nuns in 1043. Although Hemma spent her last days here, it is uncertain whether she actually ever became a nun herself.

After her death about the year 1045, she was buried at the church in Gurk. Immediately, her tomb became the destination of many pilgrimages as she had become widely known for her incredible generosity and evangelical zeal. As the miracles attributed to her multiplied, the Church beatified her in 1287.

In this century, Saint Hemma received her greatest honor when in 1938 the Catholic Church canonized her. Today, she has the distinction of sharing the same feast day with saints Peter and Paul (June 29). Recently, Pope John Paul II paid her homage when he visited the Cathedral of Gurk on June 25, 1988, and celebrated Mass before eighty thousand jubilant pilgrims.

PRAYER TO SAINT HEMMA

Saint Hemma, I ask for your prayers on this, my pilgrimage. I pray that you may join me as one great choir asking our loving Father to assist me in my life, to help me find the path to holiness, to a life filled with virtue and love. Amen.

Saint Hemma, pray for us.

ABOUT THE SHRINE

In the beautiful, green countryside of southern Austria lies the famous pilgrimage town of Gurk. Attracting visitors from throughout Europe and abroad, the village is home to the cathedral and tomb of Saint Hemma. Open year-round, the shrine provides guided tours from April until September. The Episcopal Chapel, which houses many beautiful frescoes from around 1200, can be visited only on a guided tour, which starts daily at 1 P.M. For accommodations, there is the nearby Saint Hemma Guesthouse, which is operated by the shrine. The Salvatorian Fathers and Brothers administer the cathedral, the monastery, and the parish church of Gurk. While there be sure to visit

- Cathedral • Guided tours • Tomb of Saint Hemma
- "Miraculous stone" • Reliquary of Saint Hemma • Hemma's jewelry • Lenten cloth • Episcopal Chapel

SHRINE INFORMATION

Domkustodie Salvatorianerkolleg
Domplatz 11
9342 Gurk
Tel: (04266) 8236, (04266) 8557-0
Fax: (04266) 8236-16

TOURIST OFFICE

Gurk Tourist Office
Marktgemeinde
9342 Gurk
Tel: (04266) 81-25
Fax: (04266) 81-25-5

PLACES TO STAY

Saint Hemma Gästehaus (Guesthouse)
Domkustodie Salvatorianerkolleg
9342 Gurk
Tel: (04266) 8236, (04266) 8557-0
Fax: (04266) 8236-16
The shrine operates the Saint Hemma Guesthouse.

HOW TO ARRIVE AT GURK

Gurk is about thirty-five miles north of Klagenfurt.

ROAD

Gurk is located on highway 93.

From Klagenfurt, take Route 83 north, turning left on highway 93 and heading west to Gurk (eleven miles).

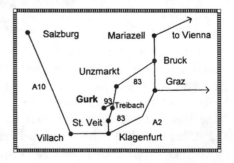

TRAIN

As Gurk is not accessible by train, the nearest railway station is at Treibach-Althofen (ten miles). From Vienna and Klagenfurt, there is frequent train service to Treibach-Althofen. From Treibach-Althofen, there is almost hourly bus service to Gurk.

BUS

There is almost hourly bus service from Treibach-Althofen to Gurk (ten miles). Taxi and other private transportation services are also available from nearby cities.

TIPS AND HINTS

To request a guided tour or stay at the Saint Hemma Guesthouse, it is best to make reservations in advance.

If traveling by train, be sure to stop at the (tiny) Treibach-Althofen railway station rather than the St. Veit an der Glan station. Although the latter is larger, it is much farther away from Gurk, and the bus service is inconvenient and much less frequent.

DID YOU KNOW?

Saint Hemma is often to referred to as "Emma."

Church of the Holy Blood

A Sign from Heaven

Although not too many cities in the world are named after Church relics, there is a small village in southern Austria that serves as an exception to this rule. What is the town? Heiligenblut (which means "Holy Blood" in German). The small village's name is derived from a tiny phial that lies inside the local parish church and is said to contain a few drops of Christ's blood.

The story begins with Briccius, a Dane who had been serving the emperor as an army commander in Constantinople. According to legend, Briccius begged God for a sign that would help end his ruler's religious doubts. Not long after the young soldier made his request to the Lord did a young Jew strike a crucifix in the Church of St. Sophia with a knife in order to test the true faith of the Christians. To the horror of the perpetrator, drops of blood began issuing forth from the wound. Fleeing the church, the man later repented of his deed and asked to be christened. Word of the miraculous event quickly spread throughout the region.

According to tradition, the parish church of Heiligenblut contains a tiny phial that is said to contain a few drops of Christ's blood. Pilgrimages to the shrine began in the thirteenth century and remain today as popular as ever. *(Tatyanna)*

When the emperor heard the news, he requested that the phial containing the holy blood be brought to him. Struck by the sight, the ruler placed the sacred object under guard and viewed it as a "sign from heaven." Hearing of the emperor's profound conversion, Briccius returned home and relieved himself of his army duties. In honor of his exceptional service to the state, the ruler granted Briccius any favor he requested. When the young soldier asked for the phial, the emperor reluctantly agreed. However, after Briccius had ridden off with the precious relic, the emperor dispatched riders to overtake Briccius and recover the treasure.

Warned by an inner revelation of the impending threat, Briccius veered off the path, cut a wound in his right leg, and hid the relic there. Miraculously, the laceration healed quickly, and the Dane continued on his journey, never to be apprehended by the emperor's soldiers. When he reached the modern-day village of Heiligenblut, he fell under a snowdrift and froze to death.

Later, several peasants discovered the Dane as they went out to collect their hay during the winter. What caught their sight were the three ears of corn peeping out of the snow. When the villagers cleared away the snow, they found the corn was sprouting from the breast of the dead man. Convinced that this corpse revealed something supernatural, the peasants fetched "untrained" oxen and yoked them in front of their sledges, leaving the animals to indicate where to bury the body. The point at which they stopped is the site of today's Heiligenblut Church.

When they buried the man, the corpse is said to have lifted its wounded leg three times from the grave before the priest noticed the wound and the phial, together with the text. After gathering all the items, the priest forwarded the objects to the archbishop of Salzburg. With the text in hand, the prelate learned the history of both the man and phial.

After the archbishop returned the holy blood to the parish church, the village adopted the name Holy Blood (Heiligenblut). Before long, vast numbers of the faithful began making the journey there to pray before the sacred relic. Today, the church continues to receive an endless stream of visitors who come to pray and meditate on the life of Jesus Christ—and the blood he shed for the remission of all sins.

PRAYER TO OUR LORD

Lord, you are all. You are a star I look up to, a rock on which I stand, a leader I trust, a staff I walk by, bread that gives me life, a spring where I rest myself, a goal I strive for. Lord, you are everything. Amen.

ABOUT THE SHRINE

Heiligenblut offers a place of breathtaking beauty in the midst of the Alpine Mountains. Surrounded by tremendous scenery, Heiligenblut's church (the Church of the Holy Blood) sits aloft a hill that rises over the small village. World famous for its winter activities and ski slopes, Heiligenblut receives visitors and pilgrims throughout the year. Near the main altar, in the elaborate six-sectioned, slender tabernacle, lies the relic of the Holy Blood. Along with spending time at the shrine, you may wish to go hiking, biking, or walking in the nearby pastures, meadows, forests, and cascades or around the lakes. While there be sure to visit

- Heiligenblut's Church • Relic of the Holy Blood • High Altar
- Reliefs, paintings, motifs, and statues • Surrounding countryside and mountains

SHRINE INFORMATION

Katholisches Pfarramt
St. Vinzenz
9844 Heiligenblut/Großgleckner

TOURIST OFFICE

Tourismusverband
9844 Heiligenblut
Tel: (04824) 2001-21
Fax: (04824) 2001-43
E-mail: heiligenblut-glockner@netway.at
Website: www.permedia.co.at/glockner

PLACES TO STAY

For a full listing of hotels, pensions, and guest rooms in Heiligenblut, contact the tourist information office or visit the website.

HOW TO ARRIVE AT HEILIGENBLUT
Heiligenblut is about twenty-five miles north of Lienz.

ROAD
From Lienz, take 107 north to Heiligenblut.

From Zell am See, head south to Heiligenblut, in the direction of Lienz.

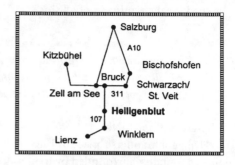

TRAIN
Heiligenblut is not accessible by train. The nearest train stations are in Lienz and Zell am See.

BUS
There are several daily bus departures from Lienz and Franz Josefs Höhe to Heiligenblut.

TIPS AND HINTS
Be sure to visit Heiligenblut's tourist office website at www.permedia.co.at/glockner

As the doors to the Church of the Holy Blood are sometimes locked, it is often a good idea to stop by the tourist office on the main street (near the Hotel Post) to check the current hours for visiting.

DID YOU KNOW?
The faithful have been making pilgrimages to the shrine since the thirteenth century.

Heiligenkreuz Abbey

An Authentic Monastic Experience

Amidst the great number of Austrian abbeys, Heiligenkreuz ranks among the best of them. Situated near Vienna, the monastery annually welcomes thousands of pilgrims and tourists who come to delve into an authentic monastic environment. With a choral prayer held in Latin, the monks offer visitors an experience unlike that found in many other places.

The origin of the monastery dates from 1133, when Leopold III donated some land to the Cistercians for a monastery to be built just south of modern-day Vienna. The reason behind the ruler's decision to have an abbey constructed here was to establish a house for prayer and monastic life and to have a burial place for his dynasty. There were also political motives for the establishment of a monastery. Leopold knew the Cistercians would make for great local farmers, fish breeders, winegrowers, and foresters because of their belief in the value of manual work.

In the following centuries, Heiligenkreuz did play an important role in the area, both in regards to its economy and cultural contributions. Although the abbey prospered in different ways during the Middle Ages, the monastery also suffered from setbacks, such as the Turkish invasions. Nevertheless, the abbey always regrouped in good time.

In German, the monastery's name of *Heiligenkreuz* means "Holy Cross." The abbey received this title because of a relic it had received in the twelfth century from Duke Leopold V of Austria. The sacred object, which originally came from the Crusader King of Jerusalem, was said to be a true piece of the cross upon which Christ had been crucified.

Today, Heiligenkreuz continues to top the list of most popular abbeys to visit in Austria. One of the biggest annual events at the monastery occurs every September 14. On this day, large groups of pilgrims arrive for the celebrations and activities associated with the Feast Day of the Triumph of the Cross.

ABOUT THE SHRINE

One of the oldest Cistercian Abbeys in Austria, the monastery of Heiligenkreuz lies just fifteen miles west of Vienna. A bustling community of fifty monks, the abbey remains as active today as it has been for centuries. Guided tours of the abbey are available between Easter and September, and visitors are welcome to attend the solemn choir prayers of the monks during the summer months. (The prayers are sung in Latin/Gregorian chant, each day at noon and 6 P.M.) While there be sure to visit

• Cistercian Abbey • Abbey Museum • Guided tours

SHRINE INFORMATION

Zisterzienserabtei Heiligenkreuz
Gastamt
2532 Heiligenkreuz
Tel: (02258) 87-03, (02258) 87-03-125, (02258) 22-86, (02258) 22-82
Tel/Fax: (02258) 8703-125, (02258) 8703-123, (02258) 8703-114,
   (02258) 22-82-171

Tourist Office

Tourismusverband Heiligenkreuz
c/o Gemeindeamt
Haus Nr. 15
2532 Heiligenkreuz
Tel: (02258) 22-66, (02258) 22-86

Places to Stay

Most pilgrims visiting the abbey stay overnight in nearby Vienna and make a day-trip to Heiligenkreuz. For more information on places to stay in Vienna, see *Cathedral of St. Stephen*. For those who would like to stay in Heiligenkreuz however, it is possible to stay at the abbey guesthouse:

Zisterzienserabtei Heiligenkreuz
Gästehaus
2532 Heiligenkreuz
Tel: (02258) 87-03, (02258) 87-03-125, (02258) 22-86 (02258) 22-82
Tel/Fax: (02258) 8703-125, (02258) 8703-123, (02258) 8703-114,
 (02258) 22-82-171

How to Arrive at Heiligenkreuz

Heiligenkreuz is about fifteen miles southwest of Vienna and ten miles northwest of Baden.

Road

From Vienna, head west on A21, following the signs to Salzburg and Linz, exiting at the signs indicating Heiligenkreuz.

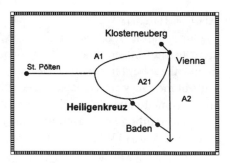

Train

Heiligenkreuz is not accessible by train. The nearest train stations are in Vienna (Sübahn-hof), Baden, and Mödling.

Bus

From the Südtirolerplatz in Vienna, take bus #1123, #1124, or #1127, marked *Alland,* to Heiligenkreuz (the trip takes about ninety minutes).

From Baden, take either bus #1140 or #1141 to Heiligenkreuz.

(To arrive at Baden from Vienna, take either the Baner Bahn bus, which leaves every fifteen minutes from the State Opera, or take the Schellbahn bus from the Vienna Südbahnof train station, which leaves every thirty minutes).

There is also daily bus service from Mödling to Heiligenkreuz.

TIPS AND HINTS

Keep in mind that it is possible to stay at the abbey's guesthouse; however, it's best to make reservations beforehand if possible.

Every Sunday morning at 9:30 A.M. there is a solemn high Mass with Gregorian chant.

DID YOU KNOW?

Heiligenkreuz has more relics of the Holy Cross than any other site in Europe except Rome.

$$\begin{array}{c} + | | + \\ \hline + | | + \end{array}$$

Klosterneuburg Abbey

A Popular Getaway Trip

Situated close to Vienna, Klosterneuburg makes for a popular getaway trip to a nearby monastery. Recognized for its rich history and art treasures, the abbey is considered by many to be the most significant monasteries in Austria. One of its greatest treasures is its world-famous enamel altar created in 1181.

The legendary origin of the abbey dates from the fifteenth century. According to the story, Leopold III of Austria was standing with his wife, Agnes, on the balcony of his castle on his wedding day when all of a sudden a strong gust of wind blew the veil off his bride's face. After searching for the head covering for quite some time with no luck, the people then gave up. However, nine years later, when Leopold was out hunting, he came across a brilliant light in the fields. Walking up close to it, he saw that the gleam was emanating from the veil. In the midst of the light appeared a vision of the Virgin Mary, directing Leopold to build a monastery in this place.

Although the legend is rather charming, it does not coincide with the abbey's actual history—except for the fact that Saint Leopold was its founder in 1113. Ceremonies for the laying of the foundation stone of the new monastery church took place on June 12, 1114. On September 29, 1136, shortly before Saint Leopold's death, the abbey church was consecrated.

In the following years, Klosterneuburg became a religious and cultural

Considered by many to be the most significant monastery in Austria, Klosterneuburg is blessed with a rich history and tradition. Inside the monastery church, pilgrims can visit the abbey's world-famous enamel altar, created in 1181. *(Author)*

powerhouse in the area. One of the greatest moments for the abbey took place on January 6, 1485, when Leopold was canonized. Thereafter, the monastery and abbey church containing the saint's sacred remains became a famous place of pilgrimage.

Although Klosterneuburg suffered from several invasions by the Turks, the abbey always rebounded. During the fifteenth century, many of the monks devoted themselves to humanistic studies and scientific research in the fields of geography and astronomy. In this century, the abbey received a significant honor when their church received the title of "Basilica Minor."

Today, the monastery continues to welcome thousands of pilgrims and tourists each year. Many of them come to visit the shrine's greatest attractions, such as its cathedral, cloister, St. Leopold's Chapel, and the residential apartments of the emperors. After their tours, many of the people often like to finish off their visit with a stop at the monastery's famous old restaurant: *Stiftskeller*.

ABOUT THE SHRINE

Considered one of the most significant abbeys in Austria, the Klosterneuburg monastery is famed for its history, art treasures, library, and cathedral. Located just outside Vienna to the north, the abbey receives visitors and pilgrims from all parts of the world. It is open all year with daily guided tours of the monastery. The abbey also operates an excellent restaurant, the Stiftskeller, where visitors can dine on classic Austrian specialties (the abbey restaurant can accommodate up to one thousand people). While there be sure to visit

> • Klosterneuburg Abbey • Cathedral of the Monastery • St. Leopold's Chapel (with the Verdun Altar) • Cloister • Abbey museum • Abbey library • Guided tours of the wine cellars • Abbey restaurant

Shrine Information
Stift Klosterneuburg
Stiftsplatz 1
3400 Klosterneuburg
Tel: (02243) 411-212, (02243) 411-154
Fax: (02243) 227-10

Tourist Office
Fremdenverkehrsverein
Niedermarkt
3402 Klosterneuburg
Tel: (02243) 320-38, (02243) 320-72
Fax: (02243) 267-73

Places to Stay
Most pilgrims visiting the abbey stay overnight in nearby Vienna and make a day-trip to Klosterneuburg. For more information on places to stay in Vienna, see *Cathedral of St. Stephen.*

How to Arrive at Klosterneuburg
Klosterneuburg is about eight miles north of Vienna.

Road
From Vienna, take Route 14 northwest, following the south bank of the Danube to Klosterneuburg.

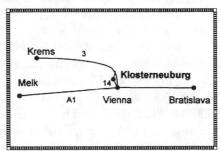

Train
From the Vienna Heiligenstadt train station, there is hourly service to Klosterneuburg-Kierling.

Bus
From the Westbahnhof train station in Vienna, take the U-Bahn (subway service) heading for Heiligenstadt, where you can then board bus #239 or #341 to Klosterneuburg.

U-Bahn (Subway)
From the Westbahnhof train station in Vienna, take the U-Bahn heading for Heiligenstadt, where you can then board bus #239 or #341 to Klosterneuburg. The U-Bahn station nearest to the abbey is Klosterneuburg-Kierling.

TIPS AND HINTS

Be sure to take advantage of the abbey's great restaurant. If possible, call or fax ahead for current hours of operation.

Every year on November 15, Saint Leopold's Day is celebrated in Klosterneuburg with music, banquets, and a parade.

Although guided tours of the monastery take place throughout the year, the museum can only be visited between May 1 through November 15.

DID YOU KNOW?

Every year on the anniversary of Leopold's death, the monastery of New Clausterberg (founded by the saint) distributes two large doles to the poor who come to receive it.

$$+\!\!\parallel\!\!+$$
$$+\!\!\parallel\!\!+$$

Our Lady of Maria Taferl

Three Centuries of Blessings

Attracting more than two hundred thousand pilgrims each year, Our Lady Maria Taferl is the second largest Marian shrine in Austria. Aside from its spectacular scenic environment, the pilgrimage church's popularity springs from its wonderful story of origin.

According to archaeological research, the hilltop of Maria Taferl appears to have been first used as a Celtic place of sacrifice in prehistoric times. In an attempt to wipe out all pagan practices, the Christians upon their arrival in the area fixed a small wooden cross to the oak tree in front of an ancient Celtic sacrificial stone. They nailed the cross to a board ("Taferl"), and placed a representation of the crucified Christ on it, flanked by figures of the Virgin Mary and Saint John. From this statuary, the place soon became known as Beim Taferl ("At the Board")—later, the name was changed to Maria Taferl.

The beginnings of the pilgrimage church date from the seventeenth century. On January 14, 1633, a cattle-herder from the nearby village of Kleinkrummnussbaum decided to chop down the rotting oak tree upon which the crucifix hung. In several failed attempts, the man's axe slipped twice and struck both of his legs. Only then did he see the crucifix that was affixed to the tree. In horror at having unwittingly committed a sacrilege, he knelt down and prayed for forgiveness. According to his report, the blood flowing from his wounds ceased at once, and he regained enough strength to return home under his own power.

For the next ten years, no other special events occurred at the site. However, in 1642 the local magistrate replaced the decayed crucifix with a small statue of Our Lady of Sorrows. After performing this act of generosity, his fits of depression disappeared almost immediately.

In 1658 the first supernatural event was reported on the hilltop—a miraculous light was seen. In 1659 there were twenty-five such apparitions, in 1660 three, and one in 1661. In total, the villagers had reported thirty such apparitions—four of which were lights and twenty-six were figures.

In the apparitions, the townspeople saw pilgrims, clad in white, walking alone, in small groups, and in processions. With each apparition, a number of people reported cases of miraculous healings. Word soon reached Church authorities, and after a long period of careful observation

A place of pilgrimage for centuries, the hilltop shrine of Our Lady of Maria Taferl received its greatest honor recently when in 1947 Pope Pius XII raised the church to the dignity of a basilica. Inside the sanctuary, above the high altar, rests the miraculous image of Our Lady of the Seven Sorrows. *(Maria Taferl Pfarramt)*

and deliberation, the local bishops authorized a full inquiry. Fifty-one witnesses in total were examined under oath between December 15 and 17, 1659.

Although the bishops never issued a final decision, the place continued to grow in popularity. On March 19, the Feast of Saint Joseph, 1660, divine services were held for the first time as eight Masses were celebrated before a congregation of more than one thousand pilgrims. On April 25, 1660, a church official from nearby Passau laid the foundation stone of the new pilgrimage church. The shrine continued to receive vast numbers of visitors in the following years, except during the Josefine era when pilgrimages were forbidden by the government and during the two world wars.

In spite of these setbacks, the pilgrimage church has since become the second most visited Marian shrine in the country. Maria Taferl received its greatest honor in 1947 when Pope Pius XII raised the church to the dignity of a basilica. Inside the sanctuary, above the high altar, rests the miraculous image of Our Lady of the Seven Sorrows. Today, the shrine continues to serve as a source of many blessings, as it has for the past three centuries.

PRAYER TO OUR LADY OF MARIA TAFERL

My Queen! My Mother! I give you all myself, and to show my devotion to you, I consecrate my eyes, my ears, my mouth, my heart, my entire self. Wherefore, O loving Mother, as I am your own, keep me, defend me, as your property and possession. Amen.

Our Lady of Maria Taferl, pray for us.

ABOUT THE SHRINE

Perched above a hill overlooking the Danube River, Maria Taferl offers the visitor not only spectacular scenery but also a place of great Marian pilgrimage and devotion. Located in a small town, the sanctuary welcomes more than two hundred thousand pilgrims each year from around the world. One of the greatest highlights for visitors is praying before the miraculous image of Our Lady of Sorrows. Maria Taferl has a number of hotels and inns for the visiting pilgrims. While there be sure to visit

• Our Lady of Sorrows Basilica • Miraculous image of the Virgin Mary (above the high altar)

SHRINE INFORMATION

Katholisches Pfarramt
3672 Maria Taferl
Tel: (07413) 278
Fax: (07413) 278-24

TOURIST OFFICE

Marktgemeinde Maria Taferl
Bezirk Melk (Niederösterreich)
3672 Maria Taferl
Tel: (07413) 302
Fax: (07413) 302-4

PLACES TO STAY

Maria Taferl has plenty of guest rooms and hotels for visiting pilgrims. Contact the tourist office for a full listing of places to stay.

HOW TO ARRIVE AT MARIA TAFERL

Maria Taferl is about seventy miles from Vienna, ten miles from Melk, and eight miles from Emmersdorf a.d. Donau. (Emmersdorf a.d. Donau is located near Melk, just across the bridge.)

ROAD

From Vienna, take A1 west to Melk, then crossing the bridge, take Route 3 west to Marbach. Once at Marbach, follow the signs to Maria Taferl (two miles uphill).

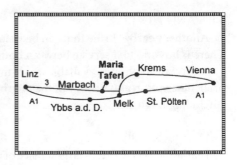

From Linz, take Route 3 east to Marbach. Once at Marbach, follow the signs to Maria Taferl (two miles uphill).

TRAIN

Maria Taferl is not accessible by train. The nearest railway stations are at Ybbs a.d. Donna and Emmersdorf a.d. Donau. From Vienna and Melk there is daily train service to Ybbs a.d. Donna; and from Krems there is daily train service to Emmersdorf a.d. Donau. To arrive at Maria Taferl from the railway stations, see the bus information below.

BUS

From Ybbs a.d. Donna railway station, take bus #7720 to the Ybbs a.d. Donna bus station (two miles), then change and take bus #7721 to Marbach bahnhof (bus stop). Once at Marbach, take the taxi to Maria Taferl. (See Taxi information below.) Note, however, that if the bus schedule is inconvenient, taxi service is always available from the Ybbs a.d. Donna railway station to Maria Taferl.

From Emmersdorf a.d. Donau railway station, there are two early morning bus departures for Maria Taferl. Taxi service is also available from here.

From Melk, there is one morning and one late afternoon bus departure for Maria Taferl.

TAXI

In the tiny town of Marbach, there is only one taxi service to Maria Taferl (two miles). From the Marbach bus stop, walk about two hundred yards west along the main road until you see the sign "Taxi-Radtaxi." Gabriele is the taxi driver who provides day and night service to Maria Taferl. Her house is around the corner, and you must knock on the door (house #3) to ask her for the taxi service.

Taxi-Radtaxi
(Gabriele Hader)
House #3
3671 Marbach/Donau
Tel: (07413) 371

TIPS AND HINTS

Another nearby shrine that can be visited in the same day is Melk Abbey. There is bus and taxi service between both sanctuaries.

Information phones, available inside the shrine, provide an excellent, but brief, description and history of the pilgrimage church in various languages (including English).

DID YOU KNOW?

Maria Taferl is Austria's largest place of pilgrimage dedicated to Our Lady of Sorrows.

Our Lady of Mariazell

Great Mother of Austria

Located high up in the mountains of Austria, surrounded by picturesque mountains, green meadows, and dense forests, lies the most famous shrine in honor of the Blessed Virgin Mary in all of Central Europe, Our Lady of Mariazell. So popular has been the shrine through the centuries that few other churches or sanctuaries can claim as many ex-votos of different nationalities as Mariazell.

According to legend, on the evening of December 21, 1157, as a Benedictine monk named Magnus was walking through the forest looking for a place to build a monastery, his journey came to a halt as a huge rock formation barred his progress. As the rocky barrier was too steep to climb over and too wide to go around, the monk knelt down and prayed to the Blessed Virgin Mary for guidance. After praying for a short while, he heard a thundering rumble, and the rock barrier split in two, leaving an opening wide enough for him to pass through. After walking a short distance, the monk stopped, took out of his knapsack a small wooden statue of the Virgin Mary, and placed it on a white branch of a tree. Then, with the help of some neighboring people, the monk built a small chapel in which he enshrined the statue.

Within a few years, word spread throughout the countryside of the monk's miraculous statue of the Virgin Mary. As the numbers of people visiting the small shrine each year grew, so did the size of the chapel. The first enlargement took place in the year 1200, when a church replaced the chapel. In 1335 Henry I expanded the church, after being cured of a serious sickness through the intercession of the Virgin Mary. Then, in 1363, Louis I of Hungary replaced the first church with a larger one in thanksgiving for a victory. Finally, in 1377 Louis I built the Chapel of Grace (Gnadenkappelle). Then in 1643 Emperor Ferdinand III expanded the church into the present-day basilica. The fame of the shrine grew with each passing year, and by 1699 the church began receiving almost four hundred thousand pilgrims a year. At the pilgrimage site, the faithful began to lovingly invoke the Virgin Mary under the title Our Lady of Mariazell.

The statue itself represents the seated figure of the Virgin Mary holding the Infant Jesus with her right hand as he sits upon her lap. In the Child's hands are an apple and a fig, symbolizing Christ's redemption of the human race. Both the Virgin and the Infant Jesus are dressed in splendid garments and are wearing gold jewel-encrusted crowns.

Recognized as the most celebrated Marian shrine in Central Europe, Our Lady of Mariazell has been the destination of thousands of pilgrimages since the twelfth century. Almost unrivaled in the number of ex-votos left by visitors of different nationalities, the world-famous basilica features above its high altar the enshrined miraculous image of the Virgin Mary. *(Basilika Mariazell)*

The Lady Chapel, which contains the statue, is located over the exact spot where the monk Magnus first established his cell in the year 1157. During the last reconstruction of the basilica, the remains of the original linden tree were discovered. Recent evidence supports that this is the tree on which Magnus first placed the miraculous statue in his woodland hermitage.

Ever since that first day when Magnus placed the statue on the white branch, countless pilgrims have been making their way to Mariazell. Many honors have been bestowed upon the shrine through the years and upon those who journey there. At the 750th anniversary of its foundation in 1907, Pius X granted a plenary indulgence to all those who visited the shrine. Also in 1907 the statue of Our Lady of Mariazell received an official coronation, and the church was designated a papal basilica.

The Hungarian people were the first to make pilgrimages to Mariazell. Croatians, Slovaks, Bohemians, Germans, Russians, and many others from Central Europe were the next to make the pilgrimage to the Austrian shrine of Our Lady of Mariazell. Eventually, Our Lady received the titles "Magna Mater Austriae, Magna Hungarorum Domina, and Magne Slavorum

Genitum Mater" (Great Mother of Austria, Great Lady of Hungarians, and Great Mother of the Slavic People).

Today, the shrine continues to receive pilgrims from around the world. Recognized as the most frequented Marian pilgrimage site in Central Europe, Our Lady of Mariazell celebrated its eighth centennial of the shrine in 1957 and received Pope John Paul II as a pilgrim on September 13, 1983. With each passing year, the shrine continues to establish itself as one of the world's premier pilgrimage sites dedicated to the Virgin Mary.

PRAYER TO OUR LADY OF MARIAZELL

O Mary, we call upon you. You are the Great Mother of Austria, the Mother of the Slavic people. You offer a safe haven for the exiled; you bring freedom and consolation to prisoners. We ask you, holiest of all virgins, to guard innocence and purity. Helper in all needs, assist us in danger when we call upon you. O Mary, guardian of the German lands, we pray that you may banish the scourges of war and bring peace to all believers. Through your powerful intercession, console the disillusioned, bring back the erring, comfort the sick, and give hope to sinners. Great Mother Mary, Our Lady of Mariazell, bless and protect the people of the nations who honor you. Amen.

Our Lady of Mariazell, pray for us.

ABOUT THE SHRINE

Serving as the national shrine of Austria, Hungary, and Bohemia, Mariazell is the most celebrated Marian pilgrimage center in Central Europe. Located at the center of the city on *Hauptplatz*, the beautiful and brilliant basilica dominates the skyline. Inside the shrine is the Chapel of Miracles, which houses the famous statue of the Madonna. Both a summer resort and winter playground, the small city of Mariazell attracts pilgrims and visitors throughout the year. The feast of Our Lady of Mariazell is celebrated on September 13. While there be sure to visit

• Basilica • Chapel of Miracles (Gnadenkapelle) • Statue of the Madonna • Treasury • Mariazell's devotional gift shops

SHRINE INFORMATION

Superiorat Mariazell
Kardinal Tisserant Platz 1
A-8630 Mariazell
Tel: (03882) 2595-0
Fax: (03882) 2595-20

TOURIST OFFICE

Tourismusverband Mariazeller Land
Hauptplatz 13
A-8630 Mariazell
Tel: (03882) 2366
Fax: (03882) 3945
E-mail: tv-mzl@vip.at

PLACES TO STAY

Marienheim
Pater-Heinrich-Abel. Platz 3
8630 Mariazell
Tel/Fax: (03882) 25-45

Herzmarien Karmel
Karmelweg 1
8630 Mariazell
Tel: (03882) 26-19

Salvatorheim
Abt-Severin-Gasse 7
8630 Mariazell
Tel: (03882) 22-16-0
Fax: (03882) 22-16-11

Haus St. Franziskus
Heimweg 3
8630 St. Sebastian
Tel: (03882) 60-23

Kleine Schwestern Jesu
Dr. Lueger-Gasse 18
8630 Mariazell
Tel: (03882) 27-25

HOW TO ARRIVE AT MARIAZELL

Mariazell is about eighty miles southwest of Vienna.

ROAD

From St. Pölten, head south on Route 20 to Mariazell.

From Graz, head north to Bruck a.d. Mur, then take Route 20, which leads north into Mariazell.

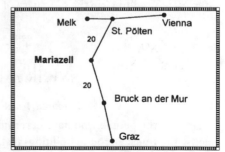

TRAIN

Mariazell is accessible by train. However, it is important to note that all trains bound for Mariazell originate *only* in St. Pölten—fifty miles to the north. From Vienna and Salzburg, there is frequent daily service to St. Pölten. Once at St. Pölten, change trains and take the narrow-gauge train to Mariazell (the trip takes approximately 2.5

hours). Upon arrival at the Mariazell train station, a local bus takes the passengers into town (five minutes). The train station is about a fifteen-minute walk from the basilica and Hauptplatz (the center of Mariazell).

BUS

Mariazell is accessible by bus. From Vienna's Wien Mitte bus station, there are approximately six daily buses to Mariazell. The trip takes approximately two to four hours—depending on the number of scheduled stops.

There are several daily bus departures from St. Pölten to Mariazell (1.5 hours). If the train schedule between St. Pölten and Mariazell is inconvenient, the bus is a good option. In addition, there are several daily bus departures from the Graz railway station to Mariazell (three hours). There are also several daily bus departures from Mürzzuschlag—which serves as an important railway station between Vienna and Graz. (1.5 hours).

TIPS AND HINTS

The most solemn ceremonies at Mariazell are observed on August 15, the Feast of the Assumption of the Blessed Virgin Mary, and on September 8, the Nativity of the Blessed Mother. During the summer, large crowds gather together on Saturday evenings for the great torchlight processions to the church. Processions are also held on the evenings before the Church's most important holidays and feast days.

Mass is celebrated several times in the morning and once in the evening.

DID YOU KNOW?

The popularity of Our Lady of Mariazell shrine as a pilgrimage place was once so great that one emperor, who had ruthlessly suppressed all the monasteries, refused to strip the sanctuary of Mariazell of its many treasures.

Melk Abbey

Nine Hundred Years in the Spotlight

Few are the people who have never heard of Melk Abbey. Recognized as one of the finest Baroque buildings in the world, the monastery has long served as an important spiritual and cultural center of Austria. Today, more than one million tourists and pilgrims annually visit the renowned abbey.

First used as a residence by the Babenberg family that ruled Austria, the monastery was later handed over in the eleventh century to the Benedictine monks by Leopold II. In the following years, the abbey's influence in matters of religion and learning spread far and wide. However, during the sixteenth and seventeenth centuries, Melk experienced a few rocky times, because of the Reformation and Turkish invasions.

In 1702 construction of the abbey in Baroque style began. Among the sites at the monastery that received extra special treatment was the

For more than nine hundred years, Melk Abbey has served as one of Austria's most important spiritual and cultural centers and the goal of thousands of pilgrims. *(Author)*

church. Richly embellished and lavishly garnished, the golden abbey sanctuary is today filled with a vast array of marble sculptures and brilliantly colored frescoes. Although it suffered damage in a 1947 fire, the church has since been completely restored.

Today, the Benedictine monks of Melk continue to live and work in the abbey as they have for more than nine hundred years. Currently, they remained engaged in two traditional apostolates: education and parochial work. Upon a visit to the monastery, pilgrims and tourists may still see the black-robed monks walking about doing their business.

ABOUT THE SHRINE

One of the finest attractions in all of Austria, Melk Abbey is situated west of Vienna on the Danube River. The abbey is open every day of the year. From Palm Sunday to All Saints' Day (April–October), visits are possible with or without a guided tour. Although tours for individuals in English are as needed, there are usually one or two group tours taking place each day (in English). From All Saints' Day to Palm Sunday (November—March), visits are possible only with a guided tour. Tours for individuals are offered in German twice a day. It is encouraged that groups requesting a guided tour always book in advance. While there be sure to visit

• Melk Abbey • Stiftskirche (Golden Abbey Church) • Monastery museum • Guided tours • Monastery restaurant

SHRINE INFORMATION
Stift Melk
3390 Melk
Tel: (02752) 523-12 (April-October extension: 232)
Fax: (02752) 523-12-249, (02752) 523-12-52
To request a guided tour, contact the abbey at this address.

TOURIST OFFICE
Tourismusbüro
Babenbergerstraße 1
3390 Melk
Tel: (02752) 52307-32, (02752) 523-07-33
Fax: (02752) 52307-37

PLACES TO STAY
For a full listing of hotels, pensions, and guesthouses in Melk, contact the tourist office.

HOW TO ARRIVE AT MELK
Melk is about fifty-five miles west of Vienna.

ROAD
From Vienna, take Autobahn A1 west, exiting at the signs for Melk. Another option from Vienna is to take Route 3 west to Melk (this trip is about thirty minutes longer but runs alongside the Danube River).

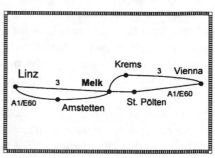

TRAIN
From Vienna's Westbahnhof train station, there are frequent daily departures to Melk (the trip takes about one hour). From the train station in Melk, it is a short ten-minute walk to the abbey.

BUS
Melk is accessible by bus; however, the train service is much more efficient.

BOAT
If you have the time, you can take the 5.5-hour boat ride from Vienna to Melk (or vice versa) on the Danube River.

TIPS AND HINTS

The Mauthausen Concentration Camp is not far from Melk Abbey. Hitler and his associates operated this slave-labor and death camp from 1938 to 1945.

The abbey operates an excellent restaurant where visitors can dine.

DID YOU KNOW?

Melk has gained such a fabulous reputation in Austria through the centuries that it has been mentioned in a number of poems, including the famous German epic poem *The Nibelungenlied*.

+‖+
+‖+

Christ Child of Loreto

An Apostle of Mercy

Tucked away in a tiny chapel on a side street in Salzburg lies an ancient miraculous statue of the Child Jesus. It is here, at the Loreto convent, where Capuchin nuns devoutly guard and watch over the precious ivory image.

Although Austria is now the present-day home of the statue, this has not always been the case. The image originally came from Switzerland and gained popularity through the hands of a holy Capuchin priest, Fr. John Chrysostom Schenk. Given the statue by his superior, the priest kept it close to him wherever he traveled. So affectionately did Father Schenk think of his Child Jesus image that he built a wooden case for it—making it much easier to carry the statue around on his apostolic errands.

Using the image daily in his ministry, he found it especially powerful in his work with the sick. As he often loaned the statue out to those in need, people were amazed at how the image always seemed to be miraculously returned to the priest in good

Dating from the seventeenth century, the wonder-working statue of the Christ Child of Loreto is now enshrined above a side altar in the Convent Chapel of the Capuchin nuns on a side street of Salzburg. *(Loreto Kloster)*

time. Patients loved seeing Father Schenk and his beloved statue—as it always gave them much hope.

On November 25, 1634, the priest died a most holy death. However, the legacy of the miraculous statue continued. As the image had gained such great notoriety through the priest's errands of mercy, the faithful desired that the statue be enshrined in a church for public veneration.

Eventually, the Capuchin nuns in Salzburg received the honor of placing it in their chapel. Engulfed in precious jewels, the tiny statue is today surrounded by a magnificent tabernacle decorated with golden angels and silver clouds. Pilgrims and faithful alike still honor the Christ Child under the title Miraculous Child Jesus of Loreto.

PRAYER TO THE HOLY INFANT CHILD

Divine Infant Jesus, I want to give you my hands today. I want to serve you with all my heart and make you known and loved. Doing your will is the source of my inner peace and joy.

Divine Infant, I give you my hands to touch those I meet with your love and peace. I ask you to heal those in pain, to encourage the hopeless, to console the sorrowing, to provide for those in want. I ask you to reach out to the lonely. I especially plead for the many people suffering from great poverty and injustice.

Miraculous Infant, I believe that you love me and know all of my needs. I place them in your precious hands, especially my present concerns (mention here). *I trust in your love and care. I want to honor and praise you, now and forever. Amen.*

O most gracious Infant Jesus, I prostrate myself before your holy image, to offer my fervent thanks for the blessings you have bestowed on me. Henceforth my entire confidence lies in you. Everywhere I will proclaim your mercy and generosity, so that your great love and deeds may be acknowledged by all. May devotion to your holy infancy increase in the hearts of all Christians, and may all who experience your assistance persevere with me in showing unceasing gratitude to your most holy infancy, to which be praise and glory forever. Amen.

ABOUT THE SHRINE

Open year-round, the small chapel containing the miraculous image of the Christ Child lies on Paris-Lodron-Strasse Street in the heart of Salzburg—near the famous Mirabellgarten. As the church is poorly marked and can be easily missed, look for the small sign "Loreto Kirche" next to the brown doors (the outside of the chapel is a rather musty yellow). Inside the small church, on the right side, is the side chapel containing the Christ Child statue. Mass is celebrated daily at the Capuchin shrine. While there be sure to visit

- Loreto church • Miraculous image of the Christ Child • Porter (and possibly get a blessing from one of the nuns with the Christ Child statue)

SHRINE INFORMATION

Loretokloster
Paris-Lodron-Strasse
5020 Salzburg
Tel: (0662) 87-11-63

TOURIST OFFICE

Salzburg Information
Fremdenverkehrsbetriebe der Stadt Salzburg
Auerspergstr. 7
5020 Salzburg
Tel: (0662) 88-987-0, (0662) 88-987-313, (0662) 88-987-430
Fax: (0662) 88-987-32, (0662) 88-987-435
E-mail: tourist@salzburginfo.at
Website: www.salzburginfo.or.at or www.salzburginfo.at

PLACES TO STAY

Erzb. Priesterseminar
Dreifaltigkeitsgasse 14
Postfach 66
5024 Salzburg
Tel: (0662) 877-495, (0662) 877-495-0
Fax: (0662) 877-495-62
Home to the Salzburg seminary, the Priesterseminar has fifty single and ten double guest rooms for men and women.

Christkönigkolleg
Kapitelplatz 2a
A-5020 Salzburg
Tel: (0662) 84-26-27
Sixteen beds from July to September, and eight beds during the academic year.

Johanesschlössl (Apostolhouse) of the Palatine
Mönchsberg 24, P.O. Box 501
5010 Salzburg
Tel: (0662) 84-65-43 (ext. 72 or 78)
Fax: (0662) 84-63-47-86
Has twenty-five single rooms, ten double rooms.

Institute St. Sebastian
Linzer Gasse 41
5020 Salzburg
Tel: (0662) 88-26-06, (0662) 87-13-86, (0662) 87-59-36
Fax: (0662) 875-936-85, (0662) 871-386-85
St. Sebastian has approximately ninety beds, with special offers for students
and youths. On every floor there is a kitchen and washing machine.

HOW TO ARRIVE AT SALZBURG

Salzburg is located in north-central Austria.

ROAD

Several major highways connect with Salzburg, including
A8 (west), A1 (east), and A10
(south).

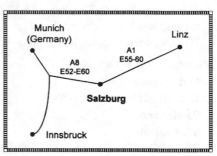

TRAIN

Salzburg's main train station
(Hauptbahnof) has excellent
connections with cities throughout Austria and the rest of Europe.

BUS

Salzburg is accessible by bus from cities throughout Austria; however, the
train service is often much more convenient.

SALZBURG CITY BUS AND TRAM (STREET CAR) SERVICE

The Loreto Chapel (Loretokirche) is located on Paris-Lodron-Strasse near
the famous *Mirabellplatz*. The north terminal of the city bus system (Terminal Nord) is within short walking distance of the shrine.

TIPS AND HINTS

Located two doors down from the Loretokloster church entrance is the
porter. Knock here (on the porter's door), and someone will come and pro-

vide you with assistance. Let him or her know you would like to see their small gift shop and to receive a blessing from one of the nuns with the Christ Child statue, if possible.

While in Salzburg, you can take advantage of the city's many different activities and events—including the numerous indoor and outdoor musical performances. Also, there are a number of Catholic sites to visit, including the cathedral, Noonberg Convent, St. Peter's Abbey, and Franciscan Church.

DID YOU KNOW?

Another famous image representing the Christ Child lies in Prague, Czech Republic. It is often referred to as the Infant Child of Prague.

Our Lady of Maria Plain

A Shrine of Inspiration

With a spectacular view overlooking Salzburg city, the hilltop shrine of Maria Plain has served as a top pilgrimage destination for more than three hundred years. So awesome is the presence inside the Sanctuary of Maria Plain that Mozart chose this place to write his *Coronation Mass for the Blessed Virgin Mary.* Drawing visitors from throughout Europe and abroad, the pilgrimage church is home to a beloved miraculous image of the Virgin Mary.

The story begins in sixteenth-century Germany, where a great fire broke out in a family's bakery. When the owners surveyed the damage afterward, they found everything

Welcoming pilgrims from around the world, the seventeenth-century hilltop shrine of Maria Plain offers its visitors not only breathtaking views of Salzburg and the mountains but also an opportunity to pray before a miraculous portrait of the Virgin Mary. *(Author)*

destroyed—except for their precious painting of the Blessed Virgin. Miraculously, the image had been completely untouched by the fire, yet everything else around it had been devastated.

Twenty years later, the nobleman Rudolf of Gaming brought the picture to Maria Plain. First, he placed it in a small chapel on the hill. However, so many pilgrims came to pray at the site that a larger church had to be built. In 1671 the bishop commissioned the construction of a shrine. Three years later, he consecrated it in a solemn ceremony attended by numerous pilgrims. Outside the church, a number of small chapels had been constructed along the pathway to the sanctuary. From the beginning, the Benedictine monks assumed responsibility for the care and upkeep of the shrine.

Through the years, Maria Plain has been a place of numerous healings for the faithful. In thanksgiving for prayers answered, pilgrims have placed numerous votive pictures around the shrine, attesting to the truth of their claims.

One of the most recent highlights took place in 1983, when Pope John Paul II visited the shrine and prayed before the holy image. Today, the shrine continues to welcome pilgrims and tourists from around the world who come to pray before the miraculous portrait.

PRAYER TO MARIA PLAIN
"ACT OF CONSECRATION TO THE MOTHER OF GOD"

Mother of God, Immaculate Mary, to you I consecrate my body and soul, all my prayers, works, joys, and sufferings, all that I am and possess. With an eager heart I dedicate myself to you in love. I give you complete freedom in making use of me for the salvation of all people. From now on I wish to do everything with you, through you, and for you. I know that by my own strength I shall accomplish nothing. You, however, can do everything that is the will of your Son, and you are always victorious. Grant then, Help of Christians, that my family, my parish, and my country may truly be the Kingdom of your Son and yours. Amen.
Our Lady of Maria Plain, pray for us.

ABOUT THE SHRINE

With a commanding view extending sixty miles over the city of Salzburg to the Alpine Mountains, Maria Plain offers some of the most spectacular scenery in Austria. Located on a hill just outside of Salzburg, the shrine welcomes thousands of pilgrims every year. Inside the sanctuary, above the main altar, lies the cherished image of the Virgin Mary. Along with the basilica, pilgrims can visit the small chapel where the miraculous picture of Our Lady was kept when it was first brought to Maria Plain. While there be sure to visit

• Basilica • Miraculous image of the Virgin Mary • Small outdoor chapels • Information phone (providing the story of the shrine in

English and other languages) • Chapel (where the picture was
first kept until the larger shrine was built)

SHRINE INFORMATION

Superiorat Maria Plain
Plainbergweg 38
5101 Maria Plain—Bergheim
Tel: (0662) 450-194
Fax: (0662) 450-194-12

TOURIST OFFICE

See *Christ Child of Loreto* for tourist office information.

PLACES TO STAY

Gasthof Maria Plain
Plainbergweg 33
5101 Maria Plain
Tel: (0662) 450-701
Fax: (0662) 450-701-19
Situated next door to the shrine, the Gasthof Hotel is located approximately
one to two miles outside of Salzburg.

HOW TO ARRIVE AT SALZBURG

For directions on how to arrive at Salzburg, see *Christ Child of Loreto.*

HOW TO ARRIVE AT THE BASILICA OF MARIA PLAIN FROM DOWNTOWN SALZBURG

Situated on top of a hill in the
outskirts of Salzburg, the Basilica
of Maria Plain is not connected
by any bus or train service. The
only options for arriving at the
shrine are by private transportation, taxi service, or foot, making the twenty-minute walk uphill from the nearest bus stop/
train stop.

BUS SERVICE FROM DOWNTOWN SALZBURG
TO THE BASE OF MARIA PLAIN HILL

From the Salzburg train station, take bus #6 to the Plainbrücke bus stop.
Upon arrival at Plainbrücke, exit the bus, and as you face the yellow building
Schweiger Gasthof zu Plainbrücke, turn right and cross the small bridge to

Plainbergweg Street. To reach the basilica from here, turn right on Plainbergweg Street, following the green and white signs pointing in the direction of Maria Plain. The walk uphill to the shrine takes approximately twenty to twenty-five minutes. (There is also a local train service that drops passengers off near this bus stop; however, if you choose to take this train, *you must be very careful to get on the correct one.* If you take the wrong train to Maria Plain, you will end up completely on the other side of the city of Maria Plain—nowhere close to the basilica. To prevent this from occurring, be sure to clarify your destination with the train personnel at the Salzburg Railway Station beforehand by letting them know you would like to visit *Wallfahrtsbasilika Maria Plain*—the Pilgrimage Basilica of Maria Plain.)

TIPS AND HINTS

If you are in good physical condition, walking up the hill from the bus or train stop to the Basilica of Maria Plain makes for a very pleasant journey. Along the upper part of the path to the shrine are a number of small outdoor chapels where you can spend time praying or meditating.

While in Salzburg, you can also visit the shrine of the *Christ Child of Loreto*, the cathedral, and other important Catholic sites. As the city of Salzburg has so much to offer in the way of concerts and events, it is worth spending several days here.

Information phones are available inside the shrine, providing an excellent, but brief, description and history of the pilgrimage church in various languages (including English).

DID YOU KNOW?

In 1952 the shrine of Maria Plain had one of the greatest honors bestowed on it when the pope declared the church a "Basilica Minor."

Eucharistic Miracle of Seefeld

Then he took a loaf of bread, and when he had given thanks, he broke it, and gave it to them, saying, "This is my body, which will be given for you. Do this in remembrance of me."
LUKE 22:19

Although Seefeld is renowned throughout the ski world as a winter sports playground, it's the parish church that brings the religious devout to the village each year. Here, in the fourteenth century, a eucharistic miracle occurred, changing the life of the local faithful forever.

The story of the event begins in 1384, on the night of Holy Thursday. Knight Oswald Milser, a guardian of the nearby castle, attended Mass on this special day. He was a man of immense egoism and arrogance and held his position in the military with great personal pride. Unfortunately, it was these attributes that caused him to commit a great sacrilege, which led to a eucharistic miracle. The local newspaper of that time reported the event:

> Oswald Miller came down with his followers to the parish church of Seefeld. He demanded—and a refusal could mean death—the large Host; the small one he regarded as too ordinary for him. He surrounded the frightened priest and the congregation with his armed men. At the end of the Mass, Milser, his sword drawn and his head covered, came to the left of the high altar, where he remained standing. The stunned priest handed him the Host, upon which the ground under the blasphemer suddenly gave way. He sank up to his knees. Deathly pale, he grasped the altar with both hands, the imprints of which can be seen to this day.

Although the local chronicler didn't provide many more details, other sources did provide a fuller description of what took place afterward. It is said that the knight, filled with terror, begged the priest to remove the host from his mouth. Once he did so, the ground became firm again. Without wasting time, the humiliated knight rushed to the monastery of Stams, where he confessed his sin of arrogance. In the following two years until his death, the knight continued performing penances in reparation for his great sacrilege. Having his wish granted, he was later buried near the entrance of the chapel of the Blessed Sacrament.

There also are a number of other details that are recorded in the church documents. After the miracle, one knight donated a silver monstrance to enshrine the

The parish church of Seefeld, near Innsbruck, is the site of a eucharistic miracle. On Holy Thursday, 1384, the ground suddenly gave way under a knight when he approached the altar and demanded a larger host. *(Author)*

miraculous host. Also, the site became so popular that they had to build a hostel to accommodate all the visiting pilgrims. As the numbers grew, the church was quickly outgrown. In response, Duke Freidrich commissioned the building of a larger church in 1423. One century later, Emperor Maximilian I added to the pilgrimage site by erecting an adjoining monastery. Built in 1516, the abbey housed the Augustinian monks until 1807. Also demonstrating a special love for the miracle, Archduke Ferdinand II of Tyrol constructed the Chapel of the Holy Blood inside the church.

Today, what can still be seen at the shrine? Near the altar, the faithful can view the hole in the ground where the knight sank up to his knees. The original stone altar of the miracle, with the imprints of Oswald's hands, can also be seen. (Although a new altar has been built over the original one, it was designed so that visitors can still easily view the altar of the miracle and the knight's hand prints.) In the sanctuary, near the high altar, you will also find the monstrance with the miraculous host. A look around the church will also reveal many frescoes and paintings depicting the miraculous event.

One of the most recent monumental moments at the shrine took place in 1984, when the church celebrated the six hundredth anniversary of the extraordinary event. Today, the sanctuary continues to serve as one of the most popular pilgrimage destinations for miracles of this kind. Here, the faithful can renew their faith in Jesus—and his true presence in the Eucharist.

PRAYER TO OUR LORD IN THE BLESSED SACRAMENT

Lord Jesus Christ, present here in your constant gift of the Blessed Sacrament, I come before you now as your child. I offer you praise, honor, and thanksgiving. I offer you my love and my life. You are the refreshing waters, O Lord; You are the Bread of Eternal Life, the rest for my soul. I know, here in the presence of your wonderful Sacrament, you are with me in a very special way.

I have come before you today as a humble pilgrim, seeking the loving protection of your holy Mother. I know she is my Mother also, given to me by you as you suffered on the cross. Please guide me, dear Jesus, to be aware each day of all you have done for me, of all you continue to do for me while I am on this earth.

As I continue my pilgrimage here at this shrine so loved by your Mother, remind me often of this visit with you in your Blessed Sacrament. I truly desire to live my life always in your sight and before your dwelling place. Amen.

ABOUT THE SHRINE

Surrounded by majestic mountains and a lush green countryside, Seefeld offers the visiting pilgrim a place of unparalleled beauty and tranquillity. At the center of the village, next to Dorfplatz, is the famous pilgrimage church of St. Oswald. Inside the shrine, marble steps lead up to the Chapel of the Holy Blood, where the miraculous host lies. At this same spot, to your left, is an old book that gives a historical account of the miraculous event in a vast number of languages. Frescoes and paintings throughout the church also depict the event. Near the altar is the grate that sits above the infamous sunken ground—the result of the knight's stubborn attitude. While there be sure to visit

- St. Oswald Church • Chapel of the Holy Blood • Monstrance for the Miraculous Host • Indentations in the altar from the knight's hands—still visible today • Sunken ground (covered by a grate) • Information phone (describing the events and church in different languages) • Frescoes and paintings • Hiking in the nearby mountains and countryside

SHRINE INFORMATION

For more information about the shrine, contact the Seefeld Tourist Office.

TOURIST OFFICE

Tourismusverband Seefeld
A-6100 Seefeld (Tirol)
Tel: (05212) 23.13
Fax: (05212) 33.55
E-mail: info@seefeld.tirol.at
Website: http://tiscover.com/seefeld

PLACES TO STAY

For a full listing of hotels, pensions, and guest rooms in Seefeld, contact the tourist information office or visit the website. For visitors who would like to stay in nearby Innsbruck, there are several places of Catholic housing:

Haus Marillac
Rennweg 40
6020 Innsbruck
Tel: (0512) 572-313
Fax: (0512) 572-313-10

Barmherzige Schwestern
Schwester Pia Maria
Rennweg 40
6020 Innsbruck
Tel: (0512) 587-176-15

Haus Der Begegnung
Tschurtschentaler Strasse 2a
6020 Innsbruck
Tel: (0512) 587-869
Fax: (0512) 587-869-11

HOW TO ARRIVE AT SEEFELD

Seefeld is fifteen miles northwest of Innsbruck.

ROAD

From Innsbruck, head west on Route 171, then continue north to Seefeld on Route 177.

TRAIN

Seefeld is accessible by train. From Innsbruck, there are frequent daily departures to Seefeld (forty minutes). From Munich, there are also daily departures to Seefeld, passing through the resort town of Garmisch-Partenkirchen.

BUS

There is regular bus service to Seefeld; however, most visitors arrive by train. From Innsbruck's Hauptbahnhof, there are approximately twelve daily bus departures to Seefeld (forty-five minutes).

TIPS AND HINTS

Famous for its year-round activities and events, the city receives pilgrims and visitors throughout the year (Seefeld is very popular for its winter activities, such as skiing).

The train ride to Seefeld from Innsbruck offers some of the most spectacular scenery of any place in Europe—take advantage of it, if possible!

Information phones are available inside the shrine, providing an excellent, but brief, description and history of the pilgrimage church in various languages (including English).

DID YOU KNOW?

The knight's velvet mantle that he had worn during the Holy Thursday Mass was made into a chasuble and later given to the monastery of Stams.

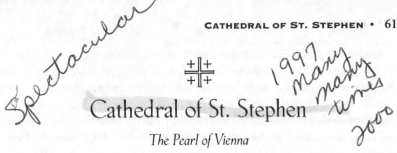

Cathedral of St. Stephen

The Pearl of Vienna

Serving as the landmark of Vienna, the Cathedral of St. Stephen has long possessed a close affinity with its people. Affectionately called "Steve," the massive church serves as a symbol for the freedom and independence of the city and its inhabitants. Today, several million tourists and visitors come annually to visit this historic religious sanctuary and monument.

Construction on the first St. Stephen's Church began in the latter half of the twelfth century. Interestingly, as there was no room left inside the walls of Vienna, the erection of the sanctuary began outside the city limits. Ten years later, the bishop of Passau consecrated the newly built church.

In 1230 a complete reconstruction of the shrine began; however, this proved to be futile as a raging fire destroyed much of St. Stephen's in 1258. Plans to rebuild the church were immediately put into place, and by 1263 the ecclesiastical authorities set the reconstruction process in motion. After another fire in Vienna partially destroyed St. Stephen's in 1276, the church representatives commenced construction on the present-day Gothic cathedral in 1304.

In the following centuries, the massive religious structure was richly embellished with beautiful chapels, famous artwork, and renowned sculptures. Unfortunately, the cathedral experienced a number of

Every year several million pilgrims and tourists visit the renowned Cathedral of St. Stephen in Vienna. The shrine is home to not only a number of spectacular paintings and sculptures but also the famous miraculous image of Our Lady of Máriapócs. *(Author)*

invasions in subsequent years. The worst occurred in 1945, when German troops set the surrounding houses on fire. Sparks from the flames set St. Stephen's roof on fire as well, which eventually led to its collapse and the destruction of almost half the church. Between 1945 and 1952, a full restoration of the cathedral took place.

Among the church's chief attractions is the miraculous image of the Weeping Madonna of Máriapócs (see *Our Lady of Máriapócs*). An object of great veneration, the portrait shed tears in 1696 before hundreds of people on several occasions in the small village of Máriapócs in Hungary. When the emperor heard of the miracle, he ordered the painting to be brought to Vienna and had it enshrined in the cathedral in the midst of great pomp and ceremony.

Today, St. Stephen's has once again regained its rightful place as one of the premier cathedrals of Europe. Welcoming visitors from around the world, the colossal church remains one of the most famous tourist destinations in Austria.

PRAYER TO OUR LADY OF MÁRIAPÓCS

O weeping Virgin Mother, refuge of sinners, we call upon you to petition your Divine Son to obtain for us the forgiveness of our sins and an abundance of blessings for us and for those for whom we pray. Alleviate our sufferings, cure our ills, console us in our sorrows, help us to lead a virtuous life, and guide us to eternal life.

O weeping Virgin, Mother of God, remember us before your Son, our Lord Jesus Christ, now, and at the hour of our death. Amen.

ABOUT THE SHRINE

Situated at the heart of Vienna, the cathedral is the ultimate destination for several million tourists and pilgrims every day in this capital city. Home to many different treasures, the shrine's greatest possession (the miraculous image of Our Lady of Máriapócs) lies just inside the front entrance to the right. Visitors are also drawn here for the cathedral's magnificent architecture. Open throughout the year, the cathedral provides daily tours of the shrine and its catacombs. To arrive at the cathedral by the U-Bahn, take the subway to Stephenplatz. To attend Mass with the famous Vienna Boy's Choir, you can visit the nearby Burgkapelle (Hofburg Palace Chapel) where the boys perform throughout the year—with the exception of July and August. While there be sure to visit

• St. Stephen's Cathedral • Miraculous image of Our Lady of Máriapócs • Magnificent altars

SHRINE INFORMATION

Tourismuspastoral
Stephansplatz 6/6/70
1010 Wien
Tel: (1) 515-52-3375
Fax: (1) 515-52-3366
The Pastoral Tourist Office, operated by the Vienna Archdiocese, provides excellent information for pilgrims visiting the city.

Dompfarre St. Stephen (St. Stephen's Cathedral)
Stephansplatz 1
1010 Wien
Tel: (1) 515-52-3530

TOURIST OFFICE

Vienna Tourist Board
Obere Augartenstrasse 40
1025 Wien
Tel: (1) 211-14
Fax: (1) 216-84-92
E-mail: wtv@info.wien.at
Website: http://info.wien.at/

PLACES TO STAY

Stephanushaus
Ungargasse 38
1030 Wien
Tel: (1) 717-03
Fax: (1) 717-03-812
Operated by Catholic Sisters, St. Stephen's House provides excellent accommodations near the city center.

Benediktushaus
Freyung 6a
1010 Wien
Tel: (1) 534-98-900
Fax: (1) 534-98-12
Ten double rooms, ten single rooms; open year-round.
Serving as the guesthouse of the Benedictine nuns' abbey, the Benediktushaus provides exceptionally nice accommodations in the heart of the city.

Hotel "Don Bosco"
Hagenmüllergasse 33
1030 Wien
Tel: (1) 711-84-555, (1) 711-84-0
Fax: (1) 711-84-112
Open only from July to September, the Don Bosco Hotel offers excellent
accommodations in a very pleasant atmosphere.

Kardinal-König-Haus
Lainzer Straße 138
1130 Wien
Tel: (1) 804-75-93
Fax: (1) 804-97-43
E-mail: bh-lainz@ping.at

Pallotti-Haus
Auhofstrasse 10
1130 Wien
Tel: (1) 877-10-72
Fax: (1) 877-10-72-29
E-mail: pallottihaus@xpoint.at

Don Bosco Haus
St. Veit-Gasse 25
1130 Wien
Tel: (1) 878-39
Fax: (1) 878-39-414
E-mail: donbosco@magnet.at

Marianneum
Hetzendorfer Straße 117
1120 Wien
Tel: (1) 804-33-01
Fax: (1) 804-33-01-17

Marienheim der Schulbrüder
Anton-Böck-Gasse 20
1210 Wien
Tel: (1) 291-25
Fax: (1) 290-18-39

Seminarzentrum Am Spiegeln
Meyrinkgasse 7-9
1230 Wien
Tel/Fax: (1) 889-30-93
E-mail: AmSpiegeln@compuserve.com

Exerzitienhaus der Schwestern vom göttlichen Erlöser
Kaiserstraße 23-25
1070 Wien
Tel: (1) 523-41-81
Fax: (1) 523-64-44-833

Katholisches Bildungshaus Schönstatt am Kahlenberg
1190 Wien
Tel: (1) 320-13-07
Fax: (1) 320-13-07-302

How to Arrive at Vienna

Vienna is located in eastern Austria, near the Hungarian border.

Road

Vienna is connected by several major highways, including A1 (west), A2 (south), A4 (east), and A22 (northwest).

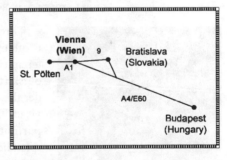

Train

Vienna has four major railway stations:

1. Wien Westbahnhof—Provides train service to and from western Austria, Western Europe, and many Eastern European cities.
2. Wien Südbahnhof—Provides train service to and from southern Austria, Italy, Slovenia, and Croatia.
3. Franz Josef Bahnhof—Provides mostly local train service, with a few international connections, such as to Prague and Berlin.
4. Wien Mitte—Provides mostly local train service.

Bus

Vienna is accessible by bus from all major cities throughout Europe. The city bus station is located at Wien Mitte train station. However, it is usually most convenient to arrive at Vienna by train from long-distance cities.

TIPS AND HINTS

With many Catholic guesthouses to choose from, consider using Vienna as a home base to visit other shrines in the surrounding area. For example, you can spend nights in Vienna while taking day-trips to nearby sanctuaries and abbeys, such as Melk, Klosterneuburg, Maria Taferl, and Göttweig.

Any visit to Vienna can easily last several days to a week. With a number of religious and secular sites to visit, as well as a vibrant city life, Vienna has much to offer the pilgrim tourist.

DID YOU KNOW?

Famous musical composers, such as Mozart, Joseph Haydn, and Anton Bruckner, performed at St. Stephen's Cathedral.

$$✛$$

Our Lady of the Bowed Head

"All those who implore my protection, devoutly honoring this picture, will obtain their petitions, and will receive many graces."
OUR LADY OF THE BOWED HEAD

The seventeenth-century miraculous image of Our Lady of the Bowed Head is enshrined in a side altar of the Carmelite Convent Chapel in the northern outskirts of Vienna. *(Author)*

Throughout the world the Virgin Mary is often invoked under a number of different titles. In a Carmelite convent on the outskirts of Vienna, she is beseeched under the heading "Our Lady of the Bowed Head." The title stems from a miraculous portrait of the Virgin Mary that rests in a splendid side chapel.

In 1610 a Discalced Carmelite friar by the name of Blessed Dominic of Jesus of Mary was out searching for possible locations for a new monastery. While visiting an abandoned, run-down house, he came across a pile of debris lying in a weed-filled yard. After at first ignoring the wreckage, he then felt an interior impulse to sift through the trash, and something caught his attention while he was carefully examining the garbage.

Underneath a layer of dirt and filth was a beautiful oil painting depicting the Virgin Mary.

Possessing a great love for the Mother of God, Dominic immediately took out his handkerchief and brushed off the portrait. So great was his sadness at seeing the ill-treated picture that he decided to take it home, repaint it, and keep it as an object of personal veneration.

One evening, after having swept his cell, Dominic noticed that some dust had settled upon his treasured picture. Deeply regretful for his actions, he tenderly wiped the picture as he lovingly said, "O purest and holiest of Virgins, nothing in the whole world is worthy of touching your holy face, but since I have nothing but this coarse handkerchief, deign to accept my good will."

While he continued to clean the picture, the face of the Virgin Mary became animated before him. Smiling and nodding her head in appreciation, Our Lady then spoke to him: "Fear not, my son, for your request is granted." (Dominic had earlier petitioned the Virgin Mary about a particular favor.) "It will be accomplished and will be part of the recompense that you are to receive for the love that you bear my divine Son and myself."

She then asked Dominic to express to her with confidence any favor he might desire. Falling on his knees, he prayed for the deliverance of a particular soul in purgatory. After hearing him, the Virgin Mary assured Dominic his prayers would be answered if sacrifices and several Masses were offered for the soul.

A short time after Dominic had fulfilled Our Lady's requests, the Virgin Mary appeared to him again as he prayed before the miraculous image. This time, she was with the soul of the person Dominic had desired to deliver from purgatory. After the benefactor thanked the Carmelite friar for his prayers and sacrifices, the Virgin asked Dominic about his other hopes and desires. The friar responded by asking Our Lady if she would listen mercifully to the prayers of all those who honored the picture and invoked her aid. The Virgin offered her assurance:

> All those who implore my protection, devoutly honoring this picture, will obtain their petitions and will receive many graces. Moreover, I shall hearken in a special manner to the prayers that shall be addressed to me for the relief of the souls in purgatory.

With this request granted, Dominic knew he must make the portrait available for public veneration. After receiving permission, he placed the miraculous image in an oratory connected to the Church of Santa Maria della Scala.

For the rest of his life, the portrait became a centerpiece of devotion, and the faithful and the number of favors received through it were many. So popular was the portrait that several reproductions were made available for public veneration elsewhere.

After Dominic's death, the Duke of Bavaria asked the Carmelite Order if they could loan the portrait to him. Knowing that he had been a close friend of Dominic, they agreed. Hence, Brother Anastasius, who had been a traveling companion of Dominic for fifteen years, carried the portrait to Munich. Along with transferring the sacred image, the young brother wrote a document attesting to all that he had heard from Dominic concerning the picture and the miraculous events relating to it. He signed it under solemn oath on August 7, 1631.

For the next year, the portrait made a small pilgrimage of its own. The duke transferred it to the Carmelite Fathers of Munich, who then in turn loaned it to the Emperor Ferdinand II. A great benefactor of the Carmelite Order, the emperor promptly placed the image in the Imperial Court of Vienna in 1631. Soon afterward, he and his wife hung the precious image in the private chapel of the palace. Over time, the portrait became richly decorated as the royal family never ceased to shower it with gifts.

Upon the death of the emperor, Eleanor, the emperor's wife, entered the Discalced Carmelite Order and joined the convent she had founded in Vienna. She brought the miraculous image with her and placed it over the high altar. The portrait remained there until her death in 1655, upon which the beloved image was returned to the Carmelite friars.

Once again, the miraculous picture became available for public veneration. Immediately, crowds of pilgrims came to venerate the holy image. Numerous were the favors received and prayers answered.

On December 14, 1901, the portrait made its last pilgrimage trip. When the Carmelite friars moved into the new church and monastery in northern Vienna, they brought with them the holy picture. Here, they built a special altar in honor of the miraculous portrait—*Our Lady of the Bowed Head*. Ever since then, the faithful have been coming in large numbers to honor the Virgin's picture and implore her protection…and receive many graces.

PRAYER TO OUR LADY OF THE BOWED HEAD

Oh Mary, Mother of our Lord, and our Mother also! You gave your assurance to your servant Dominic: "I will grant the request of those who seek my protection and devoutly honor my image, I will give them my blessing, and will grant special hearing to prayers said for the comfort and delivery of the souls in purgatory." Look upon me, oh Mother of Mercy,

I too am coming to you today with my concerns and present them to you with childlike trust. May you turn your gracious face and compassionate heart toward me as I beseech your guidance and protection, O kind, mild, and sweet Virgin Mary. Amen.

Our Lady of the Bowed Head, pray for us.

ABOUT THE SHRINE

In the northern section of Vienna, on Silbergasse Street, lies the Carmelite church with the miraculous image of Our Lady of the Bowed Head. The picture is located inside the sanctuary to the left, near the main altar. Another prominent attraction is the tomb of Blessed Dominic, which lies to the right of the main altar. Mass is celebrated daily at the shrine. While there be sure to visit

* Carmelite church • Our Lady of the Bowed Head miraculous image • Blessed Dominic's tomb • Frescoes and paintings

SHRINE INFORMATION

Karmelitenkonvent
Silbergasse 35
1190 Wien
Tel: (1) 320-3340
Fax: (1) 320-5364-33
E-mail: karmel@ocd.vienna.at
website: http://members.vienna.at/ocd or http://www.karmel.at/wien/

TOURIST OFFICE

See *Cathedral of St. Stephen* for more information about tourist offices in Vienna.

PLACES TO STAY

See *Cathedral of St. Stephen* for more information about places to stay in Vienna.

HOW TO ARRIVE AT THE CARMELITE CHURCH

The Carmelite church, containing the image of Our Lady of the Bowed Head, lies in the northern section of Vienna. (For directions on how to arrive at Vienna, see *Cathedral of St. Stephen*.)

FROM THE VIENNA WESTBAHNOF TRAIN STATION

Take U-Bahn #6 (subway) to Nussdorferstr, exit the subway, and then take streetcar #38 to Silbergasse (in the direction of Grinzing). Upon exiting the streetcar at Silbergasse, you will see the large Carmelite church with the two towers (it is the biggest church in the area—you can't miss it). From here, take the five- to ten-minute walk up Silbergasse Street to the Carmelite church.

TIPS AND HINTS

With a visit to the shrine's Internet home page, you can also link to a number of other Carmelite websites.

Near the entrance of the Carmelite church are various postcards, photos, and materials about Our Lady of the Bowed Head.

DID YOU KNOW?

Emperor Ferdinand I cherished the miraculous image so much that, it is said, he even took the picture with him on all his travels.

$$+\!\!\parallel\!\!+$$
$$+\!\!\parallel\!\!+$$

Church of St. Wolfgang

A Pilgrimage Church of Art

Ever since the tenth century, the Church of St. Wolfgang has served as a place of pilgrimage. Drawing visitors and the faithful alike from all over, the sanctuary features a virtual museum and gallery of magnificent religious artwork.

According to legend, the lakefront church stands on the site where Saint Wolfgang built a hermitage in the tenth century. After the saint's death, the faithful began making pilgrimages to his former residence. As the place became too small to accommodate the great number of visiting pilgrims over the years, the first church was erected in the fourteenth century at the site.

During the construction of the new sanctuary, the designers embellished the entire interior with splendid works of art. The result was a church with a world-class winged high altar, accompanied by lavish pulpits, statues, and paintings. Today, the church remains a place of pilgrimage as much for its interior aesthetic beauty as for the sanctuary's geographical placement in a summer and winter resort area.

PILGRIMAGE PRAYER

God of our journey, be with us on this pilgrimage, and guide our feet along your path of life. Be our companion day and night; may we feel your presence at our side. Keep us safe, and give us your blessing, that our journey, begun in faith, may reach its true completion through Christ our Lord. Amen.

ABOUT THE SHRINE

St. Wolfgang is another Austrian city blessed with outstanding scenery and stunning views. Situated high in the mountains, next to a crystal-blue lake, St. Wolfgang serves as both a summer and winter holiday resort. The pilgrimage church is located at the main streets of Pilgerstrasse and Michael Pacher Strasse. The shrine receives pilgrims and visitors throughout the year.

While there be sure to visit

• Church of St. Wolfgang • Winged high altar

SHRINE INFORMATION

Pfarrkirche St. Wolfgang
A-5360 St. Wolfgang
Tel: (06138) 2574

TOURIST OFFICE

Kurdirektion St. Wolfgang
A-5360 St. Wolfgang
Tel: (06138) 2239-0
Fax: (06138) 2239-81
E-mail: info@stwolfgang.gv.at
Internet: http://www.salzkammergut.at/wolfgangsee

PLACES TO STAY

Contact the tourist office for a full listing of places to stay in St. Wolfgang.

HOW TO ARRIVE AT ST. WOLFGANG

St. Wolfgang is about thirty-five miles east of Salzburg.

ROAD

There is only one road to St. Wolfgang. From Salzburg, head east on 158 to Strobl, then follow the signs to St. Wolfgang. From Bad Ischl, head west on 158 to Strobl, then follow the signs to St. Wolfgang.

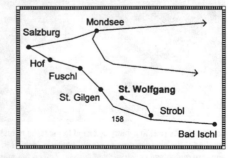

TRAIN

St. Wolfgang is not accessible by train. It is accessible only by bus, taxi, or car. Locally, however, there is a scenic train that services Strobl, St. Gilgen, and Schafberg.

BUS

St. Wolfgang is accessible by bus. There is frequent bus service from Salzburg (Hauptbahnhof), Bad Ischl (Bahnhof), and St. Gilgen (with a change of buses in Strobl).

FERRY

Locally, there are ferry services to St. Wolfgang from Strobl and St. Gilgen. These ferries stop at the village center (the Markt) and at the Schafberg railway.

TIPS AND HINTS

The Eurail Pass covers many of the bus services to St. Wolfgang.

DID YOU KNOW?

In 976 the bishop of Regensburg, Germany, founded the town of St. Wolfgang—and that bishop was none other than Saint Wolfgang himself.

+╬+

Zwettl Abbey

A Royal Cathedral in Cistercian Guise

Serving as one of the oldest monasteries in Austria, the Abbey of Zwettl is renowned for its richness in history and tradition. Among the monastery's chief attractions for visitors today is its church. Often referred to as "a royal cathedral in Cistercian Guise," the abbey's magnificent sanctuary features artwork and architecture of international distinction.

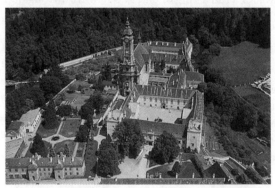

Founded in 1138 by one of the leading ministerial families of the Austrian princes, Zwettl Abbey was built as a new spiritual center to counter the threat of the Bohemians. The Monastery of

Founded in the twelfth century by one of the leading ministerial families of the Austrian princes, Zwettl Abbey is located in the northern region and countryside of Austria. Among the monastery's greatest attraction is its magnificent church, which is often referred to as "a royal cathedral in Cistercian Guise." *(Stift Zwettl)*

Heiligenkreuz, near Vienna, served as its motherhouse. Although the facts are straight about why and how it was founded, one legend relates that the Virgin Mary appeared on New Year's Eve to Hermann, the first abbot, and told him to build a monastery at the spot of the blossoming oak tree in the wintry countryside.

During the Middle Ages, the abbey thrived and experienced prosperous times. However, that all came crashing down at the time of the Reformation. But with the Catholic Counter Reformation, the religious and artistic life of the monastery soon recovered.

Despite the ensuing periods of various reforms by emperors and socialist regimes, the abbey maintained its traditional monastic way of life. Today, despite suffering several setbacks, the abbey has been able to preserve its unique religious and cultural heritage.

In this century, Zwettl has continued to contribute to the world and the Church by opening the Monastery Education Center in 1924 and the "Priests' Welfare Society" in 1953. One of the abbey's most recent highlights came in 1988, when it celebrated its 850th anniversary.

ABOUT THE SHRINE

Situated in the beautiful countryside of northern Austria, the Stift Zwettl Abbey provides a peaceful setting and atmosphere for its many visitors throughout the year. Pilgrims can visit the abbey, pray in the church, and take recollective walks in the nearby fields. While there be sure to visit

• Monastery • Abbey church • Abbey gift shop (Klosterladen)

SHRINE INFORMATION

Bildungshaus Stift Zwettl
3910 Zwettl
Tel: (02822) 550-25, (02822) 550-26
Fax: (02822) 550-30
E-mail: bildungshaus@stift-zwettl.co.at or info@stift-zwettl.co.at
Website: www.stift-zwettl.co.at

TOURIST OFFICE

Stift Zwettl Waldviertel
3910 Stift Zwettl
Tel: (02822) 550-0
Fax: (02822) 550-50

Stadtamt Zwettl
Gartenstraße 3
3910 Zwettl
Tel: (02822) 24-14-29

Fremdenverkehrsverband "Waldviertel"
Dreifaltigkeitsplatz 1
3910 Zwettl
Tel: (02822) 22-33

PLACES TO STAY

The abbey operates a guesthouse with accommodations. For more information or to make reservations, contact the shrine office.

HOW TO ARRIVE AT STIFT ZWETTL

Zwettl is about seventy miles northwest of Vienna; Stift Zwettl is about
three miles from Zwettl. (Most transportation services such as trains and
buses connect only with the city of Zwettl—and not the town of Stift Zwettl.
The only way to reach Stift Zwettl is by taxi or local bus from Zwettl.)

ROAD

From Vienna, take 4 north to
Horn, then head east on 38 to
Rastenfeld. From Rastenfeld, con-
tinue on 38 in the direction of
Zwettl, following the signs to Stift
Zwettl via Rudmanns. Another
option from Vienna is to take 3
and 37 to Rastenfeld via Krems.

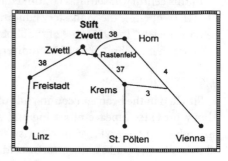

TRAIN

Zwettl is accessible by train. From Vienna (Heiligenstadt and Franz-Josefs
railway stations), there is daily service to Zwettl. Upon arrival at Zwettl, you must
ask the train personnel at the small railway station to call a taxi for you, as there
is no local bus service from the Zwettl train station to Stift Zwettl (two miles).

BUS

From Linz, there is regular bus service to Zwettl. From Zwettl, you can
take either a taxi or the local bus to Stift Zwettl (two miles).

TIPS AND HINTS

Keep in mind that by using the Internet, you can easily communicate
with the abbey for making reservations or acquiring further information
(see shrine information).

DID YOU KNOW?

Austria is often called the "country of monasteries" because of the great
number of abbeys that lie within its borders.

Croatia

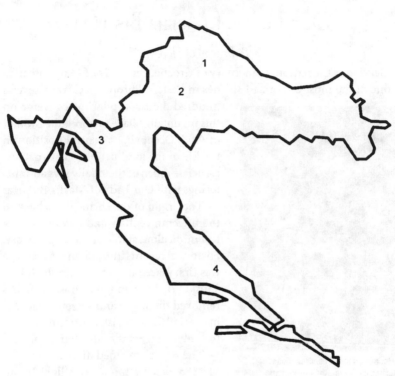

1. Eucharistic Miracle of Ludbreg
2. Our Lady of Marija Bistrica
3. Our Lady of Trsat
4. Our Lady of Sinj

Isle of Krk / *beautiful*

Oct 2000 w/ Rudica, Antun, Tony, + Tina

✠

Our Lady of Marija Bistrica

A Beacon of Hope

Serving as the national sanctuary of Croatia, Our Lady of Marija Bistrica is one of the most celebrated shrines in Eastern Europe. Each year, several

Welcoming several hundred thousand pilgrims each year, the brilliant and spectacular sanctuary of the national shrine of Croatia is home to a fifteenth-century miraculous statue of the Virgin Mary. *(Nacionalno Svetište Majke Božje Bistričke)*

hundred thousand pilgrims converge on this mountain village to honor the Mother of God. Occupying a central position in the life of the local people, the Croatians associate much of their daily joys and sufferings with Our Lady of Marija Bistrica.

The origin of the shrine dates back to the fifteenth century and owes its legacy to a miraculous statue of the Virgin Mary. Historical records indicate that the image was first placed in a chapel on the hill of Vinski Vrh. Later, in 1545, church officials removed the statue and secretly placed it in the wall of the parish church in Bistrica, to protect it from the advancing Turks.

The statue remained hidden there until 1588, when a miraculous light began emanating from the site. After breaking down part of the wall, the parishioners found the all-but-forgotten statue. The image remained on display for public veneration for the next seventy years. In 1650 the parishioners placed it again in the wall, but this time behind the main altar in the church. Thirty-four years later, it was uncovered again and made available for the faithful thereafter.

In the following years, the image became such a part of the country's heritage that in 1715 the Croatian National Parliament built a great altar in the church of Marija Bistrica. In 1731 the Parliament had the church expanded and consecrated to Our Lady of the Snows. Today's present-day shrine was built between 1879 and 1882. As healings had become such an integral part of the sanctuary, twenty-two paintings of these miracles were placed in the church.

In this century, the shrine has witnessed several spectacular moments, such as the golden crowning of the miraculous statue and the proclamation of Our Lady as Queen of the Croats. In 1923 Pope Pius XI bestowed upon the church a great honor in designating it a "Basilica Minor." On August 15, 1971, the International Marian Congress took place at the shrine, and on that occasion the bishops' conference proclaimed Marija Bistrica the Croatian National Pilgrimage Center. In 1974 the first Croatian Marian Congress was held at the sanctuary. In 1984 extraordinary celebrations took place in Marija Bistrica to honor thirteen hundred years of Christianity in Croatia, the third centenary of the finding of the miraculous statue, and the hosting of the National Eucharistic Congress. In September 1998, Pope John Paul II returned here to pray with his people.

In its centuries-long history, Our Lady of Marija Bistrica shrine has continued to serve as a beacon of hope to the faithful. People come from everywhere to present their petitions to the Virgin Mary and to kneel before the black wooden figure of the smiling Madonna with the infant Jesus. Here at the shrine, all human experiences seem to take on a special meaning in light of the Virgin Mary's motherly love and protection.

PRAYER TO OUR LADY OF MARIJA BISTRICA

Immaculate Mother of Jesus, we honor you as God's chosen one, beautiful, beloved, and free from all sin. Keep watch over us, pray that we rise above our sins and failings and come to share the fullness of grace. Be a mother to us in the order of grace by assisting us to live in your obedience, your faith, your hope, and your love. Amen.
Our Lady of Marija Bistrica, pray for us.

ABOUT THE SHRINE

Lying amidst the rolling hills and beautiful countryside of northern Croatia, the shrine welcomes pilgrims from around the world. A small village, Marija Bistrica offers visitors warm hospitality in the usual Croatian tradition. With lots of activities and events at the shrine, especially on September 9, the Feast of Our Lady of Marija Bistrica, this sanctuary is a must for anyone visiting this part of Europe. While there be sure to visit

• Our Lady of Marija Bistrica Shrine • Miraculous statue of the Virgin Mary • Stations of the Cross • Fountain called "Spring of Water and Light" • Eucharistic and Marian processions • Shrine gift shop

SHRINE INFORMATION

Nacionalno Svetište Majke Božje Bistričke
Trg Republike 24
49240 Marija Bistrica
Tel/ Fax: (049) 469-156, (049) 468-350

TOURIST OFFICE

Turistička Zajednica Općine Marija Bistrica
Ured Turističke Marija Bistrica
49240 Marija Bistrica
Tel/ Fax: (049) 468-380

PLACES TO STAY

Hotel Kaj
P.Z. "BUDUĆNOST"
49240 Marija Bistrica
Tel/ Fax: (049) 469-026, (049) 469-006

HOW TO ARRIVE AT MARIJA BISTRICA

Marija Bistrica is about twenty miles north of Zagreb.

ROAD

From Zagreb, head east on Mak-
simirska Street, turning left at the
junction indicating Kašina and
Marija Bistrica. Continue north
to Marija Bistrica via Kašina, following the signs.

TRAIN

Marija Bistrica is not acces-
sible by train. The nearest major railway stations are in Zagreb and Varaždin.
From Zagreb and Varaždin, there is frequent bus service to Marija Bistrica.

BUS

Marija Bistrica is accessible by bus. From Zagreb or Varaždin, there is
frequent bus service to Marija Bistrica.

TIPS AND HINTS

Consider spending some extra time at Marija Bistrica, as it is a place filled
with a number of special activities and celebrations—especially on weekends. In the evening, the town has a delightful atmosphere for visiting the
local restaurants and cafés.

DID YOU KNOW?
One of the shrine's most extraordinary moments occurred during its construction. A fire broke out that destroyed the whole interior of the church—all except for the great altar and the miraculous image of Our Lady.

Our Lady of Sinj

Croatia's Beloved Mother

A picturesque little town dominated by a fortress on a hill, Sinj is home to a beloved shrine housing a miraculous icon of the Blessed Virgin Mary. Serving as the largest sanctuary in southern Croatia, Our Lady of Sinj receives several hundred thousand pilgrims each year. For more than three centuries, the people of this southeastern European country have shown a great filial affection for the beautiful image of the Mother of Mercy that lies inside the shrine.

Serving as one of the country's greatest spiritual centers, Our Lady of Sinj welcomes several hundred thousand pilgrims each year. Situated atop a hill in a beautiful setting, the shrine is home to a miraculous icon of the Virgin Mary dating from the seventeenth century. *(Svetište Gospe Sinjske)*

Painted probably toward the end of the sixteenth century, the portrait has played a large part in the lives of local Catholics. According to tradition, Our Lady of Sinj has saved the citizens from war and invasion many times. The faithful have always related their lives and work, famine and wealth, defeats and victories, health and sickness, to the holy image. This unity between the local Catholic community and the Virgin Mary gives special attraction to the shrine at Sinj.

The shrine dates several centuries back. In 1687, as the Franciscans and the faithful fled from the Turkish Empire to the district of Cetina, they carried with them the holy picture of the Virgin Mary from Rama (Bosnia). Unable to reach their destination, the Franciscans were forced to settle first at Dugopolje, then at the ancient abbey of St. Stephen—just outside of modern-day Split. In time, the people were able to return to Sinj, where the priests ministered to them.

As early as 1699 the Croatian people desired to build a chapel at the foot of the small fortress of Kamicak to house the image of the Virgin Mary. However, their plans were deferred as war broke out and the enemy captured one of their most prominent leaders, Pavao Vuckovic. When he returned unharmed in 1705 from Istanbul, he immediately set into motion plans for the construction of a new church at Sinj. Five years later, with the completion of the church walls, the archbishop of Split celebrated public Mass in front of the picture. In 1714, as a final touch was put on the church, another war broke out. This new combat against the Turks became known as the War of Sinj.

From August 8 to 14 the powerful Turkish army led a merciless assault on the tiny fortress in Sinj. While the handful of soldiers fought bravely, the Franciscans and local people appealed unceasingly in prayer to Our Lady of Sinj. With the holy image of the Virgin placed inside their fortress, the soldiers regrouped and placed their trust in Mary. This conviction filled them with fresh force to resist the enemy that greatly outnumbered them.

On the eve of the Feast of the Assumption, the Turks decided to take the fortress by storm. However, rather than successfully overpowering the Sinj soldiers, the enemies suffered a devastating defeat as they hurriedly had to retreat. And so it happened, on the feast day of the Virgin Mary, that not a single enemy soldier set foot in the half-destroyed fortress. With thankful hearts, the defenders descended to the burnt church, carrying the holy image of Our Lady of Sinj. Here, they prayed in thanksgiving with the people for the miraculous preservation of their town.

In 1716 the popularity of the portrait had become so great that the local bishop crowned the image of the Virgin Mary. Five years later the Franciscans placed the picture in the chapel of the restored church. Devotion to the holy image continued to grow so much that crowds of ten thousand pilgrims were not uncommon on special feast days at the shrine. Many visitors often left behind votive gifts in thanksgiving or for prayers answered. These became quite numerous over time.

Before long, devotion to Our Lady of Sinj had reached the far corners of the country. The Franciscans who posted posters and distributed brochures about the holy image had spread much of the word. They had also created special songs and begun preaching from the pulpit about the Virgin under this title.

The people especially turned to Our Lady of Sinj in difficult moments, including times of plague (1732, 1764, 1784, and 1816), famine, and war. In

1769 a disastrous earthquake damaged Sinj and the church. However, with an unshakable trust in the Virgin's providence, the people helped in its reconstruction. Grateful for the received graces, the devout embellished the holy portrait with a lavish, silver frame and built a grand marble altar.

In 1887 enormous celebrations took place at the shrine in honor of the two hundredth anniversary of the picture's arrival from Rama. Because of brochures, medallions, and pictures of the Virgin of Sinj, the icon's notoriety grew immensely throughout southeastern Europe. After World War I, with the printing of the book *The Virgin of Sinj*, the shrine received its greatest publicity. After World War II the pilgrims visiting the shrine from neighboring countries and other parts of the world became very numerous.

Today, devotion to Our Lady of Sinj flourishes in many countries, especially in communities where a large number of Croatians are gathered. In the United States, certain congregations in Chicago have long been known for their veneration of the Virgin under this title. Other countries such as Argentina, Australia, and New Zealand have large communities of Croatians who celebrate the feast days associated with Our Lady of Sinj.

In Croatia, devotion to Our Lady under this title remains stronger than ever. Each calendar year is filled with an abundant number of celebrations, processions, festivities, and special ceremonies in honor of the Virgin. The pilgrim visiting the Croatian sanctuary today can experience that same filial devotion to Our Lady of Sinj that filled the shrine three centuries ago.

PRAYER TO OUR LADY OF SINJ

O Virgin Mary, Our Lady of Sinj, we dedicate ourselves to your service. We concentrate our minds, hearts, and bodies and promise to work always for the glory of God and the salvation of all people. We pray for the Church throughout the world. Protect the young and help the aged, save sinners and console the dying. You are our hope, Mary, Mother of Croatia and the whole world. Pray to your Son for us so that we may be filled with selfless charity and deep faith. Ask Jesus for those things that we cannot obtain through our own actions, and help us in this, our present necessity. May we always see the Will of the Father in our lives. We ask you this, sweet Spouse of the Holy Spirit, so that we may come to your Son in grace. Amen.

Our Lady of Sinj, pray for us.

ABOUT THE SHRINE

In southern Croatia, the shrine of Our Lady of Sinj serves as one of the country's great spiritual centers. An important spiritual site, the shrine annually receives thousands of pilgrims from throughout Europe and other parts of the world. Inside the sanctuary lies the precious image of the Madonna. With a warm climate, the shrine remains active throughout the year and receives visitors and pilgrims continuously. While there be sure to visit

- Our Lady of Sinj shrine • Portrait of the Madonna (Mother of Mercy)

SHRINE INFORMATION

Svetište Čudotvorne Gospe Sinjske
Šetalište A. Stepinca 1
21230 Sinj
Tel: (021) 821-374
Fax: (021) 824-301

TOURIST OFFICE

Turistička Zajednica Grada Sinja
Turistički ured
Vrlička ulica 50
21230 Sinj
Tel/Fax: (021) 826-352
E-mail: tzg-sinja@st.tel.hr

PLACES TO STAY

Hotel Alkar
21230 Sinj
Tel/Fax: (021) 824-474, (021) 824-505, (021) 824-474, (021) 824-448

Hotel Sv. Mihovil
21240 Trilj
Tel: (021) 831-770

Motel Matanovia Dvori
Glavice
Tel: (021) 824-570

Motel Masle
Brnaze
Tel: (021) 821-477, (021) 822-248

HOW TO ARRIVE AT SINJ

Sinj is about eighteen miles northeast of Split.

ROAD

From Split, take E71 northeast to Sinj via Dicmo and Brnaze.

TRAIN

Sinj is not accessible by train. The nearest major railway station is in Split. From Split, there is regular bus service to Sinj.

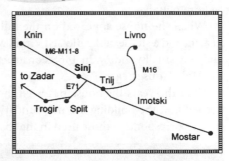

BUS

Sinj is accessible by bus from all major cities in Croatia. From Split, there is regular bus service to Sinj.

TIPS AND HINTS

From nearby Split, you can take the boat across the water to Ancona, Italy, and visit the world-famous shrine of the Holy House of Loreto.

DID YOU KNOW?

So beloved is the shrine in other parts of the world that a Jesuit Croatian missionary erected seven chapels in honor of the Virgin of Sinj in Benghazi, India.

+||+
+||+

Our Lady of Trsat

Queen of the Adriatic

The shrine of Our Lady of Trsat in northern Croatia owes its fame and existence to the Holy House of Loreto. According to legend, Trsat is the site where the angels temporarily moved the Virgin Mary's home from Nazareth, until they finally laid it on a hill in eastern Italy. In subsequent years, the local Croatian bishop commissioned the building of a sanctuary in his diocese to commemorate the landing of the Holy House in Trsat.

The story of the angelic transfer relates that in 1291 angels first transported the house from Nazareth to Croatia. Here it remained for three years until the night of December 12, 1294, when angels moved it again, this time to Italy. During that night shepherds near Recanati, Italy, saw a house being moved across the sea and watched it settle on the land four miles away. The house remained there for a short while, but after bandits proved to be a hindrance, the same "angelic hands miraculously moved it again," this time to Loreto, Italy.

When the house appeared on the hill in Loreto it had only an altar, a hearth, and a statue of the Blessed Virgin Mary. It also had only a single door and one small window. In 1468 construction of a great basilica to enclose the Holy House began.

Over the years the house has been thoroughly examined. Research has proved that the building has no foundation, and the materials used in the house correspond to those used in the "basement" of the home still in place

at the Basilica of the Annunciation in Nazareth. After measuring the foundation where the Holy House had stood in Nazareth, these measurements were found to match perfectly with the House of Loreto. Also, various graffiti cuts of Jewish-Christian origin found in the stones resembled those found at Nazareth. The same ex-

Our Lady of Trsat shrine was built in commemoration of the angelic transfer of the Holy House of Loreto from Jerusalem to Italy in the thirteenth century and today serves as one of Croatia's most famous places of pilgrimage. *(Author)*

perts also determined that the walls of the house were the originals and that the structure had never been rebuilt.

The Holy House of Loreto is one of the most sacred spots in all of Christianity. First, tradition strongly asserts that the Blessed Virgin was conceived and born in this home. Second, it is the place where Mary grew up and received the angel's invitation to be the mother of our Lord. Within these walls Mary spoke the words that echoed throughout heaven and earth, "Here am I, the servant of the Lord; let it be with me according to your word" (Luke 1:38). Third, it is where the child Jesus grew and "increased in wisdom and in years, and in divine and human favor" (Luke 2:52).

The history surrounding the Holy House's arriving and departing from the shores of Croatia is also rather extensive. During the year of its angelic transport to Italy, Count Nicola I (Frankopan) sent an embassy accompanied by the parish priest to Nazareth with the task of checking all points of tradition telling about the transfer of the house. In the early fourteenth century, Nicola placed a chapel on the site of the Holy House's resting spot. In

1367 Pope Urban V donated a miraculous painting of the Virgin Mary to the Croatian Loreto pilgrims. The precious image of the Madonna was soon lovingly invoked as Our Lady of Trsat, Mother of Mercy. In subsequent centuries, royalty and peasantry alike showered gifts upon the holy shrine.

The twentieth century has brought to the sanctuary many celebrations and honors. In 1930 Pope Pius XI bestowed upon the pilgrimage church the designation of "Basilica Minor." In that same year, Our Lady of Trsat became a recognized feast day in the local Church calendar. In 1990 the shrine celebrated its 700th anniversary. A few months later the Croatian Parliament issued a document confirming that the Trsat Sanctuary is a "multiple monument of the Croatian Catholic creed, history, and civilization." In 1993 the City Council of Rijeka declared that the shrine's feast day (May 10) be solemnly celebrated and enlisted in the City Statute. Such is the honor and prestige of Our Lady of Trsat, Queen of the Adriatic.

PRAYER TO OUR LADY OF TRSAT, QUEEN OF THE ADRIATIC

O Glorious Mother, Queen of the Adriatic, I come to you today as your child, as your devoted pilgrim. I kneel before you in your shrine with joy and gratitude for the gift of being here before your lovely image, so revered, so wonderful.

Mary, kind and gentle Mother, I bring you today my heart, filled with love for your divine Son, my spirit, filled with the hope of all Christians, and my mind, filled with desire for a deeper knowledge of my most loving Father.

When I consider those many pilgrims who have prayed here in your shrine, the many before me who have experienced your help and consolation, I feel much peace and joy.

Bless me, dear Mary, and bless and pray for all my dear ones and their intentions. Pray also for the intentions of those around me here in the shrine. Be to all of us, for all our lives, a source of love and consolation. Amen.

Our Lady of Trsat, Queen of the Adriatic, pray for us.

ABOUT THE SHRINE

An international shrine in a number of ways, Our Lady of Trsat serves as an important place of pilgrimage for Croatians, Italians, and thousands of others around the world. As an important link in the story of the Holy House of Loreto, the sanctuary receives several hundred thousand visitors each year. Located near the Adriatic Sea, the shrine is easy to reach from downtown Rijeka—a large city in northern Croatia. A place of constant pilgrimage and celebrations, the sanctuary receives the most visitors on special Marian feast days. While there be sure to visit

- Trsat Madonna shrine • Miraculous image of Our Lady of Trsat
- Votive Gifts Chapel • Gift shop

SHRINE INFORMATION

Franciscan Monastery of Trsat
Frankopan Square 12
51000 Rijeka
Tel: (051) 217-018, (051) 217-018
Fax: (051) 217-347

TOURIST OFFICE

Turistička zajednica Grada Rijeka
Turistički informativni centar
Užarska br. 14
51000 Rijeka
Tel: (051) 335-882, (051) 213-145
Fax: (051) 214-706, (051) 333-909
E-mail: tz-rijeka@ri.tel.hr

PLACES TO STAY

Bonavia
Dolac 4
51000 Rijeka
Tel: (051) 333-744
Fax: (051) 335-969
Four-star hotel with restaurant.

Kontinental
A.K. Miošića 1
51000 Rijeka
Tel: (051) 216-477
Fax: (051) 216-495
Three-star hotel with restaurant.

Neboder
Strossmayerova 1
51000 Rijeka
Tel: (051) 217-355
Fax: (051) 216-592
Two-star hotel.

Jadran
Šetalište XIII divizije 46
51000 Rijeka
Tel: (051) 216-600
Fax: (051) 217-667
Three-star hotel.

Lucija
Kostrenskih boraca 2/2
Kostrena
51000 Rijeka
Tel: (051) 289-004
Fax: (051) 216-760
Three-star hotel.

HOW TO ARRIVE AT RIJEKA

Rijeka is about one hundred miles southwest of Zagreb. To get to Our Lady of Trsat shrine from downtown Rijeka, take bus #1 to *Trsat Madonna*.

ROAD

From Zagreb, head southwest on M12 and E65 to Rijeka. From Trieste, head east on M12 and E61.

TRAIN

Rijeka is accessible by train. From Zagreb and Trieste, there are daily departures to Rijeka.

BUS

Rijeka is accessible by bus. From Zagreb and Trieste, there are daily departures to Rijeka. Note that the bus service to Rijeka is very efficient and oftentimes more convenient than the train service.

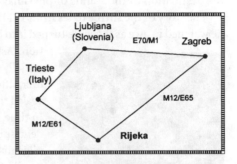

TIPS AND HINTS

To make the best of your pilgrimage trip, you can visit Our Lady of Trsat sanctuary and the Holy House of Loreto on the same journey. For more information about the Loreto shrine in Italy, see the book *Catholic Shrines of Western Europe: A Pilgrim's Travel Guide* by Kevin J. Wright (Liguori Publications, 1997).

DID YOU KNOW?

According to tradition, on his travels to Siria in Croatia, Saint Francis of Assisi suffered a shipwreck and consequently was forced to disembark on the coast of Croatia near Trsat. On that occasion Francis experienced a vision of a transfer of the Virgin's house and saw that the home would later be guarded by his spiritual followers—the Franciscan brothers.

Fr Gosip
5-18-01
Very special showing + I w/able to touch relic
crazy
stuff

Eucharistic Miracle of Ludbreg

Croatia's Prized Possession

Among all the pilgrimage sites in Croatia, Ludbreg ranks as one of the country's most impressive. Sharing a history similar to that of Lanciano and Santarém, the town is home to a renowned eucharistic miracle that has been the destination of thousands of pilgrimages.

The story of the shrine dates from 1411. As a local priest celebrated Mass, he watched in awe as the wine turned into blood at the moment of consecration. Astonished by the event, the priest initially kept the incident a secret. However, after further reflection, he later revealed the miraculous event to the bishop. In time, word about the remarkable incident spread throughout the region, and pilgrims began to journey to Ludbreg to pray before the sacred relic. On April 14, 1513, Pope Leo X issued a "bulla," a written document that confirmed the miraculous appearance of the holy blood of Jesus Christ in the chapel of Ludbreg castle.

Through the years, Ludbreg has remained an important part of the Croatian Christian tradition because of the miraculous event that took place here. In 1739 the Croatian Parliament promised to build a shrine devoted to the eucharistic miracle. However, as it is often the case, it took many years before they fulfilled their pledge. In 1994, with great pomp and ceremony, the new shrine was finally consecrated in honor of the Eucharistic Miracle of Ludbreg.

Ranking as one of Croatia's most impressive pilgrimage destinations, Ludbreg is home to a renowned fifteenth-century eucharistic miracle. Today, the precious sacred relic lies enshrined in a beautiful monstrance in the parish church of the Holy Trinity. *(Turistička Zajednica Grada Ludbreg)*

ABOUT THE SHRINE

There are two places to visit in Ludbreg related to the eucharistic miracle. First, there is the local parish church of the Holy Trinity, which houses the precious relic. Second, there is the new small outdoor chapel built in honor of the miraculous event. Surrounded by the Stations of the Cross, the new shrine serves as a gathering point for pilgrims. Many of the festivities and pilgrimage Masses take place here. One of the most popular days of pilgrimage to Ludbreg occurs on the first Sunday in September. While there be sure to visit

- Parish church of the Holy Trinity • Eucharistic Miracle of Ludbreg • New outdoor chapel built in honor of the eucharistic miracle • Stations of the Cross

[handwritten: orig chapel where miracle happened]

SHRINE INFORMATION

Ludbreg Catholic Church Office
P. Zrinskog 4
42230 Ludbreg
Tel: (042) 811-116

TOURIST OFFICE

Ludbreg Tourist Office
Trg Sv. Trojstva 14
42230 Ludbreg
Tel: (042) 810-690, (042) 661-690
Fax: (042) 810-623, (042) 661-623

[handwritten: The relic is not available to see every day; only on days of religious significance.]

PLACES TO STAY

Hotel Crnkovic
P. Zrinskog 9
42230 Ludbreg
Tel: (042) 810-727, (042) 663-255
Fax: (042) 661-727

Hotel Putnik *[handwritten: → ate lunch here]*
Trg Sv. Trojstva 27
42230 Ludbreg
Tel: (042) 810-477, (042) 661-477, (042) 661-656
Fax: (042) 661-575

HOW TO ARRIVE AT LUDBREG

Ludbreg is about fifty miles north of Zagreb and fifteen miles east of Varaždin.

ROAD

From Varaždin, head east to Ludbreg (fifteen miles).

TRAIN

Ludbreg is accessible by train. From Varaždin and Zagreb, there is regular service to Ludbreg.

BUS

Ludbreg is accessible by bus. From Varaždin, there is hourly bus service to Ludbreg.

TIPS AND HINTS

During the days prior to the major religious celebration of the first Sunday in September, Ludbreg becomes an active town. Almost all the streets and squares fill up with plenty of religious, cultural, and sporting events and an abundance of entertainment, food, and drinks.

DID YOU KNOW?

The Croatian Parliament once called the Eucharistic Miracle of Ludbreg the "greatest treasure of the Croatian Kingdom."

Czech Republic

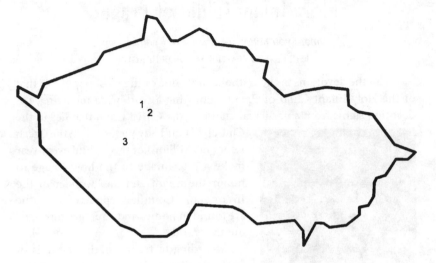

✝✝✝

Holy Infant Child of Prague

"The more you honor me, the more I will bless you."
THE HOLY INFANT CHILD OF PRAGUE

Of all the devotions in the Catholic faith, one of the most popular is that of the Holy Infant Child of Prague. Enjoying a worldwide following, the devotion stems from a particular statue of the Christ Child that lies in the

Church of Our Lady Victorious in the Czech Republic. Millions of the faithful every year make a pilgrimage to the holy image to honor the Infant and the "wonder of the Incarnation." Countless replicas of the statue are found in homes and churches throughout the world.

According to tradition, the statue is of Spanish origin and was first given to a princess by her mother as a wedding gift. Eventually, the image made its way to Prague when the bride, Maria Maxmiliana Manriquez de Lara, married a Czech nobleman in 1556. Later, the daughter of Maria received the statue as a wedding gift also. On being widowed in 1628, she donated the holy image to the Discalced Carmelites of Prague and the Church of Our Lady Victorious. When the novices of the Carmelite monastery received the new statue, they quickly

Every year several million pilgrims visit the world-famous church of Our Lady Victorious in the Czech Republic, which features the renowned statue of the Holy Infant Child of Prague. Object of one of the most famous and beloved devotions, the statue is one of the most recognizable religious images in the Catholic faith. *(Bosí Karmelitáni)*

grew attached to it. One of the novices, Cyril of the Mother of God (1590–1675), eventually became a great apostle of the Infant Child.

When the Thirty Years' War broke out and the monastery's novitiate was moved to Germany in 1630, devotions before the statue were unfortunately discontinued. In the ensuing years, troubles continued as King Gustavus Adolphus of Sweden took possession of the Prague churches, ransacked the Carmelite monastery, and disposed of the holy image. For the next seven years the statue lay forgotten until Cyril, now an ordained priest, returned to Prague in 1637.

With hostile armies still in control of the city and the monastery suffering setbacks, the prior of the community called the monks together to offer prayers. Upon hearing his request, Father Cyril remembered the favors received through the intercession of the Infant and searched the monastery in hopes of finding the lost statue. Eventually, he found it behind the main altar, amidst cobwebs and scattered debris. With great sorrow, Cyril then placed the dusty image in the community's oratory in hopes of renewing the long-forgotten devotions.

One day, while kneeling before the statue in prayer, Father Cyril heard these words: "Have pity on me, and I will have pity on you. Give me my hands, and I will give you peace. The more you honor me, the more I will bless you." At that moment, Father Cyril looked up and noticed for the first time that the Infant was missing his hands. Later, the holy priest begged the prior to fix the statue, but it was to no avail.

Providentially, a wealthy man who had fallen gravely ill came to Prague and offered to restore the statue. However, rather than fixing the old statue, the Carmelite prior took the easy way out and used the old man's funds to buy a new one. The first day of its display, a falling candlestick shattered the new statue. This incident was an indication to Father Cyril that the wishes of the Infant must be fulfilled literally. Subsequently, the original statue became the object of veneration again. However, when additional funds for the necessary repairs proved to be in jeopardy, Father Cyril heard the words: "Place me near the entrance of the sacristy, and you will receive aid." When this was done, a stranger stopped by the church a few days later and donated the amount of money needed to repair the statue.

Years later, when the prior contracted a disease that was epidemic in Prague, the Carmelite friar promised to spread devotion to the Infant if he were cured. Not long after he said these words, the prior began to experience a miraculous recovery. After returning to good health, the prior kept his promise and reinstituted general devotion to the Infant Child.

The seventeenth century proved to be a favorable one for the holy image. In 1641 a magnificent altar to the Blessed Trinity was built to serve as the first home of the miraculous statue. Three years later a new chapel for the Infant was blessed on the feast of the Most Holy Name of Jesus. (This has remained the principal feast day of the miraculous Infant ever since.) In 1648 the archbishop of Prague gave the first-ever ecclesiastical approval of the devotion when he consecrated the chapel and gave permission to priests to say Mass at the chapel altar. Finally, in 1655 the statue was solemnly crowned.

Almost one hundred years later, the statue was moved to a magnificent chapel inside the church of Our Lady Victorious. Over time, a traditional practice of clothing the statue several times each year in the proper liturgical color developed. For example, during the Christmas season the statue is clothed in a dark green robe made of velvet and richly decorated with golden embroidery.

Today, young and old alike continue to cherish and adore the Holy Infant Child of Prague. Serving as one of the most famous and beloved devotions in the world, the statue is one of the most recognizable religious images in the Catholic faith. The holy image's popularity has reached to the far corners of the earth, touching the hearts of all the faithful.

PRAYER TO THE HOLY INFANT CHILD
(by Father Cyril, O.C.D.)

Jesus, you decided for me to become a child, and I'm coming to you full of trust. I believe that your attentive love forestalls all my needs. Even for the intercession of your holy Mother, you can meet my necessities, spiritual as well as material, if I pray according to your holy will. I love you with all my heart, all of my strength, I beg you pardon if my weakness makes me sin. I repeat with the Gospel "Lord, if you want you can heal me." I leave you to decide how and when. I'm ready to accept suffering, if this is your will, but help me not to become hardened to it, but rather to bear fruit. Help me to be a faithful servant and for your sake, holy Child, to love my neighbor as myself. Almighty Child, unceasingly I pray to you to support me in my necessities of the present moment (mention them here). *Grant me the grace to remain in you, to be possessed and to possess you entirely, with your parents, Mary and Joseph, in the eternal praise of your heavenly servants. Amen.*

ABOUT THE SHRINE

The world-famous Infant Child of Prague statue is located in the Church of Our Lady Victorious on Karmelitská Street in downtown Prague. Several million pilgrims from every part of the world visit the shrine each year. The statue itself is situated on the marble altar to the right in a crystal box in the middle of the church. The Discalced Carmelites (both sisters and brothers) are the custodians of the shrine. The sanctuary is open every day of the year, and there is daily Mass. On weekends, in addition to the regular Czech Masses, there is a Spanish Mass (Saturday 7:00 P.M.), English Mass (Sunday noon), and Italian Mass (5:30 P.M./6:30 P.M. summer). While there be sure to visit

- Church of Our Lady Victorious • Infant Child of Prague statue
- Shrine museum • Religious articles shop

SHRINE INFORMATION
Bosí Karmelitáni
Kláster Prazského Jezulátka
Karmelitská 9
11800 Praha
Tel: (02) 57-316-780
Fax: (02) 90-022-435
E-mail: pragjesu@login.cz
Website: http://karmel.at/prag-jesu

TOURIST OFFICE
Prazská informacní sluzba
Old Town Square 22
119-02 Praha

American Hospitality Center
Na mustku 7
119-02 Praha

PLACES TO STAY

Dum sv Krystof
Zabehlicka 72-60
10600 Praha
Tel: (02) 769-371-4
Fax: (02) 769-629
E-mail: Krystof@comp.cz

Pension Unitas
Bartolomejska 9
Praha
Fax: (02) 232-7709

Family Pension
Tel/Fax: (02) 900-20-905
Tel: (02) 524-600
E-mail: zoya@phraha.czcom.cz

HOW TO ARRIVE AT THE CHURCH OF OUR LADY VICTORIOUS
The Church of Our Lady Victorious is located on Karmelitská street in Prague. The nearest metro station is *Malostranská*. Take tram #12 or #22 to arrive at *Malostranská*. The shrine is within short walking distance of the metro station. Prague itself is located near the center of the Czech Republic.

ROAD
Prague is connected by several major highways, including D5/E50 (west), E50/E55 (south), D11/E67 (east), and D8/E55 (north).

TRAIN

Two of the major Prague railway stations are:

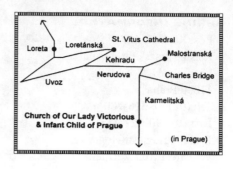

1. Praha hlavni nádraží (also called Wilsonovo nádraží)– Recognized as Prague's main railway station; most international trains arrive and depart from here.

2. Masarykovo nádraží—Many domestic trains arrive and depart from here (as well as from Praha hlavní nádraží).

BUS

Prague has international bus connections to most major European cities. Buses arrive and depart from Florenc.

TIPS AND HINTS

Mass is said in English on Sundays at noon and in Spanish on Saturdays at 7:00 P.M.

The shrine also operates a "souvenirs expedition service" so that people from any part of the world can order religious articles directly from them. They have an extensive listing of Infant Child of Jesus statues, greeting cards, rosaries, candles, medals, necklaces, and so on. Their service is a nonprofit extension of the apostolic mission of the shrine, and all proceeds go to help restore churches in the Czech Republic. To obtain a catalog of their products, contact the shrine at the following address/fax number:

Sanctuary of the Infant Jesus of Prague
Souvenirs Expedition Service
Karmelitská
11800 Praha
Czech Republic
Tel: (02) 530-752
Fax: (02) 900-224-35

DID YOU KNOW?

The Infant's wardrobe consists of more than seventy outfits, donated from all over the world.

✠

St. Vitus Cathedral

Crown of the Kingdom

2000 Gorgeous on hill above our Lady Victorio

Referred to as the "Crown of the Kingdom," St. Vitus Cathedral in Prague is the largest and best-known church in the country. An architectural wonder, the cathedral is also home to the chapel and relics of the first Czech saint—Saint Wenceslas. Through its centuries-long development, the St. Vitus Cathedral has become the tangible symbol of the nation's identity and religious culture.

Founded in the fourteenth century by King Charles IV, the foundation stone for the cathedral was solemnly laid on November 21, 1344. The first master-builder of the splendid Gothic cathedral was the French architect Matthew of Arras. After his death, Peter Parler and his sons continued the work. In 1367 the holiest shrine of the Czech lands was consecrated inside the cathedral—the Chapel of St. Wenceslas. The choir with chapels and the main tower were erected in the fifteenth century, and in 1770 the Baroque roof was constructed. Construction of the west part of the church began in 1873 and was completed in 1929.

Today, the cathedral features some of the country's most prized possessions. Among its most famous belongings are the Czech kings' tombs, the Coronation Jewels, and a number of outstanding artworks. In front of the altar is the tomb with urns for the members of Ferdinand's family. (Ferdinand I was elected King of Bohemia in 1526 and became the founder of the Habsburg dynasty.) From the Chapel of the Holy Rood, the stairs lead to the Royal Crypt of Charles IV, his successors and wives, members of the Premysl dynasty, and other sovereign families.

The number one attraction inside the cathedral, however, is without a doubt the Chapel of St. Wenceslas. A magnificent representation of Czech art of the Gothic Age, the sanctuary features more than 1,300 precious stones and jewels adorning its walls. Extremely rich in painting decorations, the chapel also houses the saint's relics.

Born in 907 near Prague, Saint Wenceslas was the grandson of Borivor, the first Christian duke. Reared in the faith by his grandmother Blessed Ludmilla, the young Wenceslas quickly developed in the virtues of piety, meekness, modesty, and fortitude. With an ardent love for the Christian faith, he took over as ruler of Bohemia at the tender age of eighteen. Experiencing many difficulties serving as a Christian duke, he was later betrayed by his pagan brother Boleslaus, who killed him with a company of assassins in 935. Almost immediately, the people began declaring Wenceslas a saint. Boleslas, terrified of the many miracles occurring at the martyr's tomb, translated the body of the Christian duke three years later to the Church of St. Vitus. The son of Boleslas, who later ascended to the royal throne, became a faithful imitator of his uncle Saint Wenceslas and became one of the greatest princes of his time.

PRAYER IN HONOR OF SAINT WENCESLAS

Lord, you taught your martyr Wenceslas to prefer the kingdom of heaven to all that the earth has to offer. May his prayers free us from our self-seeking and help us to serve you with all our hearts. We ask this through our Lord Jesus Christ, your Son, who lives and reigns with you and the Holy Spirit, one God, forever and ever. Amen.
Saint Wenceslas, pray for us.

ABOUT THE SHRINE

The largest of the churches in Prague, St. Vitus Cathedral is located in the famed Prague Castle. The shrine attracts thousands of visitors every year for its history, beauty, and architecture. Of the many beautiful chapels, the one not to be missed is that of Saint Wenceslas. The shrine is open every day of the year, and guided tours are offered in several different languages. The feast of Saint Wenceslas is celebrated on September 28. While there be sure to visit

- St. Vitus Cathedral • Chapels, including St. Wenceslas Chapel
- Royal Crypt • Choir

SHRINE INFORMATION

There is no shrine information office.

TOURIST OFFICE

See *Holy Infant Child of Prague* for tourist office address.

PLACES TO STAY

See *Holy Infant Child of Prague* for more information about places to stay.

HOW TO ARRIVE AT ST. VITUS CATHEDRAL

St. Vitus Cathedral is located near the center of Prague—it is the most visible monument in the city.

METRO (SUBWAY)

The nearest metro station to St. Vitus Cathedral is *Malostran-ská*. Take tram #12 or #22 to arrive at *Malostranská*. The shrine is within short walking distance of the metro station.

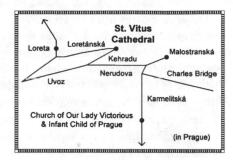

TIPS AND HINTS

With the purchase of a ticket, you can have access not only to the cathedral but also to its tower, the St. Wenceslas Chapel, the catacombs, and a number of other important sites inside the shrine. It is definitely worth buying a ticket.

Alongside the cathedral, on the outside, is an excellent spot for taking photographs of Prague. The view from the ledge offers a great view of the city.

DID YOU KNOW?

Peter Parler, the renowned master mason and architect of St. Vitus Cathedral, also built the famous Charles' Bridge in Prague.

Our Lady of Svatá Hora

A Holy Mountain in the Center of the Czech Republic

Serving as one of the oldest and most sought-after Christian destinations in the Czech Republic, the hilltop sanctuary of Svatá Hora features a renowned miraculous image of the Virgin Mary. Overlooking the ancient mining town of Příbram, the holy shrine is also home to world-class artworks and architecture. So popular has been the place of pilgrimage that the shrine has received the nickname Svatá Hora, or Holy Mountain.

Ranking among the country's greatest sanctuaries, the hilltop shrine of Svatá Hora features a renowned miraculous statue of the Virgin Mary and a spectacular basilica that is filled with magnificent frescoes and paintings. *(Svatá Hora—Proboštský Úřad)*

The shrine dates from seven centuries ago. According to tradition, the first chapel resided at the site in the thirteenth century. The knight Malovec had built it on the mountaintop in honor of the Mother of God. The story relates that he constructed the chapel in 1260 as a sign of thanksgiving to the Virgin Mary for hearing his prayers and delivering him from robbers. By the early part of the fifteenth or sixteenth century, a little sanctuary with a tower and bells had also been erected at the spot.

Shortly after the second chapel's establishment, the small church received its first major prized possession. A statue, believed to have been the artwork of the first archbishop of Prague, was transferred to the mountaintop sanctuary. The sculpture, modeled after the famous Klodzka Madonna, depicted the Virgin Mary and the Child Jesus. Later referred to as the *Svatá Hora Madonna*, the artwork had previously served as an altarpiece at the prelate's private chapel.

Some hermits who lived in nearby huts began to look after the church. In time, the sanctuary began to attract a great number of pilgrims who had heard of the many favors received by those who visited it. The person who helped most of all to spread the statue's fame was the blind Prague beggar Jan Prochazka, who came here on June 10, 1632, to pray for the return of his sight. After three days of fervent prayers, his sight was miraculously restored. As word spread throughout the village and the rest of the country about the extraordinary event, the faithful began flocking to the shrine in droves. Many processions and events began taking place at the sanctuary. One person in particular, Jan Prochazka, made it his mission to take care of the chapel until his death.

In 1647 the Jesuits, in the nearby town of Brenice, took over the administration of the chapel. In one of their first moves, they connected their house to the shrine with sixteen crosses—and later, stone wayside shrines. To cope with the greater number of pilgrims, the Jesuits quickly embarked on a major project. They built a larger shrine and placed the Svatá Hora Chapel inside the main church. The premises were constructed with the notion of the entire sanctuary would be a Marian castle.

With the completion of the church in the latter half of the seventeenth century, the shrine became the most famous one in the country. Not only did the faithful continue to come in larger numbers, but so also did the artists. Prominent painters and sculptors were entrusted with the decoration of the new church.

Svatá Hora then became not just the most famous place of pilgrimage in Bohemia but also a virtual treasure chest of superb artworks. Along with adorning itself with spectacular architecture, the shrine also built up its wealth of several hundred sensational religious statues and pictures. Everyone from goldsmiths to metal workers and stonemasons to carpenters contributed to the extraordinary work.

In 1773 the archdiocese of Prague took over the administration of the sanctuary for the next seventy years. Then, in 1861, the Prague archbishop placed the care of the shrine in the hands of the Congregation of the Most Holy Redeemer (the Redemptorists). The new religious order remained here until April 13, 1950, when they were violently removed during the suppression of monasteries in the country. After forty years, in 1990, they returned to Svatá Hora by decree of the local cardinal.

With its inspiring architecture, the Svatá Hora sanctuary continues to attract visitors from all over the world and has since set the pattern for other places of pilgrimage. In 1905 Pope Pius X conferred on it the title of "Basilica"—symbolizing it as a royal palace of the Queen of Heaven. Today, Svatá Hora is becoming one of the most popular places of pilgrimage in Central Europe.

PRAYER IN HONOR OF SVATÁ HORA VIRGIN MARY

Lord Jesus, you have given us the Virgin Mary, whom we have been venerating for centuries at this place as the Mother, always ready to help us. Grant, we beseech thee, that her motherly intercession will strengthen the faith in our families, increase the number of spiritual vocations, bless our nation, and guide us safely to the eternal joy where you live and reign forever and ever. Amen.

Svatá Hora Virgin Mary, intercede for us!

ABOUT THE SHRINE

Situated at the top of a hill, the holy shrine of Svatá Hora is within short walking distance of the small city of Příbram. Among the sanctuary's greatest attractions are its basilica, the miraculous image of Our Lady, and the numerous frescoes and paintings that fill the walls of the shrine. The main "Coronation" pilgrimage takes place every year on the third Sunday after the Feast of the Descent of the Holy Spirit, and a second large pilgrimage on the Sunday after the Feast of the Assumption (August 15). The Congregation of the Most Holy Redeemer (the Redemptorists) administers the shrine. While there be sure to visit

- Basilica • Miraculous image of Our Lady of Svatá Hora
- Coronation chapel of the Visitation • Silver altar • Gift shops

SHRINE INFORMATION

Proboštský úřad na Svaté Hoře
261 80 Příbram II-591
Tel: (0306) 263-51
Fax: (0306) 247-44

TOURIST OFFICE

There is no tourist office in Svatá Hora.

PLACES TO STAY

Contact the shrine information office for more information about reserving overnight accommodations in the guesthouse.

HOW TO ARRIVE AT PŘÍBAM

Příbram is about thirty miles south of Prague.

ROAD

From Prague, head south on highway 4, then turn and head west on 18 to Příbram.

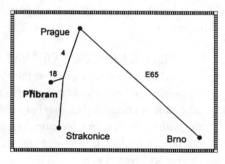

TRAIN

Příbram is not accessible by train. The nearest major railway station is in Prague.

BUS

From Prague, take bus #18 from the Na Knížecí bus station (near Metro Anděl to Příbram. Upon arrival in Příbram, exit at the second bus stop—Jiráskovy Sady. From here, take either the short walk to the shrine (ten minutes) or the local bus service to the bottom of Svatá Hora Hill and walk the final five minutes. The entire bus trip takes about an hour, and there are regular departures from Prague to Příbram.

TIPS AND HINTS

Most people stay overnight in Prague and make a day-trip to Svatá Hora.

In summer on Sundays at 1 P.M., pilgrims can take part in the Stations of the Cross, sung litanies, Holy Benediction, and the farewell ceremony.

Did You Know?

Our Lady of Svatá Hora is not the only pilgrimage site in the Catholic world nicknamed "Holy Mountain." In Ireland, there is also the pilgrimage site Croagh Patrick—better known as "Saint Patrick's Holy Mountain." For more information about Croagh Patrick, see *Catholic Shrines of Western Europe: A Pilgrim's Travel Guide* by Kevin J. Wright (Liguori Publications, 1997).

Germany

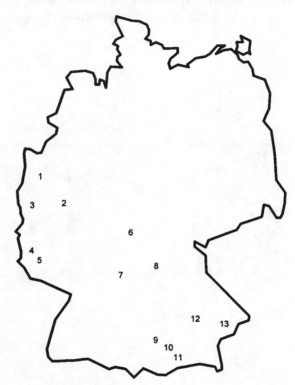

1. Our Lady of Kevelaer
2. Cathedral of Cologne
3. Cathedral of Aachen
4. St. Matthias Abbey
5. Cathedral of Trier
6. Cathedral of Fulda
7. Eucharistic Miracle of Walldürn
8. Our Lady of the Vineyard
9. Ottobeuren Abbey
10. Wies Church
11. Oberammergau & the Passion Play
12. Eucharistic Miracle of Erding
13. Our Lady of Altötting

Cathedral of Aachen

A Royal Spiritual Center of Christendom

Inseparably linked with the reign of Charlemagne, the Cathedral of Aachen offers a spectacular look back into history. Once the royal spiritual center of Christendom, the church served as the site of the crowning of all the Holy Roman Emperors from 936 to 1531.

Built around 800, the Imperial Cathedral became part of Charlemagne's plans to establish a permanent residence at the heart of the huge empire. To further enhance his new place of worship, Charlemagne sent a few of his people to Jerusalem and Constantinople to acquire major relics on his behalf. In 799, according to historical records, the patriarch of Jerusalem donated to him "relics from the place of the Lord's Resurrection." The *Four Great Aachen Relics*, as they are commonly called, consisted of the garment worn by Mary during the night of Christ's birth, the swaddling clothes of the Infant Jesus, the bloodstained loincloth the Lord wore on the cross, and the cloth used at the beheading of John the Baptist. After Charlemagne's death, the following emperors also did their part to embellish the enormous "octagon" church and palace.

Once the royal spiritual center of Christendom, the world-renowned Cathedral of Aachen is a "must-see" for anyone visiting Germany with its many sacred objects, including the Four Great Aachen Relics. *(Author)*

In 1265 a magnificent reliquary containing the mortal remains of Charlemagne was placed in the cathedral. Once this was installed, it became the focal point of the renowned church. Shortly after, the *Four Great Aachen Relics* were also enshrined in an elaborate reliquary.

When Charlemagne had his church consecrated, he dedicated it to the Mother of God. For this reason, the cathedral has always demonstrated a visible outward sign of devotion to the Virgin Mary. One example of this is the statue of Our Lady of Aachen, which has resided in the cathedral since the fourteenth century. The source of numerous miracles, the image has been engulfed in magnificent garments over the years in thanksgiving for prayers answered.

Today, the cathedral remains the destination of many pilgrimages, just as it has for the past millennium and during the years of royal coronations. Among the greatest highlights for visitors is seeing the two "little shrines," or reliquaries, that contain the remains of Charlemagne and the four great relics.

ABOUT THE SHRINE

The world-renowned Cathedral of Aachen is a "must-see" for anyone visiting Germany. Home to many sacred objects, the shrine welcomes millions of pilgrims and visitors each year. The Cathedral Treasury is also a "can't miss" pilgrimage sight. Charlemagne's throne, one of the most venerable monuments in Germany, can be seen, but only with a guide (ask for one at the treasury or call ahead). While there be sure to visit

- Aachen Cathedral • Cathedral Treasury • Shrine of Our Lady
- Shrine of Charlemagne • Charlemagne's Throne

SHRINE INFORMATION

Cathedral of Aachen
Domkapitel: Aachen
Klosterplatz 2
52062 Aachen
To book a tour of the cathedral and treasury for groups:
Tel: (0241) 47-70-91-27
Fax: (0241) 47-70-91-50

TOURIST OFFICE

Aachen Tourist Information
Postfach 2007
52022 Aachen
Tel: (0241) 1-80-29-60, (0241) 1-80-29-61
Fax: (0241) 1-80-29-31
E-mail: actourist@t-online.de
Website: www.aachen.de

PLACES TO STAY

August Pieper Haus
Leonhardstraße 18-20
52064 Aachen
Tel: (0241) 47-99-60
Fax: (0241) 47-99-610

Haus Eich
Eupener Straße 138
52064 Aachen
Tel: (0241) 09-20
Fax: (0241) 509-26-60

Rolleferberg
Rollefbachweg 64
52078 Aachen
Tel: (0241) 52-66-54
Fax: (0241) 52-87-32

Oswald-von-Nell-breuning-Haus
Wiesenstr. 17
52134 Herzogenrath
Tel: (02406) 9-55-80
Fax: (02406) 46-32

HOW TO ARRIVE AT AACHEN

Aachen is about forty miles west of Cologne.

ROAD

Aachen is accessible by the A4 autobahn (east-west) and the A44 autobahn (north-south).

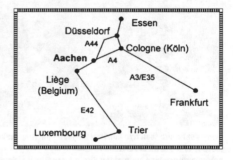

TRAIN

The Aachen Hauptbahnhof train station is accessible from all major cities in Germany and some international cities, including Paris. The trip from Cologne to Aachen takes about forty-five minutes.

BUS

Aachen is accessible by bus; however, the train service is much more convenient and efficient.

TIPS AND HINTS

If you are spending the night in nearby Cologne, Aachen makes for an easy day-trip.

DID YOU KNOW?

Every seven years, the *Four Great Aachen Relics* are publicly displayed for veneration for two full weeks. The next exposition takes place in the year 2000, marking the cathedral's 1,200th-year anniversary.

Darling

✠

love

altötting

Our Lady of Altötting

When Elizabeth heard Mary's greeting, the child leaped in her womb.
And Elizabeth was filled with the Holy Spirit and exclaimed with a loud cry,
"Blessed are you among women, and blessed is the fruit of your womb."
LUKE 1:41-42

Amidst green meadows and snowcapped mountains in the heart of Bavaria lies one of Germany's most celebrated shrines. In a small chapel in the center of Altötting is a little miraculous statue of the Blessed Virgin Mary. Through the years pilgrims from far and near have journeyed to Altötting to kneel before the image and offer their petitions. As the thousands of ex-votos at the shrine prove, Our Lady has been quite active in responding to her children's needs.

Beautiful picture

Every year more than five hundred thousand pilgrims make a sacred journey to the town of Altötting to present their petitions to Jesus before a miraculous state of the Virgin Mary. Thousands of ex-votos decorate the walls of the shrine, testifying to the numerous graces received by visitors over the years. *(Stadt Altötting)*

Two miracles seem to have played a prominent role in the life of Altötting as a place of pilgrimage. The first miracle occurred in 1489 when a three-year-old child drowned in a nearby river. Desperate to revive her child, the grief-stricken mother rushed the dead body to the altar in the nearby chapel as she pleaded for his life. When all seemed hopeless, the child opened his eyes and was restored.

The second miracle involved another young person. Falling under a heavily loaded wagon, a six-year-old child was severely crushed. In desperation, the mother brought the lifeless body to the chapel and also laid it before the statue. Again, through the intercession of Mary, God cured and restored life to the child.

As news of both stories spread, pilgrims began visiting the miraculous statue to present their own personal prayers and petitions to the Virgin Mary.

Over time, thousands of ex-votos were placed on the walls of the church, testifying to the abundant graces received by the pilgrims. Many of these ex-votos are in the form of pictures that indicate the favor received or miracle obtained. For example, some of these include pictures of the sick or crippled who were cured, the blind who received sight, children who were saved from harm, bombs that did not explode, ships that were saved from sinking, and countless other infirmities and events. So numerous have been the miracles and favors received through the intercession of Our Lady of Altötting that the entire outside perimeter of the shrine is today embellished in these physical signs of thanksgiving.

As the pilgrims come to pray, many of them also come to do penance. A tradition that has perpetuated for centuries is the "carrying of the cross." That is, a number of large wooden crosses are provided for the pilgrims who want to do penance by solemnly carrying one of these crosses around the arcade. Some perform the entire act on their knees.

While at the shrine, many visitors also take time to pray at the tomb and cell of Saint Conrad of Parzham. He is the saint most closely linked to the sanctuary of Altötting as he served as a Capuchin lay brother and porter at the nearby St. Anne's Friary.

Inside the shrine's chapel itself, you will find the miraculous image of the Virgin Mary embellished in a spectacular sight of jewels, gold, and silver. The statue itself, made of wood, is about two feet tall. On Our Lady's lap is the Christ Child, whose oversized hand is said to symbolize the large number of graces he wishes to dispense.

Through the years, the shrine has welcomed a number of prominent visitors. In 1782 the sanctuary received Pope Pius VI as a guest, and in 1814 Joseph II, the Emperor of Austria. In November 1980, the shrine was honored to receive Pope John Paul II. Today, the shrine welcomes more than five hundred thousand pilgrims each year—each of whom is a significant visitor.

PRAYER TO OUR LADY OF ALTÖTTING

O sweet Virgin Mary, thank you for bringing me here to your shrine in Altötting, in the land of Bavaria. I come to you today filled with trust amid the everyday challenges I face. To you I come seeking your motherly love and protection. You know the suffering in this world, be our comforter and friend! In illness, need, and affliction, be always by my side. When I am beset by death, do not deny me your intercession but rather present me to your loving Son. O Mother of God, I am yours forever. Amen.

Our Lady of Altötting, pray for us.

About the Shrine

The town of Altötting is located in the prealpine region between Munich and Salzburg in an area surrounded by large forests and abundant water resources. Each year the town welcomes more than five hundred thousand pilgrims to the shrine. The chapel containing the miraculous statue is located in the very center of the city in the Kappellplatz. The shrine is open year-round. While there be sure to visit

- Basilica • Miraculous statue in the Chapel of Mercy • Pilgrim Museum • Panorama of the Crucifixion • Parish church and treasury • Mary film and historical scenes • (Pilgrim) Tourist Information Office

Shrine Information

Stadt Altötting
Wallfahrts-und Verkehrsbüro
Rathaus—Kapellplatz 2a
84503 Altötting
Tel: (08671) 80-68, (08671) 80-69
Fax: (08671) 8-58-58
Website: www.altoetting.de

Tourist Office

Same as Shrine Information, above.

Places to Stay

For a full listing of hotels, guesthouses, and private rooms in Altötting, contact the Shrine Information office—or visit the website.

How to Arrive at Altötting

Altötting is about forty-five miles east of Munich.

Road

From Munich, take highway A94/B12 east to Altötting. Another possibility is to take 304 east to Altenmarkt, then take 299 north to Altötting.

From Passau, take B12 west to Altötting.

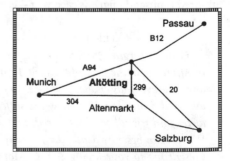

Train

Trains depart regularly for Altötting from nearby cities; the railway station is within walking distance of the shrine (ten to fifteen minutes).

Munich has almost hourly service during the day to Altötting via Mühl-dorf.

BUS

Altötting is accessible by bus from nearby towns; however, the train service is often much more convenient and efficient.

TIPS AND HINTS

Young people might consider staying in the youth hostel: in the St. Magdalene convent—which is run by the shrine.

Along with cultural attractions, the city and its surroundings offer activities for recreation and relaxation, including horseback riding, cycling, and swimming. The Alps and Lake Chiemsee are within an hour's drive. Also, music lovers will find Altötting an excellent place to visit for its classical, folk, and sacred music.

DID YOU KNOW?

Twenty-four Bavarian rulers were so devoted to Our Lady of Altötting that they arranged to have their bodily hearts set in urns in the Holy Chapel after their deaths.

Cathedral of Cologne

Germany's Jewel

Attracting more than three million visitors every year, the Cathedral of Cologne stands as one of the most magnificent and awe-inspiring churches in the world. Overpowering in its sheer massive size, the religious structure boasts a vast array of brilliant stained-glass windows, captivating artworks, and breathtaking architecture. In the center of the mammoth church lies the sanctuary's most prized possession—the shrine of the Three Magi.

The history of the cathedral began during the fourth century. In 313 Bishop Maternus built the first church in the area and celebrated Mass at the site. After a fire destroyed this sanctuary in 850, construction began on a new church, which later became known as the "old cathedral." This new structure, consecrated on September 27, 870, served as one of the most important models for medieval church architecture in Europe.

In 1164 the cathedral received its most treasured relics—the sacred remains of the Three Magi. As the shrine containing the bones of the Three

Kings became one of the most popular pilgrimage destinations in Europe, the church authorities desired that a new structure be built to properly house the holy relics.

On August 15, 1248, the foundation stone of the present-day Gothic cathedral was laid. The design of the new church was based on the style of

architecture used in the French royal cathedrals such as those at Chartres, Reims, and Amiens. In the beginning, work progressed so quickly that Mass could be celebrated for the first time in one of the splendid seven chapels in 1265. Thereafter, construction of the cathedral continued until 1560, then not a hammer or chisel was heard again in the building until 1842. In that year, a few small repairs were made—which eventually led to the completion of the enormous church thirty-eight years later. On October 15, 1880, the last stone was placed in the mammoth religious structure, thus successfully completing the construction of the cathedral, which had taken 632 years.

One of the most magnificent and awe-inspiring churches in the world, the Cathedral of Cologne serves as one of Germany's most famous national and spiritual symbols. Located at the heart of the city, the enormous shrine welcomes more than three million pilgrims and tourists every year. *(Author)*

Today, the shrine remains one of Germany's most famous national and spiritual symbols and serves as one of the country's top tourist and religious destinations. On August 15, 1998, the cathedral marked the 750th anniversary of the laying of its first foundation stone with great celebrations and festivities.

ABOUT THE SHRINE

One of the most famous spiritual edifices in the world, the Cologne Cathedral receives several million pilgrims every year. A vast church, the shrine lies at the heart of the city and can be seen from miles away. Behind the high altar lies one of the most prized possessions of the cathedral, the Shrine of the Three Magi. The cathedral is open every day of the year, and guided tours are offered daily in various languages. While there be sure to visit

• Cologne Cathedral • Shrine of the Three Magi • Cathedral Tower • Cathedral Treasury

SHRINE INFORMATION

DOMFORUM
Domkloster 3
50667 Köln
Tel: (0221) 92-5847-30, (0221) 92-5847-20
Fax: (0221) 92-5847-31

TOURIST OFFICE

Köln Tourismus Office
Unter Fettenhennen 19
50667 Köln
Tel: (0221) 2-21-33-45
Fax: (0221) 2-21-33-20

PLACES TO STAY

Dominikanerkloster Heilig Kreuz
Lindenstr. 45
D-50674 Köln
Tel: (0221) 207-140
Fax: (0221) 207-1455
E-mail: nc-mertenma2@netcologne.de

Priesterseminar
Kardinal-Frings-Str. 12
D-50668 Köln
Tel: (0221) 16003-0
Fax: (0221) 16003-410
The Priesterseminar is the Archdiocese of Cologne's seminary, which
provides very nice guest rooms for men and women.

Collegium Albertinum
Adenauerallee 19
D-53111 Bonn
Tel: (0228) 2674-0
Fax: (0228) 2674-1810
The Collegium Albertinum is a seminary in the Archdiocese of Bonn, which
provides guest rooms for men only.

St. Pantaleons-Kloster
Am Pantaleonsberg 10
50676 Köln
Tel: (0221) 31-47-15

Tagungs—und Gästehaus St. Georg
Rolandstraße 61
50667 Köln
Tel: (0221) 93-70-20-0
Fax: (0221) 93-70-20-44

Kolpinghaus International
St. Apern-Straße 32
50667 Köln
Tel: (0221) 2-09-30

HOW TO ARRIVE AT COLOGNE

Cologne is located in western Germany near the French and Netherlands border.

ROAD

Being a major city, Cologne is easily reached from all parts of Germany. The A3 autobahn runs north and south and the A4 autobahn runs east and west.

TRAIN

The Cologne train station (Hauptbahnhof) is located next to the cathedral in the heart of the city. It is connected by rail with all major cities in Germany.

BUS

Cologne is accessible by bus from many local and international cities.

TIPS AND HINTS

Located in front of the cathedral on the main plaza lies the DOMFORUM. Serving as a visitor's center for the city's churches, the DOMFORUM provides guided tours of the cathedral, arranges visits to the Treasury, and offers a wide range of information about church activities and events in Cologne. (See Shrine Information above for contact information.)

DID YOU KNOW?
In 1880 the Cathedral of Cologne was the world's tallest structure.

Our Lady of the Vineyard

A Wayside Shrine Finds Its Place in the World

Among the many larger Catholic shrines around the world, there also exist many smaller ones. Such is Our Lady of the Vineyard shrine in central Germany. Here, the faithful come to pray before a miraculous image of the Virgin Mary in the small but spectacular parish church.

The sanctuary originally began as a shrine at the side of the road, located about one mile from the small town of Dettelbach. In 1484 a local vine-grower had set up the tiny shrine by placing inside it a statue depicting the Sorrowful Mother holding the lifeless body of the crucified Christ. As street-side shrines were common throughout Europe, there was nothing unusual about the farmer's particular

Once a small wayside shrine, Our Lady of the Vineyard has since developed into a major place of pilgrimage after a young man received a miraculous healing in connection with the fifteenth-century sanctuary. *(Franziskanerkloster)*

sanctuary. His only intention in constructing it was to provide a small place of worship for those traveling past his vineyard.

Twenty years later, however, the small shrine attracted quite a bit of special attention after a local confrontation. During a fight, one of the local vinedressers had been severely beaten. The man, Nicholas Lemmerer, remained in a coma for almost a year. As he neared the point of death, he heard a voice telling him that he could recapture his health if he would promise to visit the roadside shrine located where he formerly worked and if he would offer a blessed candle. Nicholas promised to do as the voice suggested. From that moment forward, he experienced a miraculous recovery.

When he was almost completely healed, Nicholas visited the wayside sanctuary and left behind a blessed candle, as promised. When word reached the villagers about his miraculous recovery, they began visiting the small shrine in droves. So popular had the little sanctuary become that the town's magistrate commissioned the building of a chapel to house the holy image.

Despite the local official's good intentions, the chapel quickly proved to be too small for the vast number of pilgrims. Consequently, the town embarked on another project, building a larger chapel in 1520. Eventually, the local bishop placed the new church under his care and hired the most talented artisans of the area to embellish the shrine. Then he assigned the Franciscan Friars Minor as custodians of the shrine.

One of the most extraordinary stories about the shrine has been the incredible survival of the miraculous statue. During the Thirty Years' War the Swedish soldiers ransacked the church and stole everything of value from the treasury—except the image. When Napoleon's troops plundered the shrine, they also took everything of importance—except the precious image.

Today, the miraculous statue remains enshrined in a spectacular marble canopy in the center of the church. Carved of wood and adorned with an array of colors, the pietà image is about eighteen inches high. Three altars surround the sanctuary containing the image–all designed so as to allow the faithful to kneel in a complete circle around it. Each year, several thousand pilgrims still visit this small, but prominent, shrine to present their needs to Our Lady of Sorrows.

PRAYER TO OUR LADY OF SORROWS

My Blessed Mother, before you could become the Consoler of the Afflicted, you first had to know the affliction. I pause with you now and meditate on that great suffering in your life, the death and burial of your most beloved Son. O, how humble I am, dear Mary, when I see before me your Son in the tomb. He gave his life, the most perfect act of love, for all humankind and has gained for me freedom from sin. Help me to be ever aware of this scene, Mary, to be aware of the love Jesus has for me, a love so strong and so perfect. Remind me always that any suffering in my life is passing, just as the suffering you experienced passed in the joy of the Resurrection. Holy Mary, Mother of Sorrow, I mourn with you, knowing the sure and certain joy of your Son and his gift to all of us in everlasting life. Through this act of his, you have become our Mother of Consolation. Amen.

ABOUT THE SHRINE

A popular place of local pilgrimage in central Germany, the church of Maria im Sand lies just west of Würzburg. The main pilgrimage season occurs between May and mid October. The small shrine is open throughout the year, and Mass is celebrated daily. Guided tours are available on request. For bookings or group visits, contact the Franciscans at the shrine in advance (see Shrine Information). While there be sure to visit

- Maria im Sand Church • Miraculous statue of the Virgin
- Miraculous image of the Origin of the Pilgrimage • Altar of Grace • Pulpit, Tree of Jesse

SHRINE INFORMATION

Franziskanerkloster
"Maria im Sand"
Wallfahrtsweg 18
97337 Dettelbach
Monastery Tel: (09324) 9171-0, (09324) 9171-11
Pilgrimage Pastoral Care Tel: (09324) 91-72-31, 91-72-12
Fax: (09324) 9171-20

TOURIST OFFICE

Kultur-und Verkehrsamt
Im Historischen Rathaus
Rathausplatz 1
97337 Dettelbach
Tel: (09324) 35.60
Fax: (09324) 49.81

PLACES TO STAY

Franziskaner Hotel
Wallfahrtsweg 14
97337 Dettelbach
Tel: (09324) 41-91
Fax: (09324) 45-37
E-mail:AkzentHotel.Dettelbach@t-online.de
Website: www.akzent.de/hotels/ak136.htm
Franziskaner Hotel is situated next to the shrine.

Hotel Am Bach
Eichgasse 5
97337 Dettelbach
Tel: (09324) 14-80
Fax: (09324) 47-19
E-mail: AkzentHotel.Dettelbach@t-online.de
Website: www.akzent.de/hotels/ak135.htm

HOW TO ARRIVE AT DETTELBACH

Dettelbach is about ten miles east of Würzburg.

ROAD

From Würzburg, take 22 east
to Dettelbach.

TRAIN

As the nearest railway stop is
located about 1.5 miles outside of
Dettelbach in the countryside,
taking the bus instead of the train
is strongly recommended. (There

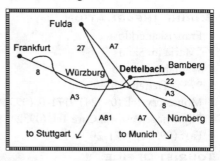

is sporadic bus service from the Dettelbach train stop and no available taxi
service.)

BUS

Dettelbach is accessible by bus. From Würzburg, take bus #8102 to Dettelbach (exit the bus at Weingartenstrasse). From the Kitzingen railway station,
take bus #8110 to Dettelbach (exit the bus at Weingartenstrasse).

TIPS AND HINTS

The shrine can easily be visited in one short afternoon. Most pilgrims
come just to spend a few moments in prayer before the miraculous image of
Our Lady.

Pilgrims visit the shrine daily, but their number is especially large on September 15, the Feast of Our Lady of Sorrows.

DID YOU KNOW?

Among the most common shrines in the world are those honoring Our
Lady of Sorrows, or Our Lady of the Seven Sorrows. Few other titles of the
Virgin Mary are used as often as these in the dedication of particular sanctu-
aries and places of pilgrimage.

Eucharistic Miracle of Erding

A Miracle in Honor of the Blessed Sacrament

Eucharistic miracle sites have long served as places of pilgrimage in the Catholic faith. Some of the more famous sanctuaries where they have occurred include Lanciano in Italy, Santarém in Portugal, and Walldürn in Germany. Wherever and whenever these miracles occur, one thing is always certain— the faithful become much more fervent in their devotion to the true presence of Jesus Christ in the Blessed Sacrament. Such is the case with the Eucharistic Miracle of Erding.

As two farmers were walking to church on the outskirts of the town called Erding, one of them asked the other why he was so fortunate in his life. Everything always seemed to "fall into place" for him and his family. Speaking of his own predicament, the first farmer began to explain his problems: "If the harvest is good, the grapes are bad. If the chestnuts do well, the olives are rotten. The cows give milk; but the sheep have little wool, and they

The chapel inside the Church of the Holy Blood is said to rest on the site where a eucharistic miracle occurred several centuries ago in front of the village people, the parish priest, and even the bishop himself. *(Author)*

don't bear lambs. I have never known good fortune; I have not even seen it from a distance. They say fortune has long hair like a horse. I have never been able to catch it."

He then continued, "I'm experiencing extreme poverty. I'm ashamed to tell you about it. There are times when, in order to save my wife and children from hunger, I do without food for myself. I'm not afraid of hard work. I've known what it's like to work through the day and into the night. And yet, I can't seem to get ahead."

Turning to his companion, the farmer concluded, "Tell me, my friend, what is the secret of your success? You seem to do well. Your life seems to be in good order. Do you have a secret charm? If so, will you share your secret with me, so that I may have some success in my life?"

The second farmer then replied that although it is not a secret or "lucky" charm, he does keep the Blessed Sacrament in a little chapel in his house. He explained that he attributes all his good fortunes, and the lesser ones, to Jesus in the holy Eucharist.

Unfortunately, the farmer with "bad luck" decided he must do the same thing by stealing a consecrated host from the church and placing it in his home. Hence, on Holy Thursday of that year, the farmer received Communion, but before swallowing it, he placed it on a clean linen cloth and left the church. While walking back home, the farmer began to feel a sense of remorse over the sacrilege he had committed. Just as he decided to turn back around and return to the church, the host slipped out of the cloth and began to float in the air. Then it fell to the earth and disappeared. Frightened by the incident, he rushed back to the church and, after Mass, confessed his horrible deed to the priest. Immediately, they set out for the site with a group of parishioners. Upon nearing the place, the priest could see the host on the ground from a distance—it was radiant and shining.

When the priest attempted to pick up the host, it became suspended in the air, only to fall to the earth and disappear as well. Following this incident, they summoned the local bishop. When he arrived, he witnessed the same scenario that the farmer and priest had experienced. But this time, when the host vanished into the ground, it never reappeared.

In honor of the miraculous event, the prelate then ordered the building of a special chapel at the site. As news spread of the incident, many of the faithful began making pilgrimages to the church. In response, the bishop bestowed special graces on those who would come to venerate the Blessed Sacrament in the church. Today, the promise still holds true.

EUCHARISTIC PRAYER

Most Sacred Heart of Jesus, truly present in the holy Eucharist, I consecrate my body and soul to be entirely one with your heart, being sacrificed at every instant, on the altars of the world, giving praise to the Father and pleading for the coming of his kingdom. Please receive this humble offering of myself. Use me as you will for the glory of the Father and the salvation of souls. Most Holy Mother of God, never let me be separated from your divine Son. Please defend and protect me as your special child. Amen.

ABOUT THE SHRINE

The Eucharistic Miracle of Erding lies in the beautiful pilgrimage church of the Holy Blood (Wallfahrtskirche Heiligenblut), which is located on Heiligenblut Street (right off of Münchener Street near the train station). The shrine is open all year. Other churches to visit in Erding include St. John's Parish and St. Paul's Church. While there be sure to visit

- Heiligenblut Church • Eucharistic miracle • Relic of the Holy Cross
- St. John's Parish • St. Paul's Church

SHRINE INFORMATION

Wallfahrtskirche "Heiligblut"
Heiligblut 4
D-85435 Erding
Tel: (08122) 67-22
Fax: (08122) 92-969

TOURIST OFFICE

The nearest tourist office is in nearby Munich:

München Tourist Office
Sendlinger Straße 1
80331 München
Tel: (089) 23-33-02-46
Fax: (089) 23-33-02-47

PLACES TO STAY

As Erding has few places to stay, most pilgrims spend the night in nearby Munich (München) or its surrounding areas. The following are a few of the Catholic guesthouses:

Kolping-Erwachsenenbildungswerk
Adolf-Kolping-Str. 1
80336 München
Tel: (085) 551-581
Accommodations possible for both individuals and groups.

St. Pius-Kolleg
Der Steyler Missionare
Dauthendeystr. 25
81377 München
Tel: (089) 71-020
Accommodations usually reserved for groups only.

Vinzenz-Pallotti-Haus
Pallottinerstr. 2
Pf. 1741
85317 Freising
Tel: (08161) 96-890
Accommodations usually reserved for groups only. Freising is located just
north of Munich (München) and a little bit east of Erding.

HOW TO ARRIVE AT ERDING

Erding is about twenty miles northeast of Munich.

ROAD

From Munich, take 388 northeast to Erding.

TRAIN

Erding is accessible by train.
From Munich, there are frequent
departures to Erding.

BUS

There is local bus service to
Erding; however, it is much more convenient and efficient to take the train.

HOW TO ARRIVE AT HEILIGENBLUT CHURCH

Upon arriving at the Erding train station, walk to the cross-street Parkstrasse and turn left. Follow Parkstrasse until it dead-ends and you must
turn right or left; at this small intersection, turn right until you reach the
restaurant La Padella. From here, turn right and walk about fifty yards to the
yellow-covered church of Heiligenblut. It is about a ten- or fifteen-minute
walk to the church from the train station.

For a shortcut to the church, follow this route:

Upon arriving at the Erding train station, walk to the cross-street Parkstrasse and turn left. Almost immediately you will see several paths to your
right in a forested area. Turn right into the forest and take the path on your
farthest left, and follow this to the yellow-covered church of Heiligenblut. It
is about a five-minute walk to the church from the train station.

TIPS AND HINTS

The pilgrimage church of Heiligenblut can easily be visited on a day-trip
from nearby Munich or Altötting (see *Our Lady of Altötting*).

When visiting the lower chapel of the shrine, you can turn the lights on for better viewing. The light switch is located near the bottom of the steps to your right.

DID YOU KNOW?

There are about sixty-seven Church-approved eucharistic miracles in the world.

Cathedral of Fulda

A Meeting Place for the Bishops

Drawing visitors from around the world, the renowned Cathedral of Fulda continues to serve as the destination of thousands of pilgrimages. What specifically attracts many of the faithful here is the tomb of Saint Boniface, which features the holy relics of this great "Apostle of the Germans."

Along with housing the remains of this beloved saint, the cathedral is next best known for being the site where the bishops gather annually for their meetings. Recognized also for being one of the most remarkable Baroque buildings in Germany, the church draws many art and architecture enthusiasts. For those inclined to musical performances, the cathedral holds organ concerts every Saturday evening during the summer months.

Born in 680, Saint Boniface grew up in what is modern-day England, where at the age of five he made the decision to become a monk. Exceptionally gifted intellectually, by the time of his ordination at age thirty he had become a distinguished scholar. After performing missionary work in the territory of Frisia (including the present-day Netherlands), he then left in 722 for the German provinces. Here, he firmly planted the Christian faith as he made a number of converts and organized a vast network of dioceses and religious orders. In Fulda he established one of the largest abbeys in the West.

During his missionary activities, Boniface had received a number of ecclesiastical titles including bishop of Mainz, primate of Germany, and apostolic delegate in Germany and Gaul. In 754 the saint died a martyr's death as he and his missionaries were attacked by a hostile band of locals in the territory of Frisia.

After his death, the relics of Saint Boniface were brought back to Fulda, where they were enshrined in the cathedral. Immediately, a number of miracles began to be reported at his tomb, making the site a major place of pilgrimage during the Middle Ages. Today, Saint Boniface is recognized as one of the Church's greatest missionaries.

PRAYER TO SAINT BONIFACE

Lord, your martyr Boniface spread the faith by his teaching and witnessed to it with his blood. By the help of his prayers, keep us loyal to our faith, and give us the courage to profess it in our lives. Grant this through our Lord Jesus Christ, who lives and reigns with you and the Holy Spirit, forever and ever. Amen.

Saint Boniface, pray for us.

ABOUT THE SHRINE

Serving as the landmark of Fulda, the cathedral is located right at the center of the city. Open every day of the year, the shrine receives thousands of pilgrims. The feast of Saint Boniface is celebrated on June 5. While in Fulda, you should be sure to visit two other worthy pilgrimage sites: St. Peter's Church (Bus line 3 to Petersberg) and the Benedictine Nun's Abbey of St. Mary. While in Fulda be sure to visit

• Cathedral of Fulda • St. Peter's Church • St. Mary's Abbey

SHRINE INFORMATION

Kath. Dompfarramt Fulda
Hinterburg 2
36037 Fulda
Tel: (0661) 73-370
Fax: (0661) 79-585

TOURIST OFFICE

Städtisches Verkehrsbüro Fulda
Stadtschloß, Schloßstraß 1
36037 Fulda
Tel: (0661) 102-345, (0661) 102-346
Fax: (0661) 102-775
E-mail: verkehrsbuero@fulda.de

PLACES TO STAY

In Fulda are two Catholic guesthouses that can be reached by the same address, phone number, and fax number:

Haus St. Lioba	Haus St. Benedikt
Steubenallee 4	Steubenallee 4
36041 Fulda	36041 Fulda
Tel: (0661) 97-09-970	Tel: (0661) 97-09-970
Fax: (0661) 97-09-972	Fax: (0661) 97-09-972

HOW TO ARRIVE AT FULDA

Fulda is about seventy miles northeast of Frankfurt.

ROAD

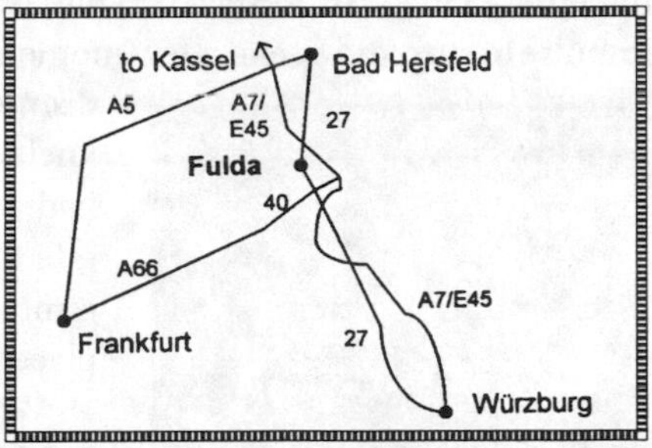

From Frankfurt, head northeast on A66 and 40, then follow the signs to Fulda. From Würzburg, head north on A7; from Kassel, head south on A7.

TRAIN

Fulda is accessible by train. There are several daily departures from the Frankfurt main train station to Fulda, as well as from Kassel.

[Map showing roads: to Kassel, Bad Hersfeld, A5, A7/E45, 27, Fulda, 40, A66, A7/E45, Frankfurt, 27, Würzburg]

BUS

Fulda is accessible by bus from several major cities, including Frankfurt.

TIPS AND HINTS

The burial place of Saint Lioba is at St. Peter's Church in Fulda.

Most tourists enjoy spending a full day in Fulda, visiting the city's splendid restaurants, museums, churches, and secular monuments.

DID YOU KNOW?

Saint Boniface was born with the name of Winfred, but after a visit to the Vatican, the pope changed his name to Boniface, which means "he who does good."

Our Lady of Kevelaer

"At this place you shall build me a chapel."
OUR LADY OF KEVELAER

Recognized as one of the preeminent Marian shrines in Central Europe, Our Lady of Kevelaer welcomes more than half a million pilgrims each year. The faithful come here from all parts of the world to kneel before a miraculous image of the Virgin Mary in the village square.

The story of the shrine began in the seventeenth century. During this time, the small town of Kevelaer had been completely wiped out by fire and desecrated by the Thirty Years' War. When the village had become a virtual wasteland, an event occurred in 1641 that changed the life of Kevelaer forever.

During Christmas season of that year a wandering peddler named Hendrick Busman, who lived in the nearby town of Geldern, was passing by the empty village of Kevelaer. While traveling through, he felt an interior impulse to stop and spend a few moments at the nearby wayside cross. After

dismounting from his horse, the merchant knelt to pray for the souls of those who had perished in the fire and to ask for a safe trip home. Then, just as he began to remount, he heard a voice saying, "At this place you shall build me a chapel."

While he felt that the voice was real, he quickly dismissed it and continued on his journey. A week later, as the same peddler passed through the village again, he felt the same interior pull to stop at the wayside cross. Again, while in prayer he distinctly heard the words of a heavenly voice directing him to build a chapel at the spot.

After hearing the voice for a third time on another day, the merchant knew he had to accept the mission. Although an interior joy swelled up within him, he also felt a great sadness as he knew he had limited funds.

Dating from the seventeenth century, the shrine of Our Lady of Kevelaer ranks among Germany's most famous places of pilgrimage, with its renowned image of the Virgin Mary and its reputation for being the site of many miracles and cures. (Wallfahrtsleitung)

As time passed, another significant event took place. The peddler's wife awoke one night to find a very bright light shining into their bedroom. In the midst of it appeared a little shrine, with a very small picture of the Virgin Mary. Immediately, she recognized the image as that of Our Lady Comforter of the Afflicted. It was the same picture that had been enshrined for many years at the famous Luxembourg sanctuary. In the apparition she also saw a couple of soldiers who were carrying with them two paper pictures of Our Lady of Luxembourg.

When the peddler heard of his wife's vision, he encouraged her to discover the whereabouts of the military men and the image. Eventually, she tracked them down and retrieved one of the pictures from an army lieutenant who was serving time in the nearby Kempen prison. When she returned home, the merchant made plans to construct the shrine in accordance with his wife's vision.

During this time, word had spread about both the peddler and his wife. After returning to his family's cottage with the picture, the merchant found his place besieged by an endless number of pilgrims who came to pray before the holy image.

Unable to accommodate all the daily requests, the merchant asked the local Capuchin Fathers to temporarily enshrine the picture in their chapel. So great were the pilgrim crowds at the Capuchin's sanctuary that their facilities also became quickly outgrown. Hence, they encouraged Hendrick to quickly finish construction on his red-brick shrine and place the image in there.

On June 1, 1641, the holy portrait was finally brought in solemn procession to the new sanctuary. As the local parish priest soon found his duties overwhelmed by the swelling number of pilgrims, the bishop assigned three more priests to assist him.

Immediately, healings became almost everyday occurrences at the shrine. During the first five years so many miracles were reported that the vicar general of the diocese instigated an investigation into the events. After an exhaustive inquiry, many of the cures were declared miraculous.

Eventually, the importance of the shrine required a more impressive structure. In 1654 the local church officials consecrated the present-day sanctuary, which encloses the original brick-pillar shrine and the miraculous picture. In the following years the sanctuary continued to grow immensely in popularity.

During the French Revolution, all pilgrimages to the shrine were suppressed. At this time, to protect the precious image from ruthless destruction, the priests placed the picture in the tower wall of the parish church. Here it remained until 1802, when pilgrimages to the shrine resumed. Ninety years later, the miraculous image was honored with a papal coronation during celebrations of the shrine's 250th anniversary.

Today, devotion to Our Lady of Kevelaer remains stronger than ever. Pilgrims can be seen throughout the year praying before the holy image, beseeching the Mother of God for her comfort and protection. Aside from Our Lady of Altötting, no other Marian shrine in Germany receives more visitors annually.

PRAYER TO OUR LADY OF KEVELAER

Mary, Mother of Jesus, I pray that I may receive a heart like yours, so beautiful, so pure, and without blemish—a heart filled with love and humility. Then I can love your Son as you love him, and I can serve him by my works of charity and mercy. Mary, I pray that I may become a messenger of the love and peace of God. Amen.

Our Lady of Kevelaer, pray for us.

ABOUT THE SHRINE

A dynamic place of pilgrimage, the shrine of Our Lady of Kevelaer has many celebrations and processions and a full program of daily activities throughout the year. Among the most prominent chapels to visit are the Chapel of Mercy (with the miraculous *Comforter of the Afflicted* picture) and the Candle Chapel. Our Lady of Kevelaer makes for the ideal Marian pilgrimage, whether you travel individually or in a group, and her feast is celebrated on June 1. While there be sure to visit

- Basilica • Chapel of Mercy • *Comforter of the Afflicted* picture
- Candle Chapel • Fountain Courtyard • Chapel of Baptism and Confession • Chapel of the Sacrament • Pax-Christi Chapel
- Consortium Sanctorum • St. Anthony's Church • Communities of Nuns in Kevelaer • Stations of the Cross • Priests' House and Pilgrimage Organization

SHRINE INFORMATION

Priesterhaus
Kapellenplatz 35
D-47623 Kevelaer
Tel: (02832) 93-380
Fax: (02832) 70-726
E-mail: WallfahrtsleitungKevelaer@t-online.de
Website: www.kevelaer.de

TOURIST OFFICE

Kevelaer Tourist Office
Verkehrsverein/Verkehrsbüro
Peter-Plümpe-Platz 12
47623 Kevelaer
Tel: (02832) 122-151, (02832) 122-152
Fax: (02832) 43-87

PLACES TO STAY

Priesterhaus
Kapellenplatz 35
D-47623 Kevelaer
Tel: (02832) 93-380
Fax: (02832) 70-726
E-mail:WallfahrtsleitungKevelaer@t-online.de
Website: www.kevelaer.de or www.kevelaer.de/english.htm
Note: The Priesterhaus provides housing for pilgrimage groups only.
Individual travelers should contact the tourist office for more information
about accommodations.

HOW TO ARRIVE AT KEVELAER

Kevelaer is about sixty-five miles northwest of Cologne.

ROAD

From Cologne, head north-
west on A57, exiting for Geldern
(Route 58) and continuing on to
Kevelaer via Route 9.

From Krefeld, take Route 9 to
Kevelaer.

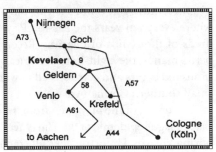

TRAIN

Kevelaer is accessible by train.
From Cologne, there are frequent departures to Kevelaer, with a change in
Krefeld.

BUS

Kevelaer is not accessible by bus.

DIRECTIONS TO OUR LADY OF KEVELAER SHRINE

To arrive at Our Lady of Kevelaer shrine from the town's train station,
walk along the main street in front of the railway station (Antoniusstr.) until
it dead-ends. From here, turn right onto Hauptstraße and you will see the
church. It is about a ten-minute walk. (On the main street in front of the
train station, there is a large map of the town, which is very helpful.)

TIPS AND HINTS

Our Lady of Kevelaer shrine can easily be visited on a day-trip from nearby
Cologne or Aachen.

To request guided tours or to obtain group accommodations at the shrine's guesthouse, be sure to contact the priest's house.

When visiting the shrine's website at www.kevelaer.de, click on the British flag for information in English. Or type in the address www.kevelaer.de/english.htm

DID YOU KNOW?

Mother Teresa visited Our Lady of Kevelaer shrine on September 19, 1987.

Oberammergau and the Passion Play

Home of the World-Famous Passion Play

Oberammergau is not a shrine but a world-famous place of pilgrimage, where every ten years the Passion Play of Christ is performed before hundreds of thousands of pilgrims. Recognized as the world's oldest running performance, the eight-hour theatrical production involves more than two thousand actors and actresses, all of whom are from the community of this small southern German village.

The origin of the play dates from the early seventeenth century, when the Black Plague epidemic of the Thirty Year's War was raging through the neighboring villages. Unfortunately, Oberammergau became a victim of the terrible illness when in 1632 an outside servant brought the disease into town. The result was that many of the village inhabitants died that year after contracting the plague.

In response, on October 27, 1633, the leaders of the community gathered together and made a vow to depict the tragedy of the Passion Play every decade thereafter. Their decision was based on several factors—one, they felt that the play would help them cope with the suffering they were enduring, and two, they hoped that by performing such a play, heaven would send blessings and protection upon their village.

Sticking to their promise, the townspeople of Oberammergau performed their first Passion Play between Eastern and Pentecost in the year 1634, on a cemetery plot next to their parish church. Amazingly, after this performance there were no more reported casualties due to the plague. And what's possibly even more remarkable, the people of Oberammergau have kept their promise of performing the play through the centuries, right up until today. (They did, however, eventually change the date of performance to the beginning of each decade.)

Lasting about eight hours, the play is divided into episodes, each introduced by an Old Testament tableau connecting predictions of the great prophets to incidents of Christ's suffering. The modern theater and open-air stage at the edge of town hold about 4,700 spectators. Through the centuries, the community has continued to enrich the play's sensitive music and spectacular costume and theatrical decorations.

Today, the tradition and spirit of the Passion Play are more alive than ever. As always, the excitement and anticipation of the next performance builds around the world as each new decade approaches. However, no matter how large the performance becomes, or how many spectators visit Oberammergau, the Passion Play remains for the people of this village a genuine and humble act of homage before God as a sign of their thankfulness.

ABOUT THE SHRINE

The great attraction in Oberammergau is, of course, the Passion Play, which takes place at the beginning of each decade (1990, 2000, 2010, etc.). However, there is much to see and do here if you visit during the "off season." For one, pilgrims and tourists can view the Passionspielhaus, the modern theater at the edge of town where the Passion Play is performed. Along with this, visitors can get a close-up look at the local artists—wood-carvers, painters, sculptors, potters—who are busy at work preparing for the next performance. These artists can be seen at the Pilatushaus on Ludwigthomstrasse street. You can also pay a visit to the Heimatmuseum (on Dorfstrasse street), which features a distinguished collection of Christmas nativity sets.

SHRINE INFORMATION

Contact the tourist office for more information about the Passion Play.

TOURIST OFFICE

Verkehrs-und Reisebüro
Gemeinde Oberammergau
Eugen-Papst-Strasse 9a
82487 Oberammergau
Tel: (08822) 92-31-0, (08822) 92-31-48
Fax: (08822) 92-31-90
E-mail: passion2000@oberammergau.de
Website: www.oberammergau.de

PLACES TO STAY

Contact the tourist office for a full listing of places to stay in Oberammergau.

HOW TO ARRIVE AT OBERAMMERGAU

Oberammergau is about fifty miles from Munich.

ROAD

From Munich (München), take A95 south (in the direction of Germisch-Partenkirchen), then turn right at Oberau onto 23 (in the direction of Augsburg) and continue northwest to Oberammergau.

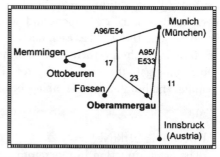

From Augsburg, take 17 (in the direction of Füssen/Germisch-Partenkirchen) south to Peiting, then take 23 southeast (in the direction of Garmisch-Partenkirchen) to Oberammergau.

TRAIN

Oberammergau is accessible by train. From Munich, there is frequent service to Oberammergau, with a change in Murnau. (This rail track is considered by many to be one of the most beautiful in Germany, as it winds itself through quiet villages and lush meadows, with excellent views of a mountain backdrop.)

BUS

Oberammergau is accessible by local bus service; however, it is often much more convenient and efficient to take the train. An unnumbered bus travels between Oberammergau and Germisch-Partenkirchen.

TIPS AND HINTS

To order tickets or learn more about Oberammergau and the Passion Play, visit the website at www.oberammergau.de

Oberammergau is an ideal place to visit in the summer or winter. The village is situated in a beautiful valley surrounded by forests, mountains, and lush green meadows.

DID YOU KNOW?

The first Passion Play of 1634 is said to have used eighty participants. (It has since grown to more than two thousand participants.)

✠

Ottobeuren Abbey

A Baroque Masterpiece

The Ottobeuren Abbey in southern Germany has received its celebrity status from its elaborate church and the monastery's longevity. Welcoming visitors from all over the world, the abbey features a vast basilica that is almost unmatched in its enchantingly beautiful artworks and majestic spaciousness.

Founded in the eighth century, the monastery has long served as a splendid seat of the Christian faith in Bavaria and as a source of development for the region's art and culture. Although the original abbey and its church were established in 764, the construction of a new one began in 1089. In the following years, monastic life at Ottobeuren flourished as the abbey continued to grow in prestige and honor.

In 1204 dedication of a new church took place as the previous one had been destroyed in a fire. During the following five centuries, the abbey witnessed both prosperous and devastating times. The eigh-

Founded in the eighth century, Ottobeuren Abbey has long served as a splendid seat of the Christian faith in the peaceful countryside of southern Germany. Welcoming visitors from all over the world, the abbey features a vast basilica that is almost unmatched in its interior beauty and majestic spaciousness. *(Abtei Ottobeuren)*

teenth century, however, brought primarily good fortune as construction began on the present-day monastery and the millennial celebrations of the Imperial abbey took place.

In 1841 the abbey received a great gift when the miraculous image of Maria Eldern was placed on one of its side altars. The statue had been the subject of many pilgrimages at its previous location. Another honor came to the monastery when in 1926 Pope Pius XI bestowed on the abbey church the title of "Basilica Minor." In 1964 the abbey celebrated the 1200th anniversary of its founding, and in 1987 the priory commemorated the 250th anniversary of the laying of the foundation stone.

Today, the abbey remains the destination of many pilgrimages. Incomparably beautiful, the church is also home to many concerts, thus assuring pilgrims or tourists of a heavenly experience upon their visit.

ABOUT THE SHRINE

The famous Ottobeuren Abbey lies in a peaceful setting in the southern German countryside, near the city of Memmingen. The highlight here is the vast basilica with its majestic spaciousness and its enchantingly beautiful interior. Regular church services, the monks' Liturgy of the Hours, and the famous basilica concerts all round off an exciting visit to the abbey. While there be sure to visit

- Ottobeuren Abbey • Museum • Chapel of St. Benedict (manger)
- Gift shop • Saint Boniface's relics • Church concerts

SHRINE INFORMATION

Kurverwaltung—Haus des Gastes
Marktplatz 14
87724 Ottobeuren
Tel: (08332) 92-19-52, (08332) 92-19-53, (08332) 92-19-50
Fax: (08332) 92-19-92

To reserve a guided tour, contact the abbey at:
Abtei
D-87724 Ottobeuren
Tel: (08332) 79-80
Fax: (08332) 79-860

TOURIST OFFICE

Contact the shrine information office (Kurverwaltung) for other information about the city.

PLACES TO STAY

Contact the shrine information office (Kurverwaltung) for a full listing of hotels and guest rooms in Ottobeuren.

HOW TO ARRIVE AT OTTOBEUREN

Ottobeuren is about sixty-five miles west of Munich.

ROAD

From Munich, take A96 west to Memmingen, then follow the signs to Ottobeuren.

TRAIN

Ottobeuren is not accessible by train. The nearest train station is at Memmingen. From Munich, take the train to Memmingen. Upon arrival at the Memmingen railway station, walk up the stairs to the bus station. Buses depart regularly from platform #1 for Ottobeuren Abbey.

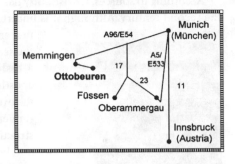

BUS

Ottobeuren is accessible by bus from local towns and cities, including Memmingen. From the Memmingen bus station, there are regular departures from platform #1 for Ottobeuren Abbey.

TIPS AND HINTS

On the bus ride to Ottobeuren, ask the driver to point out which bus stop is for the abbey. The reason for this is because Ottobeuren has several bus stops, and if you get off at the wrong one, it will be a while before you can catch the next bus to the abbey.

To obtain further information while visiting the abbey, stop by the porter's desk, which is located near the museum and gift shop.

DID YOU KNOW?

From a bird's-eye view, the entire layout of Ottobeuren Abbey represents a huge cross—and more specifically, a Romanesque body of Christ the King.

Cathedral of Trier

Guardians of the Holy Robe of Christ

Like many other grand shrines of Europe, Trier Cathedral has an impressive collection of treasures, relics, artworks, and architecture and a long and glorious history. Built in the fourth century, the church is recognized as being the oldest in Germany, dating from Roman times. Among the shrine's greatest possessions is the "Holy Robe" of Christ—the seamless garment said to be worn by Christ during his Passion.

According to sources, Christianity has existed in the area since the end of the second century. Although it is uncertain exactly when Christ's disciples first arrived, one old tradition states that the seat of the cathedral was founded by a bishop who was sent there by the apostle Peter himself. In 326, to celebrate the twentieth anniversary of his reign, the Emperor Constantine commenced construction on the Cathedral of Trier.

The history behind the Holy Robe relates that Saint Helen brought the relic back with her from the Holy Land in the fourth century. In honor of the building of the Cathedral of Trier, she entrusted the sacred object to the care of the new church.

Although the holy relic was often concealed for protection, in the sixteenth century the authorities placed it on display for twenty-three days. In that time, more than one hundred thousand pilgrims came to venerate the sacred object.

Although the Cathedral of Trier is a popular tourist destination for its artworks and architecture, it is an even more popular pilgrimage site for an altogether different reason. It is here that the "Holy Robe" of Christ, the seamless garment said to be worn by Christ during his Passion, is enshrined. *(Author)*

In 1810 the garment was publicly displayed again, this time with a crowd of 227 thousand pilgrims arriving for the seventeen days of celebrations and veneration. In 1891 more than two million pilgrims traveled to Trier and viewed the holy relic. During a three-week exposition in 1933, another two million visitors came to pay homage to the sacred object. Since 1959 the relic has remained enshrined and sealed in a glorious reliquary inside the Chapel of the Holy Robe, where pilgrims still come today to venerate it.

PRAYER TO CHRIST IN THE TOMB

Most Holy Savior, I am reminded of your death for me. As I meditate on this supreme act of love for all humankind, as I reflect on your wounds and your suffering, your sacrifice on the cross, I remember that it was through death that you gained for the world the Resurrection. Teach me, Lord, that it is through my own death to sin that I shall share in that ultimate union with you in heaven.

Lord Jesus, we praise you and bless you always. By your wounds, we are made whole. By your suffering and death, we have eternal life. Amen.

ABOUT THE SHRINE

Trier Cathedral is situated just north of the Palace Gardens in the center of the city. The most prominent treasure and relic inside the shrine is, of course, the Holy Robe of Christ. Both the cathedral and the Leibfrau Church (located next to the cathedral) are open throughout the year and receive pilgrims daily. While there be sure to visit

• Cathedral of Trier • Cathedral Treasury • Holy Robe of Christ

SHRINE INFORMATION

Cathedral of Trier
54290 Trier
Tel: (0651) 75-801
Tours of the cathedral can be arranged by contacting the sacristy at this phone number.

TOURIST OFFICE

Trier Tourist Information
Stadt und Land e.V.
An der Porta Nigra
54290 Trier
Tel: (0651) 97-80-80
Fax: (0651) 97-80-888, (0651) 44-759
E-mail: info@tit.de

PLACES TO STAY

Robert-Schuman-Haus
Auf der Jüngt 1
54293 Trier
Tel: (0651) 8105-0
Fax: (0651) 8105-434

Haus der Begegnung
Dietrichstrasse 30
54290 Trier
Tel: (0651) 97553-10

Sisters of St. Joseph Convent
Josefsstift Trier
Franz-LudwigStrasse 7
54290 Trier
Tel: (0651) 9769-0
Fax: (0651) 9769-111

Jugenbildungsstätte
Haus Sonnental
66798 Wallerfangen
Tel: (06831) 6035-0
Fax: (06831) 6927-9

Frau Thommes Jugenbildungsstätte
Marienburg
56859 Bullay/Mosel
Tel: (06542) 2077
Fax: (06542) 1591

Kolpinghaus Warsberger Hof
Dietrichstrasse 42
Tel: (0651) 975-250
Fax: (0651) 975-2540
E-mail: w-hof@t-online.de
Super clean, well run, and serves inexpensive meals in its restaurant; one block off the market square.

HOW TO ARRIVE AT TRIER

Trier is about seventy-five miles southwest of Koblenz.

ROAD

The major roads leading into Trier include the A1 autobahn north and south and Route 51 from the northwest.

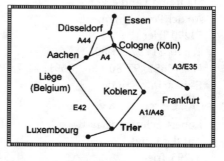

TRAIN

Trier is accessible by train and has frequent connections from many cities, including Cologne, Koblenz, and Saarbrücken. Twenty trains run from Cologne to Trier daily, making a two hour and twenty-five minute trip.

BUS

There is local bus service to Trier from nearby cities.

TIPS AND HINTS

St. Matthias Abbey is located just one short bus ride from the cathedral.

Another site worth visiting is the famous Hauptmarkt Square. Located near the cathedral, this colorful and busy marketplace is filled with people, fruit stands, flowers, painted facades, and fountains.

DID YOU KNOW?

To celebrate the twentieth anniversary of his reign, Constantine not only began construction on the Cathedral of Trier but also on St. Peter's Basilica in Rome.

✠

St. Matthias Abbey

"Then they cast lots for them, and the lot fell on Matthias;
and he was added to the eleven apostles."

ACTS 1:26

Although there is no extensive record about the life of Saint Matthias, historians have been able to piece together a rather brief but thorough description of his activities. What the saint will be most remembered for, however, is that he was the one chosen to replace Judas Iscariot—the apostle who betrayed Christ.

St. Matthias Abbey, located on the outskirts of Trier, receives thousands of pilgrims every year for one primary reason—it is here that the sacred relics of the apostle Saint Matthias are enshrined. *(Author)*

According to the Acts of the Apostles, after Christ's Ascension, the eleven apostles gathered with the Virgin Mary and other disciples in the Upper Room to wait and pray. While there, Peter opened the election for a replacement for Judas. Two candidates were chosen for their loyalty and devotion to Christ—Joseph (also called Justus) and Matthias. Sacred Scripture recalls the events:

> So they proposed two, Joseph called Barsabbas, who was also known as Justus, and Matthias. Then they prayed and said, "Lord, who know everyone's heart. Show us which one of these two you have chosen to take the place in this apostolic ministry and apostleship from which Judas turned aside to go to his own place." And they cast lots for them, and the lot fell upon Matthias; and he was added to the eleven apostles (Acts 1:23–26).

After Pentecost and the descent of the Holy Spirit, Matthias left on his own to spread the gospel of Christ. First, he spent time evangelizing in Judea before traveling to Cappadocia, in modern-day Turkey. Here, Matthias is said to have been a vital force in bringing Christianity to the area and converting a number of its residents.

From some of the writings of the Church Fathers, we can get a better glimpse of Saint Matthias. According to Saint Clement of Alexandria, Saint Jerome, and Eusebius, Saint Matthias was one of the seventy-two disciples whom Christ had sent out, two by two, during his ministry. Clement also wrote that the apostle exhausted his body by constantly mortifying it to make his spirit subject to "the Crucified."

Although there is some uncertainty as to how Matthias died, one tradition asserts that he was crucified in a manner similar to Christ. According to the Greek *Menaia* and other sources, the martyrdom took place at Colchis—an ancient country south of the Caucasus Mountains, on the eastern coast of the Black Sea.

In the fourth century, Saint Helen is said to have brought Matthias's relics to Europe from Jerusalem. Portions of the sacred remains were divided up and given to the abbey church in Trier and to the Basilica of St. Mary Major in Rome. At the monastery in Trier, the monks had the relics enshrined in a beautifully carved tomb before the high altar.

Today, pilgrims from around the world come to pray at the abbey, beseeching Saint Matthias's intercession. Among these visitors are many of the faithful who come from throughout Germany on organized walking pilgrimages from their homes and cities—some of which are more than one hundred miles away. Such is the devotion to a giant of a saint and apostle.

PRAYER TO SAINT MATTHIAS

Father, you called Saint Matthias to share in the mission of the apostles.
By the help of his prayers may we receive with joy the love you share with
us and be counted among those you have chosen. We ask this through our
Lord Jesus Christ. Amen.

Saint Matthias, pray for us.

ABOUT THE SHRINE

St. Matthias Abbey is located on the southern outskirts of Trier, just a short bus ride from the cathedral. The shrine's greatest attraction, the Tomb of the Apostle, lies in front of the main altar. Pilgrims can also visit the extensive collection of artifacts, paintings, and historical documents found in the Abbey museum. The feast of Saint Matthias is celebrated on May 14. While there be sure to visit

• Abbey • Church • Saint Matthias's tomb • Abbey museum • Gift shop • Burial crypts

SHRINE INFORMATION

Abtei St. Matthias
Matthiasstraße 85
54290 Trier
Tel: (0651) 310-79
Fax: (0651) 359-69, (0651) 374-14

TOURIST OFFICE

See *Cathedral of Trier* for more information about contacting the Trier Tourist Information office.

PLACES TO STAY

See *Cathedral of Trier* for more information about places to stay in Trier.

HOW TO ARRIVE AT ST. MATTHIAS ABBEY IN TRIER

For directions on how to arrive at Trier, see *Cathedral of Trier.*

BUS

From downtown Trier, take bus #3 to St. Matthias Abbey (Aulstrasse). It is about a ten-minute bus ride.

TIPS AND HINTS

As Trier has two major Catholic pilgrimage destinations (cathedral and abbey) and a festive city life, it is definitely worth spending at least one or two full days here.

DID YOU KNOW?

Matthias is said to have learned the practice of mortifying the flesh from Christ himself.

Eucharistic Miracle of Walldürn

"The works that I do in my Father's name testify to me."
JOHN 10:25

From time to time our Lord generously gives us extraordinary miracles to sustain and reward our faith. Such is the case with the Eucharistic Miracle of Walldürn.

In 330 while the priest Heinrich Otto was celebrating Mass, he accidentally knocked over the chalice containing the blood of Christ. As the blood spilled across the corporal, an image of the crucified Christ with eleven surrounding thorn-crowned heads appeared on the cloth. Frightened and confused by the event, the priest quickly hid the piece of linen under the altar. Not until Mass was over did he take a closer look at the corporal.

Every year two hundred thousand pilgrims make the pilgrimage to Walldürn to behold the fourteenth-century eucharistic miracle. The most striking site in the city is the towering baroque pilgrimage church, called "Holy Blood," which contains the Holy Corporal. *(Stadt Walldürn)*

Upon reexamination, Father Otto noticed that the images made visible by the blood had become decidedly sharp and clear. After venerating the holy miracle for some time, the priest hid the linen under the altar again. Not until a few days before his death did he reveal the event to anyone. When he confessed the secret on his deathbed, the Miraculous Corporal was immediately found and enshrined.

Word of the bloodstained linen spread quickly throughout the nearby villages. Soon, thousands of pilgrims were traveling to the small town to behold the Holy Corporal. Miracles, healings, and conversions were numerous among those who visited and venerated the miracle.

In 1445 Pope Eugene IV recognized the eucharistic miracle as authentic. Since then, the miracle has continued to grow in fame. Images and pictures from throughout the centuries representing the Eucharistic Miracle of Walldürn are found throughout Europe.

More than two hundred thousand pilgrims now come annually to venerate the Holy Corporal. Although the image of the crucified Christ has faded somewhat over the years, it is still visible. The major pilgrimage period, commonly referred to as the "Pilgrimage to the Holy Blood," lasts for four weeks beginning on Trinity Sunday (the Sunday after Pentecost). With an increased interest around the world in eucharistic miracles, an ever-increasing number of pilgrims, many of whom are young people, come to see the shrine each year, and today Walldürn is a bustling place of prayer.

PRAYER BEFORE THE BLESSED SACRAMENT

O Lord Jesus Christ, present here in your constant gift of the Blessed Sacrament, I come before you now as your child. I offer you praise, honor, and thanksgiving. I offer you my love and my life. You are the refreshing waters, O Lord; you are the Bread of Eternal Life, the rest for my soul. I know, here in the presence of your wonderful sacrament, you are with me in a very special way. As I continue my pilgrimage here at this shrine so loved by your Mother, remind me often of this visit upon my return home. I truly desire to live my life always in your sight and before your dwelling place. Amen.

ABOUT THE SHRINE

Walldürn is a small town situated in the German countryside in the very heart of the district formed by the cities of Frankfurt, Würzburg, Heidelberg, and Heilbronn. Throughout the year, a number of celebrations and processions take place at the shrine in honor of the eucharistic miracle. The greatest pilgrimage takes place during the Sunday after Pentecost and the four weeks thereafter. Today, the shrine continues to be operated by the Augustinian Fathers and remains open year-round. While there be sure to visit

- Church of the Holy Blood (Basilica) • Holy Corporal • Pictures and reliefs depicting scenes of the fourteenth-century eucharistic miracle

SHRINE INFORMATION

Kath. Pfarramt
Burgstrasse 26
74731 Walldürn
Tel: (06282) 520-30

TOURIST OFFICE

Walldürn Tourist Office
Rathaus, Hauptstraße 27
74731 Walldürn
Tel: (06282) 67-106
Fax: (06282) 67-103
Website: www.wallduern.de

PLACES TO STAY

Contact the tourist office for a full listing of places to stay in Walldürn.

HOW TO ARRIVE AT WALLDÜRN

Walldürn is about fifty-five miles southeast of Frankfurt.

ROAD

From Würzburg, take 27 south-west to Walldürn.

From Frankfurt, take A3 east to Junction 469 (exit 58), then take 469 south, connecting with 47 for the last part of the journey to Walldürn.

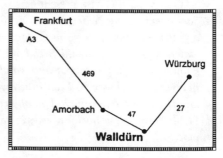

TRAIN

Walldürn is accessible by train; however, the railway station is rather small, making some connections difficult.

From Frankfurt, change trains in Aschaffenburg, and then change to a bus in Miltenberg for Walldürn.

From Würzburg, there is train service to Walldürn, but it requires several changes; oftentimes, the bus service is more convenient from Würzburg.

BUS

Walldürn is accessible by bus from select cities. There is long-distance bus service from Würzburg to Walldürn. Walldürn has no bus station but only a bus stop.

TIPS AND HINTS

If taking the train (and bus) to Walldürn, be sure to visit one of the travel-bureau agencies at the railway stations for a listing of the times and connections to the pilgrimage city.

In 1962 Pope John XXIII raised the pilgrimage church in Walldürn, containing the eucharistic miracle, to the rank of a "Papal Basilica Minor."

DID YOU KNOW?

Pope Eugene IV, who authenticated the Eucharistic Miracle of Walldürn, had confirmed another eucharistic miracle just three years earlier, that of Ferrara, Italy.

Wies Church

"In the Meadows"
GERMAN MEANING OF *WIES*

Welcoming more than one million visitors every year, the renowned Wies Church in southern Germany not only features the country's finest Rococo-style building but also holds the distinction of being home to a miraculous image of Christ. For these two reasons, the shrine today attracts not only the faithful from around the globe but also plenty of art devotees who come to view world-class paintings and frescoes.

The pilgrimage church dates from 1730, when two local friars created a wooden statue of the "Scourged Savior" to be used in the Good Friday processions. In 1732 the figure made its debut, and for the following three years it remained a part of the celebrations. However, in 1735 the congregation decided to ban the image from the processions because it was too life-like, with its bloodied and tattered appearance. Hence, the statue was placed in the attic of the monastery's innkeeper.

For a glimpse of world-class art, more than one million pilgrims and tourists annually make the journey to the small southern German town of Wies to visit the renowned local church. Inside the shrine, near the main altar, is a cherished miraculous image of the "Scourged Savior." *(Pfarramt Wieskirche)*

On March 4, 1738, the innkeeper's godmother, Maria Lory, transferred the figure to her farm in Wies, where it became an object of personal veneration. Then, on June 14, 1738, the "Miracle of Wies" took place. While praying before the holy statue, Maria and her husband saw tears form in the eyes of the Scourged Savior. Immediately, the local church authorities were contacted, and within a year a special small chapel was built in the fields to house the miraculous image. As word spread about the event, the number of pilgrimages to the little shrine increased. Many of those who came were not only from Germany but also from many other parts of Europe, including Sweden, Holland, Denmark, Norway, France, Spain, and Russia.

As a much larger church was needed to accommodate the vast numbers of pilgrims, the renowned artist and architect Dominikus Zimmermann began construction on a new pilgrimage church at Wies in 1745. Nine years later the masterpiece Rococo-style church had been completed, prompting an even greater number of visitors to the area. In time, the pilgrimage site developed into one of the country's most popular Christian destinations.

Today, the Wies Church continues to receive international recognition for its world-class art, including recently being named to UNESCO's list of Cultural Heritage Buildings. With a vast array of heavenly frescoes and statues adorning the entire interior of the shrine, the church exhibits a profound spirituality and theology almost unmatched in the world. In addition to the art, the miraculous image of the Scourged Savior continues to serve as the spiritual center of this great place of pilgrimage.

PRAYER AT WIES CHURCH

Teach us, good Lord, to serve you as you deserve: to give, and not to count the cost; to fight, and not to heed the wounds; to toil, and not to ask for any reward, but that of knowing that we do your will. We ask this through Christ our Lord. Amen.

ABOUT THE SHRINE

One of the most extravagant and flamboyant Rococo buildings in the world, the Wies Church is situated on the slopes of the Alps, in a meadow just off the Romantic Road near Steingaden—between Ammer and Lech. Along with visiting the sanctuary for its architectural and artistic wonders, most pilgrims come to spend time praying before the miraculous image of Christ as "Scourged Savior." Although the church can be visited throughout the year, it is best to stop by the tourist office to confirm that the church will be open at the time of your visit. While there be sure to visit

- Wies Church • Miraculous image of the "Scourged Savior"
- Frescoes and paintings • Wies Tourist Office

SHRINE INFORMATION

Pfarramt Wieskirche
(Clergy office of the Wies Church)
Wies 12
86989 Steingaden-Wies
Tel: (08862) 501
Fax: (08862) 414

TOURIST OFFICE

Kurverwaltung
Kaiser-Maximilian-Platz 1
87629 Füssen
Tel: (08362) 70-77, (08362) 70-78

PLACES TO STAY

Contact the tourist office for a listing of places to stay in nearby Füssen.

HOW TO ARRIVE AT WIES

Wies is about thirteen miles from Füssen.

ROAD

From Munich, head west on A96, then south on 17 to Steingaden. From Steingaden, follow the signs to Wies (three miles).

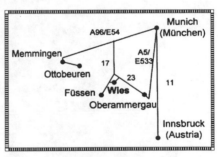

TRAIN

Wies is not accessible by train. The nearest major train stations are at Füssen and Schwangau.

BUS

Wies is accessible by bus. From Füssen and Schwangau, there are several daily bus departures to Wies. From Füssen, a bus departs every morning at 11:15 A.M. (1:00 P.M. on Sunday) for Wies and returns at 3:50 P.M. from the church. The trip takes an hour one way.

TIPS AND HINTS

Wies is about ten miles from the pilgrimage city of Oberammergau.

Days of Pilgrimage and Church Service include the Feast of Christ's Tears (first Sunday after June 14), Feast of the Guardian Angel/Anniversary of the Wies Church (first Sunday in September), and Feast of the Holy Society (second Sunday in October).

DID YOU KNOW?

Dominikus Zimmermann, the designer of the shrine, was so enchanted with his creation that he constructed a small home below the church and spent the last decade of his life there.

Greece

1. Our Lady of Tínos
2. Cave of the Apocalypse
3. Monastery of St. John the Theologian

GREECE

Cave of the Apocalypse

"Dear visitor, the place you have just entered is sacred."
INSCRIPTION AT THE ENTRANCE

One of the greatest places of pilgrimage in the Christian world is the Cave of the Apocalypse on Patmos Island in Greece. Here, inside the sacred grotto, Saint John the Evangelist wrote the famous last book of the New Testament—Revelation.

Once an insignificant island, Patmos today attracts visitors from around the globe. Before the apostle arrived on its shores, however, the place had hardly ever been mentioned in ancient literature. The

Once an insignificant island, today Patmos serves as one of the greatest places of pilgrimage in the Christian faith, as it is here that Saint John the Evangelist wrote the Book of Revelation inside the Cave of the Apocalypse in the first century. (Holy Monastery of St. John)

beginning of its fame occurred when Saint John was banished to the island and began to write his Apocalypse. We read about this in Scripture:

> I, John, your brother, who share with you in Jesus the persecution and the kingdom and the patient endurance, was on the island called Patmos because of the word of God and the testimony of Jesus. I was in spirit on the Lord's day, and I heard behind me a loud voice like a trumpet saying, "Write in a book what you see and send it to the seven churches…" (Revelation 1:9–11).

From this text and other passages, we learn that God is dictating to John what to write. The apostle describes God's voice like "the sound of many waters" (Revelation 1:15) and a trumpet, speaking behind me (Revelation 1:10). In Revelation we also hear for the first time the famous words, "I am the Alpha and the Omega…who is and who was and who is to come, the Almighty" (1:8).

Today, the Cave of the Apocalypse still possesses several traces of the apostle's presence. One piece of evidence is the divine presence of God indelibly marked upon the overhanging roof. The triple crack in the ceiling is popularly regarded as evidence of the visible presence of God in the cave at the time of his revelation to Saint John. The thrice split is taken to symbolize the Holy Trinity. Deep inside the grotto is the recess where the Evangelist is said to have placed his head for sleep. Just above and slightly to the right of this cavity, about three feet off the floor, is a small depression in the rock where the saint would place his hand when rising from his knees after praying. Nearby is also the naturally made "rock desk," used by the disciple Prochorus, who wrote down what the Evangelist dictated to him.

Although records of the Cave through the centuries are rather scanty, we do know that the Blessed Christodoulos of Latros came in 1088 and restored the holy site. It is also certain that many Christians made a pilgrimage here during the Middle Ages. When they did come, many would break off pieces of the rock so they could take home relics of the holy cave.

Today, the small grotto continues to serve as a premier place of pilgrimage. Run and operated by the Greek Orthodox Church, the shrine welcomes pilgrims from all religious traditions. For it is here that Saint John wrote the Book of Revelation—a piece of sacred writing that affects all humankind.

$$+\!\!\!+\!\!\!+$$

Monastery of St. John the Theologian

Offering a Mountaintop Experience

At the top of Patmos Island, visible from miles away, is the Monastery of St. John the Theologian. Founded by Blessed Christodoulos in 1088, the abbey was built like a fortress to protect itself from pirate raids. Belonging to the Greek Orthodox Church, the monastery is renowned for its religious and historical significance.

Considered one of the most important monuments in the Greek world from an artistic and architectural standpoint, the abbey falls into the same category as the great and wealthy monasteries that were built when monasticism reached its height in the Greek Islands. Other examples of this type of abbey are the famous monasteries of Mount St. Athos. Many of these priories were built in inaccessible spots, such as on the tops of hills, and constructed in the fashion of medieval fortresses.

Today, pilgrims can take tours through the renowned monastery. Among the most popular sites to visit are its chapels, particularly because of their

outstanding frescoes. Paintings depicting the important events in the life of Saint John are some of the most significant ones. The chapel and tomb of the founder, Blessed Christodoulos, also serve as important places of pilgrimage at the shrine.

Founded by Blessed Christodoulos in 1088, the Greek Orthodox Monastery of St. John the Theologian ranks among the country's most important monuments from an artistic, architectural, and religious point of view. The fortresslike abbey is situated at the top of Patmos Island, offering breathtaking views of the island below and the surrounding crystal-blue ocean. *(Holy Monastery of St. John)*

One of the greatest treats of visiting the abbey is spending time in the Treasury Museum. Here, the faithful can view precious icons, ancient documents, ecclesiastical ornaments, and ship pendants made of diamonds and emeralds donated by Catherine the Great. To "top off" a visit to the abbey, visitors can climb up to the roof terrace for a spectacular view extending over the island and Aegean Sea.

ABOUT THE SHRINE

While on the beautiful island of Patmos, you can visit both the Holy Cave and the hilltop Monastery of the Apocalypse (they are within ten minutes' walking distance of each other). Both places of pilgrimage are open daily, but the hours of admission usually fluctuate according to the season and arrival of cruise ships. Guided tours of the monastery are available (they usually meet the day-cruise visitors). During a visit of the monastery, the treasury-library-museum is definitely worth seeing, with its sampling of rich vestments, icons, and religious artifacts. As with the shrine on Tínos, be sure to wear proper attire for entrance into the monastery or cave. (Men must wear long pants, and women must wear skirts/no slacks; no shorts are allowed for anyone.) While there be sure to visit

• Holy Cave of the Apocalypse • Greek Orthodox Monastery of St. John • Treasury-Library-Museum • Guided tours of the monastery

SHRINE INFORMATION
Monastery of St. John
85500 Patmos
Tel: (0247) 31-398, (0247) 31-234

TOURIST OFFICE
Patmos Municipal Tourist Information Office
85500 Patmos
Tel: (0247) 31-666, (0247) 31-235, (0247) 31-058
Open during the summer months only.

Astoria Travel
85500 Patmos
Tel: (0247) 31-205, (0247) 31-975

PLACES TO STAY
There is a large variety of accommodations on Patmos Island—including
first-, second-, and third-class hotels, pensions, and rooms for rent.

HOW TO ARRIVE AT PATMOS
Patmos is about one hundred and sixty nautical miles east of Piraeus.

BOAT
From Piraeus (Athens's port), there is one daily ferry to Patmos. Daily ferry service is also available from Leros, Kálymnos, Kos, and Rhodes. Ferry service is also provided to Patmos from Ikaria (three or four times a week) and Samos (six times a week).

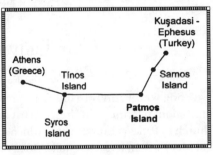

During the summer, hydrofoil services connect Patmos with Kos, Kálymnos, Leros, and Samos. (The hydrofoil service is almost twice as fast as the ferry service—albeit more expensive.)

TRANSPORTATION ON THE ISLAND

BUS AND TAXI
From the ferryboat pier (in Skála), the island's bus stop is directly ahead, a little to the left, behind the statue of Emmanuel Xanthos. Buses operate frequently between Skála and Chóra, as per the schedule posted next to the stop. Taxis are also plentiful, and there is a taxi stand at the port.

MOPEDS AND SCOOTERS

One of the best ways to discover the island and visit the shrine is to rent a moped or scooter for the day. They provide an efficient, inexpensive, and common form of transportation on the island. (And they're a lot of fun too!)

TIPS AND HINTS

During Easter, there is the famous Nipteras. It is a reenactment of the Last Supper, that's only performed on Patmos, in the square outside the Monastery of St. John, and in Jerusalem. The festivities and holy days extend from the Monday before Easter to the following Tuesday.

Those who would like to walk to the Monastery of St. John instead can take the thirty-minute uphill trek. (However, I personally prefer taking a taxi up the hill to the monastery, and then walking down to the Cave of the Apocalypse, and then continuing downward into town.)

DID YOU KNOW?

The Monastery of St. John the Theologian has a sixth-century fragment of the Gospel of Saint Luke.

Our Lady of Tínos

The Lourdes of Greece

Along with Patmos Island, Tínos ranks among the most popular places of religious pilgrimage in Greece. What makes the site so famous is the island's church of Panayía Evangelístria, which features a miraculous icon of the Virgin Mary within its sacred walls. Often referred to as the "Lourdes of Greece," the Greek Orthodox sanctuary receives thousands of pilgrims each year.

The shrine dates from 1822. In that year a nun by the name of Pelagia was favored with a number of visions of the Holy Virgin. On one occasion, Our Lady asked that the local Church authorities begin an excavation at a particular spot on the island to find an ancient icon of her that had been buried centuries ago. In Pelagia's vision, the Virgin also requested that a chapel be built at the site.

After hesitating at first, the nun eventually spoke with the bishop about her visions. To her surprise the prelate accepted her mission with enthusiasm and instructed the people of the island to help in the excavations. Although excitement filled the air during the early days of the search, it soon gave way to frustration and loss of hope as the people found nothing. At the same time, a terrible illness had broken out on the island, adding to the dismal misery of the fruitless search.

However, after the bishop gave a warm and moving proclamation about Our Lady of Tínos, the inhabitants became inspired to renew their excavations. One month later, on January 30, 1823, the workers found the icon. After hastily cleaning the holy image, they quickly ran over to the bishop's house to show him the "treasure" they had found.

Immediately, the prelate placed it on an old double-legged stand outside the church that was being built. As

Often referred to as the "Lourdes of Greece," the nineteenth-century Greek Orthodox sanctuary ranks among the most popular places of pilgrimage in Greece. Welcoming pilgrims and visitors from all walks of life, the shrine of Our Lady of Tínos features a miraculous image of the Virgin Mary. *(Author)*

word spread through the village about the finding of the icon, the people hurried to the site to venerate it. Seven years later, the holy icon was finally enshrined in the brilliant new church of Panayía Evangelístria.

In the ensuing years, numerous miracles occurred through the intercession of Our Lady of Tínos. One involved a Muslim who experienced a full and immediate recovery from an incurable disease after visiting the church and asking for the Virgin's help. On another occasion, a Greek who was living in America had become blind after a terrible sickness. In desperation, he asked the Virgin for the restoration of his sight and promised that he would offer to her the first thing he would see. After receiving a miraculous recovery, the first thing the man saw was an orange tree. Hence, faithful to his promise, the Greek donated the shrubbery to the shrine (it can still be seen just inside the church's entrance, to the right).

Today, the miracles and celebrations continue at Panayía Evangelístria. Throughout the year pilgrims can be seen walking into the shrine and kissing the holy icon of the Virgin Mary, which is covered in gold and precious stones. As one of the most popular pilgrimage sites of the Greek Orthodox faith, the sanctuary welcomes visitors from all faiths and backgrounds.

PRAYER TO OUR LADY OF TÍNOS

Our Lady of Tínos, may we turn to you as we seek to imitate your faith-filled life. May we be led by the same wisdom that God sent forth from heaven to guide you along unfamiliar paths and through challenging decisions. Keep us united in mind and heart as we go forward in joyful hope toward the grace-filled freedom that Augustine recommends. O Virgin Mother of Good Tidings, hear our prayer as we look to you for guidance. Pray for us to our loving and merciful Father, to your Son, our Lord Jesus Christ, and to the Holy Spirit, giver of all wisdom, one God, forever and ever. Amen.

Our Lady of Good Tidings, pray for us.

ABOUT THE SHRINE

Located on the beautiful island of Tínos, the town has retained its enchanting villages and lovely beaches. The shrine itself is open daily, and Greek Orthodox services are held regularly. In the crypt are a number of chapels along with a font containing water said to be miraculous. Surrounding the church are several museums and galleries with beautiful religious art. The shrine's most prized possession, however, is the miraculous icon of the Virgin Mary. Located in the church, the image (covered with gold, diamonds, and pearls) is to the left of the central aisle. Amid thousands of flickering candles hanging overhead and precious jewels decorating the sanctuary, the visiting pilgrim can kiss the sacred icon on the way into the shrine. When visiting, remember to observe the shrine's dress code (men must wear long pants, and women must wear skirts/no slacks; no shorts are allowed for anyone). While there be sure to visit

• Church of Panayía Evangelístria • Miraculous icon of the Virgin Mary • Crypt • Font • Chapels • Museums

SHRINE INFORMATION

Church of Panayía Evangelístria
84200 Tínos (Kykládes)

TOURIST OFFICE

There is no tourist office on Tínos, but a number of small travel agencies can provide excellent information about the island.

PLACES TO STAY

There is a large variety of accommodations on Tínos Island—including first-, second-, and third-class hotels, pensions, and rooms for rent.

HOW TO ARRIVE AT TÍNOS
Tínos is about eighty-five nautical miles southeast of Piraeus.

BOAT
From Piraeus (Athens's port) and Rafína, there is daily ferry, hydrofoil, and/or catamaran service to Tínos. There is also daily ferry service to Tínos from Ándros, Mykonos, and Syros. Note that the hydrofoil service is available only during the summer months.

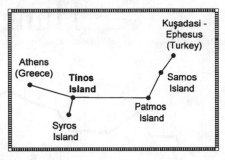

Kuşadasi -
Ephesus
(Turkey)

Athens
(Greece)

Tínos
Island

Samos
Island

Patmos
Island

Syros
Island

TRANSPORTATION ON THE ISLAND

BUS AND TAXI
Upon arrival at Tínos Island, you can find bus and taxi service to the Church of Panayía Evangelístria from the harbor (look for either the bus station or taxi stand). The shrine is also within walking distance of the harbor (ten minutes).

MOPEDS AND SCOOTERS
One of the best ways to discover the island and visit the shrine is to rent a moped or scooter for the day. They provide an efficient, inexpensive, exciting, and common form of transportation on the island.

TIPS AND HINTS
Among the biggest feast days at the shrine are January 30 (Anniversary of the Finding of the Holy Icon), March 25 (Annunciation of Our Lady), July 23 (Anniversary of the Vision of Saint Pelagia), and August 15 (Assumption of the Virgin Mary).

DID YOU KNOW?
According to Orthodox tradition, the icon is said to be one of the three icons painted by Saint Luke during the lifetime of the Virgin Mary.

Hungary

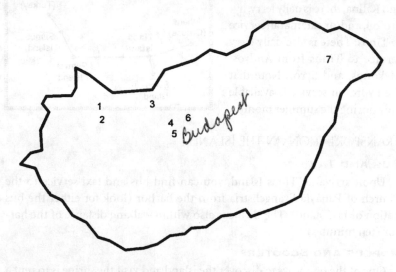

1. Our Lady of Győr
2. Pannonhalma Abbey
3. Cathedral of Esztergom
4. Our Lady of Remete
5. Basilica of St. Stephen
6. Our Lady of Máriabesnyő
7. Our Lady of Máriapócs

✠

Basilica of St. Stephen

Home of the Holy Dexter

10-23-00 - beautiful - under renovation

Serving as one of the most prominent symbols of Hungary's past and present history, the Basilica of St. Stephen in Budapest welcomes more than two million visitors every year. Featuring magnificent works of art and architecture, the shrine's greatest prize lies in a small chapel to the left of the main altar. Here, in a glass casket, lies the country's most sacred object and the basilica's major drawing card—the mummified hand of Saint Stephen (King Stephen I).

Born in 977, Stephen was the son of a Magyar prince whom he succeeded twenty years later as ruler. A devout and virtuous boy from his earliest years, Saint Stephen is said to have been baptized and tutored in the faith by Saint Adalbert. When he succeeded his father as ruler of the Magyars in 997, the saint made it his intent to develop Hungary both politically and ecclesiastically.

Seeing his work as that of a missionary, Stephen always sought to spread the

Welcoming more than two million visitors every year, the Basilica of St. Stephen not only features magnificent works of art and architecture but is also home to one of the country's most sacred relics—the mummified hand of King Saint Stephen. *(Author)*

Christian faith. During his years as king, he built churches, monasteries, and hospices for pilgrims and brought in many religious orders. He imposed taxes for the support of the Church and decreed that every tenth town in his domain should build a church and support a priest. Throughout his term, he sought to root out the pagan religions while firmly planting the Catholic Church. For his deeds and convictions, he faced constant invasions, revolts, and murder plots against him.

One of the most extraordinary moments of his life took place when he was crowned king in the year 1000 amidst great solemnity and pomp, with

159

the blessing of the Church and the pope. In a public act, the new ruler placed his entire domain under the protection of the Blessed Virgin Mary. Among the people, he was most endeared to the poor, the oppressed, helpless orphans, and widows. On one occasion, while he, disguised, was handing out alms, a group of beggars pounced on him, beat him, and stole his purse. However, this did not deter him from siding with those less fortunate.

Stephen's entire kingship was characterized by his charitable and zealous application to all the external duties of life and to the government of his kingdom. He lived his life as one uninterrupted sacrifice to God. His saintliness spilled over to his family, including his oldest son who was later canonized (Saint Emeric). Serving God to the end, the saint passed away on August 1, 1038, after receiving the sacraments of penance, viaticum, and anointing of the sick.

Today, the impact of Saint Stephen's life can still be felt in Hungary. The people of this great nation continue to honor him not only as a lawgiver and father of the nation but also as a guide and model, whose intercession can bring strength and aid in difficult times.

PRAYER TO SAINT STEPHEN OF HUNGARY

Almighty Father, grant that Saint Stephen of Hungary, who fostered the growth of your Church on earth, continue to be our powerful helper in heaven. We ask this through our Lord Jesus Christ, who reigns with you and the Holy Spirit, forever and ever. Amen.

Saint Stephen, pray for us.

ABOUT THE SHRINE

The world-renowned Basilica of St. Stephen serves as one of the most familiar symbols of the Budapest skyline. Home to many sacred treasures, the shrine's possession is the mummified hand of Saint Stephen—located in a small chapel to the left of the main altar (follow the signs saying "Szent Jobb"). The basilica's treasury is also worth a visit. Saint Stephen's feast is celebrated on August 16. While there be sure to visit

• Basilica • Treasury • Chapel with St. Stephen's sacred hand

SHRINE INFORMATION

Basilica of Saint Stephen
Presbytery
Hercegprímás u. 7
1051 Budapest

TOURIST OFFICE

Tourinform Budapest
Sütő utca 2
1052 Budapest
Tel: (1) 317-9800
Fax: (1) 317-9656
E-mail: tourinform@mail.hungarytourism.hu
Website: www.hungarytourism.hu

Dolores Travel
Kelenhegyi u. 2-4
Gellért Gyógyfürdő
1118 Budapest
Tel/Fax: (1) 385-3592

Tourism Office of Budapest
P.O. Box 215
1364 Budapest
E-mail: info@budtour.hu

Magyar Turizmus Rt.
Margit körút 85
1024 Budapest
Tel: (1) 355-1133
Fax: (1) 375-3819

PLACES TO STAY

Magyarok Nagyasszonya Társaság
Szerb Antal u. 13-17
1021 Budapest
Tel: (1) 200-1441
Fax: (1) 203-9275
Tel/Fax: (1) 275-1395

Kalocsai Iskolanővérek
Mária u. 20
1085 Budapest
Tel: (1) 266-1935, (1) 210-0505, (1) 267-6336
Tel/Fax: (1) 266-0524

Ferences Mária Misszionérius Növérek
Hermina u. 19
1146 Budapest
Tel/Fax: (1) 343-8003

Leanyfalu
Móriozzs ut. 141
Szent gellert Hàz
Tel: (26) 383-212
Fax: (26) 383-302

There are several more guesthouses located just outside of Budapest to the northwest in Piliscsaba:

Maria Szive Leanyai Társaság
Boldog Gizella Kollégium
Mátyás Kir. U. 44
2081 Piliscsaba-Klotildliget
Tel: (26) 373-903
Accommodates up to one hundred people.

Egyhazkozsegi Nóvérek Társasága
Szt. Peter Kollégium
Mátyás Kir. U. 38
2081 Piliscsaba-Klotildliget
Tel: (26) 373-764
Accommodates up to one hundred people.

Missziospapok Társasága (Lazarispák)
Szt. Vince Kollégium
Templom Tér 14
2081 Piliscsaba
Tel: (26) 375-109
Accommodates up to thirty people.

PPKE BTK
Egyetem u. 1
2087 Piliscsaba-Klotildliget
Tel: (26) 375-375
Accommodates up to forty people.

HOW TO ARRIVE AT BUDAPEST

Budapest is located in north-central Hungary.

ROAD

Several major highways including M1, M3, M5, and M7 connect with Budapest.

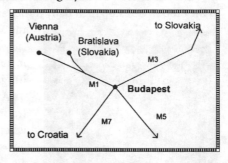

TRAIN

Budapest is easily accessible by train. The three main train stations are Keleti (Eastern), Nyugati (Western), and Déli (Southern).

BUS

Budapest is easily accessible by bus. There are three major bus stations in Budapest serving intercity, domestic, and international travel.

BOAT AND FERRY

Budapest has boat and ferry service to both domestic and international destinations, including Vienna.

TIPS AND HINTS

For a better glimpse of the sacred hand, put a 20 Ft coin into the little machine in front of it to light up the glass casket.

DID YOU KNOW?

Saint Stephen's mummified hand is referred to as the Holy Right and the Holy Dexter.

Our Lady of Remete

A Place of Healing

Throughout the world a number of shrines are built in honor of housing precious religious images or statues that are said to be the subject of numerous miracles. Such is the case with the sanctuary of Our Lady of Remete in Hungary.

The shrine dates from the eighteenth century when an Austrian woman settled in an area just outside of Budapest and hung a picture of the Virgin Mary on an oak tree near her home. With each passing day the lady would pray before the holy image, which was a replica of the miraculous picture of Our Lady of Einsiedeln from Switzerland. In time, others began to join her as they too would stop their daily duties and come over to spend time before the Virgin's picture. After the Austrian lady died, the people in the surrounding area continued the tradition of visiting the little "outdoor sanctuary."

Dating from the eighteenth century, the shrine of Our Lady of Remete welcomes thousands of pilgrims every year who come to pay homage to a miraculous image of the Virgin Mary. In 1991 Pope John Paul II made a sacred journey here to kneel before the cherished picture and present his petitions. *(Author)*

At the turn of the century, an extraordinary event occurred at the place when a woman miraculously recovered her sight while praying before the image. With great excitement and as a sign of thanksgiving, the lady commissioned the building of a small wooden chapel at the site to enclose the precious painting. In time, as word of the miraculous event spread, more and more pilgrims came to the little shrine to offer their petitions. In 1815 a stone chapel was built at the site to replace the wooden chapel. During the nineteenth century, the number of pilgrims visiting the shrine continued to grow at such a great pace that a larger church had to be built.

On October 1, 1899, the local bishop consecrated the new, present-day shrine. During the ceremony he placed the cherished image above the main altar. In subsequent years several extraordinary miracles took place at the shrine. In 1911 an English woman who prayed to Our Lady of Remete experienced the immediate and full recovery of her vision. On another occasion a Hungarian lady asked for the Virgin's help shortly before receiving an operation for her gallstones. After offering her prayers to Our Lady of Remete, she discovered that the gallstones had left her without any surgical intervention. In 1936 a university student injured in World War I experienced a sudden and complete healing of his crippled feet after praying to Our Lady of Remete.

Today, thousands are still making their way to the shrine to offer their prayers and petitions to the Virgin Mary. In 1991 Pope John Paul II joined the ranks of other pilgrims who have come to kneel before the miraculous image.

PRAYER FOR A FAMILY

O dear Jesus, I humbly implore you to grant your special graces to our family. May our home be the shrine of peace, purity, love, labor, and faith. I beg you, dear Jesus, to protect and bless all of us, absent and present, living and dead.

O Mary, loving Mother of Jesus and our Mother, pray to Jesus for our family, for all the families of the world to guard the cradle of the newborn, the schools of the young, and their vocations.

Blessed Saint Joseph, holy guardian of Jesus and Mary, assist us by your prayers in all necessities of life. Ask of Jesus that special grace that he granted to you, to watch over our home at the pillow of the sick and the dying, so that with Mary and with you, heaven may find our family unbroken in the Sacred Heart of Jesus. Amen.

ABOUT THE SHRINE

Located on the outskirts of Budapest, the shrine of Mária Remete is open daily and welcomes pilgrims throughout the year. Among the most popular sites to visit at the shrine are the miraculous image of the Virgin Mary and the outdoor Marian sanctuary. Only two short bus trips away from Budapest, Mária Remete is easy to reach. While there be sure to visit

- Mária Remete shrine • Miraculous image of the Virgin Mary
- Our Lady of Lourdes outdoor shrine

SHRINE INFORMATION

Templom Remete
Mária Remete Plebania
1029 Mária Remete (Budapest)

TOURIST OFFICE

See the *Basilica of St. Stephen* for more information on tourist offices in Budapest.

PLACES TO STAY

See the *Basilica of St. Stephen* for more information on places to stay in Budapest.

HOW TO ARRIVE AT MÁRIA REMETE

Mária Remete is about eight miles from downtown Budapest.

ROAD

From the Erzsébet Híd bridge in downtown Budapest, head northwest to Mária Remete via the streets Hegyalja, Krisztina—Alkotás, Szilágyi Erzsébet

Fasor, Hűvösvölgyi, and Máriare-
metei. The shrine is located opposite the streets Patrona and
Miatyank and is hidden by a forest of trees.

BUS

From Moszłva tér, take bus
#56 to the last station, then
change to bus #57 for Mária
Remete. On bus #57, exit at Hímes utca—the sixth bus stop. The shrine is
located across the street, hidden by a forest of trees. It is about a five-minute
walk to the shrine from the Hímes utca bus stop.

TIPS AND HINTS

To learn more about the story of Our Lady of Einsiedeln, see the book
Catholic Shrines of Western Europe: A Pilgrim's Travel Guide by Kevin J. Wright
(Liguori Publications, 1997).

As the shrine lies in a shaded area surrounded by a number of trees, it
makes for an ideal place for an outdoor picnic.

DID YOU KNOW?

More than three thousand marble plaques of ex-votos (gifts of thanksgiving) cover the entire outside base of the church.

Cathedral of Esztergom

Center of Hungarian Catholicism

Sitting atop a hill with a commanding view of the Danube River, the Cathedral of Esztergom serves as the spiritual center of Catholicism in Hungary. Welcoming pilgrims from throughout Europe and the rest of the world,
the shrine has the distinction of being the largest religious structure in the
country.

The church dates from the tenth century when the Prince of Geza ordered construction of the first cathedral at the spot. In 1010 Saint Stephen,
the king of Hungary, then converted the massive church into a basilica and
consecrated it to the Blessed Virgin Mary and Saint Adalbert.

In the following years the basilica experienced a number disasters and rebuildings. In 1188 an enormous fire destroyed the cathedral and surrounding area. Seven years later the archbishop commenced the reconstruction of the cathedral. In 1331 the huge church had to be rebuilt again, this time in the Gothic style. With each passing year, more and more chapels were added to the shrine, each one representing an earlier Hungarian Christian saint or hero, such as Saint Stephen and Maria Theresa.

In 1822 the foundation stone of the present-day basilica

Serving as the spiritual center of Catholicism in Hungary, the hilltop Cathedral of Esztergom welcomes thousands of pilgrims and visitors every year. *(Author)*

was laid. Thirty-four years later, the primate of Hungary consecrated the immense cathedral to the Blessed Virgin Mary—the patroness of the country. Today, the shrine continues to serve as both landmark and symbol of Hungary's national and spiritual heritage.

ABOUT THE SHRINE

Located on top of a hill, the vast Cathedral of Esztergom is the most visible structure in the surrounding area. Welcoming pilgrims from throughout Europe and abroad, the shrine receives thousands of visitors each year and is open daily. Among the cathedral's greatest attractions are its art and architecture. While there be sure to visit

• Cathedral • Crypt

SHRINE INFORMATION

Cathedral of Esztergom
Szent István tér 1
2500 Esztergom

TOURIST OFFICE

Tourinform Szentendre
Dumtsa J. u. 22
2000 Szentendre
Tel/Fax: (026) 317-965, (026) 317-966

Gran Tours
Széchenyi tér 25
2500 Esztergom
Tel: (033) 313-113

Komtourist
Lőrinc utca 6
2500 Esztergom
Tel: (033) 312-082

PLACES TO STAY
Beta Hotel Esztergom
Prímás-sziget
2500 Esztergom
Tel: (033) 312-555
Fax: (033) 312-853
Three-star hotel.

HOW TO ARRIVE AT ESZTERGOM
Esztergom is about forty miles north of Budapest.

ROAD
From Budapest, take highway 10 (the Panorama Highway) and head northwest to Esztergom, turning northeast on 111 at Dorog. Another route is to take Road 11 to Esztergom, following the river the entire way (this route is longer than taking highway 10, however).

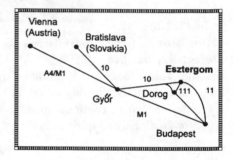

TRAIN
Esztergom is accessible by train. There are frequent departures from Budapest to Esztergom, and from Győr (via Komárom) to Esztergom. From the train station in Esztergom, take the local bus #1 to the cathedral.

BUS
There is bus service to Esztergom from nearby cities, including Budapest; however, the bus service is not so convenient or efficient as the train. From the bus station in Esztergom, take the local bus #6 to the cathedral.

FERRY
There is also ferry service from Budapest, Szentendre, and Visegrád to Esztergom between mid May and early September. There is also a hydrofoil service that runs the same route on weekends and holidays during this period.

TIPS AND HINTS

One of the best and most scenic ways to arrive at Esztergom is by taking the ferry along the Danube River.

Visiting Esztergom Cathedral is often best done by making a day-trip from Budapest or another nearby large city, such as Győr.

DID YOU KNOW?

The tomb of Joseph Cardinal Mindszenty, the famous archbishop of Esztergom and primate of Hungary who was later imprisoned for his stand against Communism, lies in the crypt of the cathedral.

$$+\!\!|\!\!+$$
$$+\!\!|\!\!+$$

Our Lady of Győr

"This is the true blood-stained cloth of the miraculous picture which shed blood and tears in this Cathedral on March 17, 1697. We offer this cloth to the glory of God and the honor of the Virgin Mary and all the saints. Győr, May 20, 1701."

INSCRIPTION ON THE BLOOD-STAINED CLOTH RELIQUARY

Serving as one of the most prominent shrines of Central and Eastern Europe, the Cathedral of Győr receives more than one million pilgrims annually from every part of the world. Inside its sacred walls lies the renowned miraculous image of the Irish Madonna of Hungary. Not a legend, the story behind this extraordinary place of pilgrimage is based on the testimony of many reliable witnesses.

The miraculous image dates from the seventeenth century and the country of Ireland. Here, the famous portrait hung for many years in the Irish Cathedral of Clonfert until the invasion of Oliver Cromwell and his army in 1649. Sparked by the desire to eliminate papal influence and establish a Protestant interest in the country, the English aggressors rounded up, arrested, and imprisoned many clergymen. Among those captured was Bishop Walter Lynch of Clonfert.

Imprisoned on an island, the bishop later escaped with other members of his group in 1652. To prevent the holy image of the Irish Madonna from falling into the hands of enemies, the prelate smuggled the picture out of the country to Belgium.

Later, he traveled to Portugal, then eventually settled in Hungary. After meeting the bishop of Győr, the local prelate appointed him as his vicar general. Here, the Irish bishop learned the Hungarian language and faithfully worked for the diocese for the next ten years.

As the situation in Ireland improved, Bishop Lynch began experiencing a strong desire to return to his homeland. However, his plans changed when he became severely ill. While on his deathbed, the prelate bequeathed the picture of the Irish Madonna to the bishop of Győr, who subsequently had the body of his Irish friend buried in the crypt of the cathedral.

On March 17, 1697, thousands of people watched as a portrait of the Irish Madonna wept bloodstained tears in the Cathedral of Győr. Hundreds of people, including the governor of the city, its mayor, all its councilmen, the bishop, priests, Calvinist and Lutheran ministers, as well as a Jewish rabbi, signed testimonies attesting to this miracle. *(Galavits József)*

With a great love already attached to the image, the Hungarian people were overjoyed to hear that the portrait would remain in their cathedral. As the news spread, many more pilgrims began making the sacred journey to the shrine to offer their petitions to the Irish Madonna of Hungary. So close did the affinity between the Virgin under this title and the Hungarians become that the faithful began attributing all their answered prayers of personal and national needs to the Irish Madonna's intercession.

In 1697 while the Hungarians enjoyed peace at home, the Irish were experiencing plenty of hardships in their homeland. The suffering worsened as Parliament passed an edict ordering the expulsion of all priests from the territory of Ireland and the British Isles. Churches were ransacked, confiscated, or destroyed, with the sole intention of erasing all traces of the Catholic faith. In its place, the National Ireland Church was established, and only members of this church were allowed to perform certain religious services.

It was the suffering of the Irish people that led to an extraordinary miracle. As thousands of parishioners were attending Mass in the Cathedral of Győr, on March 17 of that year (Saint Patrick's Day), the eyes of the Madonna began to weep bloodstained tears that ran down the canvas of the portrait. The priests took turns wiping the face of the Madonna with a linen cloth as everyone watched in awe. During the weeping, many people outside the cathedral had been summoned to witness the event.

While the painting continued to shed tears, the local church officials removed the portrait from the wall and its frame to further examine it. No explanation could be found for the phenomenon, which continued for three hours.

Among the thousands who flocked to see the miracle were Catholics, Protestants, and Jews. Many of these left testimony of what they saw, and one document in particular bears the signatures of the governor of the city, its mayor, all its councilmen, the bishop, priests, Calvinist and Lutheran ministers, as well as a Jewish rabbi. All volunteered their signatures to the document, stating that they had witnessed an undeniable miracle.

The portrait itself is a picture of the Virgin Mary gazing lovingly at her Infant Child who is peacefully asleep on a pillow. With her hands folded in prayer, she is wearing a crown and appears to be kneeling by his bedside. The baby Jesus is wearing a golden crown just like his Mother as his two arms rest above the fold of a blanket.

Today, the image of the Irish Madonna remains one of Europe's most cherished religious treasures. Sharing common histories of suffering for their faith and freedom, the countries of Ireland and Hungary will forever be bonded through the miraculous image of the Weeping Madonna of Győr .

PRAYER TO OUR LADY OF GYŐR

Our Lady of Győr, Virgin Mother, full of grace, I place myself before your holy picture with great reverence! My eyes are full of tears whenever I think of the sufferings of the Church and your followers. For them you shed tears in this place for three hours.

O Mary, through your loving and tear-filled eyes, may you see me as a devoted child of yours. Increase in me a spirit of repentance, and enliven in me a greater faith and love of your Son. Please unite all my tears with your tears and offer it as a sacrifice in order to gain mercy for me from your holy Son, Jesus Christ. Amen.

Our Lady of Győr, Our Weeping Mother, pray for us.

ABOUT THE SHRINE

The Cathedral of Győr is located at the center of the very large city near the bishop's castle, close to Káptalandomb Street. Inside the sanctuary you will find the famous altarpiece of the Weeping Icon of Mary in a side chapel to the left of the main altar. At the cathedral is also the splendid Héderváry Chapel containing a bust reliquary from one of Hungary's earliest king-saints and dating around 1400. Near the cathedral, at Káptalandomb 26 Street, is the Diocesan Treasury with its incredible collection of religious artifacts and relics. The feast of Our Lady of Győr is celebrated on March 17. While there be sure to visit

- Cathedral of Győr • Weeping Icon of Mary • Héderváry Chapel
- Diocesan Treasury

SHRINE INFORMATION

Cathedral of Győr
Káptalandomb. nr.17
Győr
Tel: (096) 320-833

Cathedral of Győr
Káptalandomb. nr.1
Győr
Tel: (096) 313-255
Fax: (096) 313-256

TOURIST OFFICE

Győr Tourist Office
Árpád u. 32
9021 Győr
Tel: (096) 317-709
Fax: (096) 328-750
Tel/Fax: (096) 311-771

Tourist—Ibusz
Szt. István u. 29-31
9021 Győr
Tel: (096) 314-224

PLACES TO STAY

Hotel Klastrom
Zechmeister u.1
9021 Győr
Tel: (096) 315-611
Fax: (096) 327-030
Hotel Klastrom, located near the Cathedral of Győr, is a three-star hotel that once served as a Carmelite cloister.

Hotel Rába
Árpád u. 34
9021 Győr
Tel: (096) 311-124
Three-star hotel.

HOW TO ARRIVE AT GYŐR

Győr is located in northwest Hungary, almost halfway between the cities of Vienna (Austria) and Budapest.

ROAD

From Budapest, head west on M1 to Győr. From Vienna, head east to Győr via A4 and M1.

TRAIN

Győr is accessible by train. From Budapest and Vienna, there is frequent train service to Győr.

BUS

Győr is accessible by bus. However, the train service is often much more convenient and efficient.

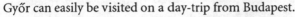

TIPS AND HINTS

Be sure to visit the shrine's gift shop, which has a number of beautiful religious objects and souvenirs of Our Lady of Győr.

Győr can easily be visited on a day-trip from Budapest.

On the Sunday following March 17 every year, there is a major pilgrimage procession to the shrine with celebrations.

DID YOU KNOW?

The linen cloth that absorbed the bloodstained tears of the Virgin Mary still exists today in the cathedral.

Our Lady of Máriabesnyő

"Dig in the wreckage...and you will find something beautiful."
OUR LADY OF MÁRIABESNYŐ

Throughout the ages a number of churches around the world have built shrines in honor of the Holy House of Loreto. In Hungary, when a family began building a replica of this particular sanctuary, they in turn discovered a miraculous image. This led to the construction of a new shrine—Máriabesnyő.

The story goes back several centuries. While a husband and wife were traveling from nearby Hatvan to their home in Gödöllő, they passed by a church in ruins on the hill of Besnyopuszta. Feeling a great sense of sorrow at seeing such a desecrated place of worship, they decided to construct a new church on top of it. As a pledge for the healing of a personal ailment, the husband chose to have the new sanctuary built in the same fashion as the Holy House of Loreto.

In the spring of 1759 construction on the new shrine began. To supervise the clearing of the wreckage and the actual building of the church, the husband and wife had hired a brick-mason. On April 19 their new employee had an experience that changed the direction of their plans. In a dream, the brick-mason heard a voice say to him, "If you dig in the wreckage of the church, near the place of the altar, you will find something beautiful." After sharing the news of his vision with a friend, they decided to dig at the place described in the dream. Before the two of them had dug very deep, they found a tiny twelfth-century sculpture of the Virgin Mary.

Often referred to as the Hungarian shrine of Loreto, Our Lady of Máriabesnyő dates from the eighteenth century when a husband and wife commissioned the building of a church on a previously desecrated site. In time it developed into a major place of pilgrimage after the finding of a miraculous image of the Virgin Mary. *(Convento dei Cappuccini)*

After their discovery, they donated the holy image to the local bishop, who had the image enshrined at the castle in Gödöllő. In the meantime, construction of the shrine finally reached completion. However, as the new sanctuary was without an image of the Virgin Mary, the Capuchin Fathers of Hatvan brought back with them a copy of the Loreto statue from Italy. In honor of the sculpture, the local Church officials crowned the image with precious jewels and placed precious clothes around the Virgin and the Child Jesus.

On August 15, 1761, the Hungarian Chapel was consecrated. Immediately, the holy shrine became a major place of pilgrimage in the area. The number of people visiting the shrine continued to grow with each passing year.

Today, the sanctuary remains a popular pilgrimage destination in Hungary. Behind the high altar, visitors can still see the famous Loreto statue that had been brought from the Italian sanctuary. The precious sculpture of the Virgin that had been discovered in the digging can also still be seen at the shrine. The image had been keep at the Gödöllő castle for a number of years, but after many requests from the faithful, the miraculous statue was returned to Máriabesnyő, in a spectacular procession on a feast day of the Blessed Virgin Mary.

In time, the entire shrine complex came to include a church, chapel, and Capuchin monastery. The settlement of the Franciscan Fathers took place on December 7, 1763. Eight years later, the bishop consecrated the newly built church and monastery. Ever since, pilgrims from both within Hungary and abroad have never ceased to come and pray before the two holy images of the Virgin Mary.

OPENING PILGRIMAGE SONG TO OUR LADY OF MÁRIABESNYŐ

We are greeting you, Our Lady of Máriabesnyő,
We bring our faithful heart to you,
You are waiting for us with open arms,
We who are coming in soiled garments,
We put down the load of our sins,
Your arms are ready to embrace us,
You dry the tears caused by our pains,
The grace of Your Son comes to us,
Because you are waiting for us,
And your Son is also waiting for us in your holy lap. Amen.
Our Lady of Máriabesnyő, pray for us.

ABOUT THE SHRINE

Located just outside of Budapest, near the city of Gödöllő, the shrine of Máriabesnyő is open daily and receives pilgrims throughout the year. Among the most important pilgrimage dates at the shrine are the feast days of the Annunciation (March 25), the Visitation (July 2), the Assumption (August 15), the Birth of the Virgin Mary (September 8), and the Immaculate Conception (December 8). Other popular days of pilgrimage include the second Sunday of May and the Feast of the Holy Trinity. While there be sure to visit

• Basilica • Statue of the Loreto Madonna • Lower chapel with Lourdes Grotto and ex-votos

SHRINE INFORMATION

Kapucinus Rendház és Plébánia
Kapucinusole tere 1
2100 Gödöllő Pf. 804
Tel/Fax: (028) 420-338

TOURIST OFFICE

Tourinform
Királyi Kastély
2100 Gödöllő
Tel: (028) 415-402
Fax: (028) 415-403

PLACES TO STAY

Mater Salvatoris
Lelkigyakorlatos Ház
Kapucinusole tere 3
2100 Gödöllő-Máriabesnyő
Tel: (028) 420-176

HOW TO ARRIVE AT MÁRIABESNYŐ

Máriabesnyő is about twenty miles from Budapest—located next to the city of Gödöllő.

ROAD

From Budapest, head northwest on 30 or M3/E71 to Máriabesnyő, via Gödöllő.

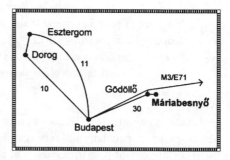

TRAIN

Máriabesnyő is accessible by train. From Budapest, there is daily train service to Gödöllő and Máriabesnyő.

BUS

Máriabesnyő is most easily accessible by bus. From Budapest and Gödöllő, there is regular service to Máriabesnyő. Once at Máriabesnyő, change to local bus service to arrive at the shrine (or make the fifteen-minute walk).

TIPS AND HINTS

Although there is a guesthouse at the shrine, many pilgrims spend the night in nearby Budapest.

DID YOU KNOW?

Our Lady of Máriabesnyő is one of the very few shrines or churches in the world that is said to possess two miraculous images of the Virgin Mary.

Our Lady of Máriapócs

The Weeping Madonna

Of all the celebrated Marian shrines in Eastern Europe, one of the most famous is Our Lady of Máriapócs. Located in a small Hungarian town, the sanctuary is home to a renowned icon of the Virgin Mary that has shed tears for its people through the centuries. Welcoming more than half a million visitors each year, the Byzantine shrine is a reflection of the life and history of the Church in Hungary.

The story of the shrine began on November 4, 1696, when an icon inside the small church of modern-day Máriapócs began weeping. As the Hungarian people were suffering terribly at the time, it was not surprising to them that the Virgin Mary was shedding tears for her people. The country was a divided nation, and the different ruling principalities were placing horrible burdens on the people.

For two full weeks, the image continued to weep. During this time a number of spectacular cures and healings were recorded. One of the most astounding occurred when a priest of a neighboring village lifted a dying child to the weeping icon. As the child reached out to touch the sacred tears falling from the Virgin's eyes, the boy experienced an immediate and full recovery. Overwhelmed, the boy's mother placed a necklace of precious stones on the icon in a sign of thanksgiving. Over time, such offerings eventually engulfed the entire image.

A month later, the supernatural

In November 4, 1696, an icon inside the small church of Máriapócs wept tears for two full weeks, during which time a number of spectacular cures and healings occurred. Although the image was eventually transferred to the Cathedral of St. Stephen in Vienna, Máriapócs received a new image in 1715 that also later shed tears and became the source of many miracles. *(Máriapócsi Kegytemplom)*

wonders continued. On December 8, 1696, as the Divine Liturgy progressed on a bitterly cold day, the icon began to weep again. The astounding miracle this time was that although the wine in the priest's chalice had frozen, the tears continued to stream down the Virgin's face despite its exposure to the icy air. The phenomenon continued for the next eleven days in the frigid weather.

Immediately, Church and secular officials began an investigation into the icon. Upon the conclusion of their in-depth inquiry, they issued a report affirming the authenticity of the tears.

When Leopold I, emperor of Austria, heard of the miraculous icon, he immediately ordered it moved to Vienna. Despite the objections of the Hungarian faithful, it was transferred in February 1697. Upon its arrival in Vienna, the icon was received with great pomp and devotion and placed over the high altar in the Cathedral of St. Stephen. (Today it is enshrined at a side altar to the right of the cathedral's main entrance.)

Nevertheless, in the course of the next forty years, close to three hundred cures and other miracles were attributed to the weeping icon the Austrians called Maria Pötsch. Outstanding among these was the defeat of the overwhelming Turkish forces at Zenta in 1697, a triumph for which the entire Austrian populace had sent up prayers to the icon of Máriapócs.

A copy of the icon, sent to Máriapócs by the Austrian emperor, began to weep between August 1 and 3, 1715. It was another time of great sadness as the Hungarians fighting for their independence were defeated by the armies of the Hapsburg emperor and sent into exile in Turkey. Some of the soldiers who had fought in this battle had come from the village of the weeping icon.

Again, a Church tribunal put the tears through a rigorous examination. The committee's outcome: the tears were authentic. The miracles obtained through devotion to the second icon of Máriapócs were not confined to cures. On one occasion an innocent man who had been charged with murder and sentenced to death was granted one last wish: to visit the shrine at Máriapócs. While there, an unseen force unshackled the prisoner's locked chains, freeing the man. The miraculous event proved his true innocence.

In time, devotion to the new image increased so much that a larger shrine had to be built to accommodate all the pilgrims. The new sanctuary was consecrated in 1756.

In this century, the icon at Máriapócs has wept again. From December 3 to 19, 1905, the holy image shed tears as poverty gripped the Hungarian people. An estimated three million people suffered from destitution, as thousands left Hungary in search of a better life elsewhere.

Again, after a scrupulous examination of the famous icon, the investigating committee declared the miraculous tears authentic. The panel of members who studied the image consisted of doctors and scientists, Catholic theologians, Protestants, and Jews.

In 1946 the shrine received an extraordinary honor when Pope Pius XII bestowed the title of Basilica on the church of Máriapócs. Cardinal Mindszenty, the famous archbishop of Esztergom and primate of Hungary who was later imprisoned for his stand against Communism, served as the principal celebrant of the liturgy to mark the occasion. The celebration also commemorated the 250th anniversary of the original icon's first weeping and the 300th anniversary of the Union of Uzhorod, which united the region's Orthodox Christians with the Church of Rome.

Soon thereafter, Communism took a death-grip on Hungary and the rest of Eastern Europe. The new leaders attempted to eradicate the Catholic faith in the country. Pilgrimages to Máriapócs were forbidden, and the roads leading to the shrine were blocked. The vehicle licenses of pilgrims wishing to drive to Máriapócs were officially recorded, and bus drivers were heavily fined. Even in later years the State Office of Church Affairs had to give an annual account of each pilgrimage, covering every detail from the number of participants to the text of the priest's sermon. As late as 1989 a report had to be submitted about Communist Party members who took part in such pilgrimages.

With the fall of the Iron Curtain in 1989, non-Communist leaders stepped into the new government roles. This opened the way for religious freedom in Hungary and the renewal of pilgrimages to Máriapócs. New signs of life were seen at the shrine as votive offerings were once again found at the altar of the icon. Since then, the number of gifts left at the shrine from the faithful for prayers answered have multiplied with each passing year.

One of the shrine's most recent extraordinary moments occurred on August 18, 1991, when Pope John Paul II visited Máriapócs. Together with the Byzantine bishops, he concelebrated the Divine Liturgy according to the Eastern Rite. In 1996 the shrine celebrated the three hundredth anniversary of the first weeping. Today, pilgrims are again flocking to the shrine in record numbers to pay homage before the miraculous image of the Virgin Mary.

PRAYER TO OUR LADY OF MÁRIAPÓCS

O most blessed Virgin Mary, Mother of mercy, adorned with miracles, whose icon shed tears at the place of your mercy in Máriapócs, we, who honor you, humbly beseech your motherly care. Save our country from all its enemies; protect the Church; and join all in one faith that, at last, the words of Christ may be fulfilled: "There shall be one fold and one shepherd." Do not deny us your intercession; and obtain for us peaceful times, health for our bodies, and peace for our souls. Obtain the grace for

us that our last hour finds us in the Christian faith and in a state of grace
so that we are enabled to gain eternal salvation. Amen.

Our Weeping Madonna of Máriapócs, pray for us.

ABOUT THE SHRINE

A very small town of two thousand people, Máriapócs lies about seven miles west of Nyírbátor in eastern Hungary and is easily accessible by road, bus, and train. At the Monastery of the Basilian Fathers stands the town's splendid Greek Catholic Church—containing the second image of the famous Weeping Madonna statue. Although the Weeping Madonna of Máriapócs does not have its own special feast day, the icon is venerated at the shrine on every Marian feast and each Sunday of May. The shrine is open every day of the year for pilgrims and visitors. As the sanctuary plays a central role in the small town, Máriapócs offers outstanding hospitality, recreation, and entertainment. While there be sure to visit

- Monastery of the Basilian Fathers • Máriapócs Catholic Church
- Statue of the Weeping Black Madonna • Processions, celebrations, and religious services

SHRINE INFORMATION

Máriapócsi Kegytemplom
Kossuth Tér 25
4326 Máriapócs
Tel/Fax: (042) 385-142

TOURIST OFFICE

Máriapócs Tourist Information Office
Tel: (042) 215-686
Fax: (042) 385-626

PLACES TO STAY

Máriapócsi Kegytemplom
Kossuth Tér 25
4326 Máriapócs
Tel/Fax: (042) 385-142

HOW TO ARRIVE AT MÁRIAPÓCS

Máriapócs is about 7 miles west of Nyírbátor and 160 miles northeast of Budapest.

ROAD

From Nyíregyháza, head east to Máriapócs via Nagykálló and Kállósemjén; and from Nyírbátor, head west to Máriapócs, following the signs.

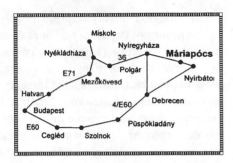

TRAIN

Máriapócs is accessible by train. All trains between Nyírbátor and Nyíregyháza stop at the Máriapócs station, where a bus will take you into town (2.5 miles).

BUS

Máriapócs is accessible by bus. From Ady Endre utca in Nyírbátor, there are frequent bus departures to Máriapócs. (Note that the bus service is often much more convenient and efficient than the train service from Nyírbátor.)

TIPS AND HINTS

Of the sixteen major annual pilgrimages, those on August 15, the Feast of the Assumption, and September 8, the Nativity of the Virgin, are the largest.

DID YOU KNOW?

During its several month "pilgrimage trip" to Vienna, the miraculous image of Our Lady of Máriapócs was greeted by people along its entire route who came to pay homage to it. In fact, large groups of the faithful delayed the carriage transporting the holy painting at each post depot for veneration.

$$\begin{array}{c}+\|+\\ \hline +\|+\end{array}$$

Pannonhalma Abbey

A World Heritage Site

One of the few shrines to receive global recognition for its spiritual and historic legacies is the Benedictine Arch-Abbey of Pannonhalma in Hungary. In December 1996, UNESCO designated the monastery and its surrounding area as a World Heritage site because of its unique religious and cultural contributions to the nation and world.

The great Pannonhalma Abbey dates from its establishment in 996. Prince Géza, the father of the renowned Saint King Stephen, invited Benedictine missionaries to Hungary to spread the gospel. Upon their arrival, they settled on the Mount of Pannonia and built their first abbey, which they dedicated to Saint Martin. Along with the priory, the monks also founded the country's first monastic school in the same century.

Saint Stephen, the first king of Hungary (1000–1038) became a great devotee of the abbey and often visited it. In 1002 the saintly king bestowed rights, privileges, land, and income on the monastery, in an attempt to help the monks spread the Christian faith west of the Danube River. In the following two centuries, as the priory grew in both prestige and influence, the abbey experienced a number of expansions. During this time the monastery became a bulwark of the Catholic and Hungarian culture.

Recently designated a World Heritage site by UNESCO, the tenth-century Pannonhalma Abbey remains one of Hungary's premier pilgrimage destinations for its spiritual and historical legacies. *(Author)*

Between 1586 and 1638 the Turks invaded the area and turned the monastery into a castle, forcing the monks to leave. After returning to the abbey in the seventeenth century, the friars experienced another invasion by the Turks, who severely damaged the abbey again. The following years, however, brought more peace, and at the turn of the century in 1700 the order celebrated the 700th anniversary of its settlement in Hungary.

In the beginning of the nineteenth century, by decree of Emperor Francis II, the monks began devoting most of their energies to their new apostolate of teaching, and they built one of the largest libraries in Europe. Since 1802 the monks have remained active in education, and after World War II they built one of the most modern boarding schools in the country.

A recent extraordinary moment for the abbey occurred in 1996, when Pope John Paul II made a pilgrimage to the mountaintop to join the monks in their celebrations for the 1,000th anniversary of the monastery's founding. Today, the abbey remains the destination of many pilgrimages and tourist trips because of its religious and historical importance.

ABOUT THE SHRINE

Pannonhalma is twelve miles south of Győr and is easily accessible by bus, train, and road. The abbey itself sits atop St. Martin Hill, with a beautiful panoramic view of the surrounding lush green countryside. Guided tours of the Abbey in the Hungarian language are available throughout the year; Guided tours in other languages are available only between March 21 and November 11. It is important to note that the abbey may be visited only with a local guide. It is best to contact the shrine information office beforehand to make arrangements for a tour guide. While there be sure to visit

- Pannonhalma Abbey • Basilica and crypt • Cloister • Library
- Picture gallery • Exhibition representing the history of the monastery • Chapel of the Blessed Virgin • Millennial Memorial

SHRINE INFORMATION

Pax Tourist Office
Vár 1
9090 Pannonhalma
Tel: (096) 570-191
Fax: (096) 570-192

TOURIST OFFICE

Tourinform Pannonhalma
Petőfi u. 25
9090 Pannonhalma
Tel/Fax: (096) 470-187

PLACES TO STAY

Pannon Pension
Hunyadi u. 7/c.
9090 Pannonhalma
Tel/Fax: (096) 470-041
Offers excellent accommodations, with an in-house restaurant.

Familia Panzió
Béke u. 61
9090 Pannonhalma
Tel/Fax: (096) 470-192
Offers excellent accommodations, with an in-house restaurant.

Pax Hotel
Dózsa György u.2.
9090 Pannonhalma
Tel: (096) 470-006
Three-star hotel.

Panoráma Kemping
Fenyvesalja u.4.
9090 Pannonhalma
Three-star hotel.

HOW TO ARRIVE AT PANNONHALMA

Pannonhalma is about twelve miles south of Győr.

ROAD

From Győr, head south on highway 82 to Pannonhalma. From Veszprém, head north on highway 82.

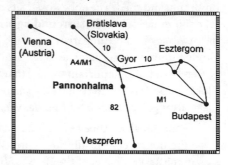

TRAIN

Pannonhalma is accessible by train. From Győr, there is frequent train service to Pannonhalma (heading in the direction of Veszprém).

BUS

Pannonhalma is accessible by bus. From Győr, the bus service is much more frequent than the train to Pannonhalma, making it an excellent option. However, make sure to take the bus that actually provides service to the abbey at the top of the hill. (Some buses provide service to the city of Pannonhalma only and do not drive up the hill to the abbey. If you happen to take one of these buses, however, you can make the pleasant twenty-minute walk uphill.)

TIPS AND HINTS

A walk around the abbey is recommended as the Millennial Memorial (1896) and the Baroque Blessed Virgin Chapel (1710) are close by.

You can easily visit Pannonhalma Abbey on a day-trip from Budapest or Győr.

DID YOU KNOW?

During the Holocaust hundreds of refugees sought shelter in the monastery under the protection of the Red Cross.

Lithuania

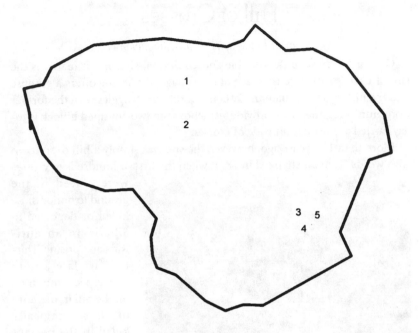

1. Hill of Crosses
2. Our Lady of Šiluva
3. Our Lady Gate of Dawn
4. Cathedral of Vilnius
5. Church of the Holy Spirit

LITHUANIA

Hill of Crosses

A Testament to the Spirit of the Lithuanian People

One of the most unforgettable and emotional sites in Lithuania is the Hill of Crosses. An intense place of pilgrimage, the shrine offers a glimpse into the history of Lithuanian Catholics and their struggles with the former Communist regime. A worldwide attraction, the two-humped hillock is today buried amidst a multitude of crosses.

More than 170 years ago, however, the site was simply a hill overgrown with weeds. That all changed in 1831, when the first of hundreds of crosses

were placed in the ground to honor those killed or deported to Siberia in an anti-Russian uprising. Thirty years later, more crosses were mounted on the hill in memory of those tragically killed in the peasant rebellion of 1863. In the ensuing years, more and more crosses were added to the site. At the end of the nine-

One of the most revered and emotional places of pilgrimage in Lithuania, the world-renowned Hill of Crosses is a symbol of the people's resistance to violence, oppression, and genocide. Despite the former Soviets' attempts to destroy the site, the area is today filled with more than fifty thousand crosses, rosaries, and other religious symbols. *(Kathleen and Valerie Kelly)*

teenth and beginning of the twentieth centuries, the faithful came here to pray in solitude or take part in religious processions. They came to present their needs to God, to mourn those who had been killed, imprisoned, or exiled, and to recall important historical events.

When Soviet authorities took power in Lithuania after World War II, the new government designated the place as "forbidden" and severely punished those who defied them. The great drama then began to unfold as authorities destroyed the crosses on the hill in an attempt to smother Christianity and erase the "fanaticism." Between 1941 and 1952 the Lithuanians suffered greatly

186

as many of their people were exiled to Siberia. Entire villages were emptied. In 1956 the people began returning to their homes.

Only a short time later, the faithful began secretly replenishing the hill with crosses again in memory of the unbearable torture they had endured and of those who had died and in gratitude for coming back. Lithuanians who returned from captivity in Siberia also put up crosses to thank God for the chance to walk the paths of their homeland and breathe its air again. In time, the Hill of Crosses with its heart-wrenching inscriptions became an open book of people's lives. The site symbolized resistance to violence, oppression, and genocide. The resurrection of the crosses on the hill told the world that the nation of Lithuania was not dead.

But once the Communist authorities discovered the freshly planted Christian symbols, they attempted in the spring of 1961 to rid the site of its religious sentiments once and for all. Under the strict guard of the Red Army and KGB, soldiers bulldozed the area, burned the wooden crosses, recycled the iron ones, and buried the stone crosses in the ground. A maple tree, planted by the people to symbolize Lithuania's independence, was also uprooted. (Ironically, however, the townspeople later returned the tree to the hill in the form of a cross.)

When new crosses began cropping up, the Soviets attempted new ways of destroying the hill. On one occasion, the Soviets flooded the place, turning the Hill into a virtual island. The Communists exhausted themselves in designing new ways to stop the faithful from planting the symbols of resurrection. They dug ditches, closed bus stops, posted signs, punished trespassers, and blocked roads. But all was in vain. Ironically, one of the new crosses erected during the night read, "Jesus, do not punish the villains for they do not know what they are doing." In total, the government bulldozed the hill three times, only to see the crosses spring up again and again. In 1975 the authorities leveled the hill for the last time.

Since then, more than fifty thousand crosses have been placed on the hill—a testament to the spirit of the people. The planting of crosses can be traced to the Lithuanian tradition of erecting crosses near roads and settlements. In fact, in the beginning of the nineteenth century, so many crosses had been placed on the sides of roads that the Minister of Internal Affairs of the Russian Empire issued an edict forbidding the erecting of them. However, the order had little effect, as the cross had already become a deeply rooted symbol in the heart of the Lithuanian people.

Recently, an extraordinary events occurred at the Hill of Crosses when Pope John Paul II celebrated Mass at the site in 1993. Today, more and more of the faithful are joining him in making a pilgrimage to the sacred spot.

Here, the incredible courage shown by the Lithuanian Catholics demonstrates the power of faith in God. For every visitor, the Hill of Crosses serves as a sacred monument to human existence—past, present, and future.

PRAYER OF THE CROSS

Jesus, you became an example of humility, obedience, and patience and preceded me on the way of life bearing your cross. Grant that, inflamed with your love, I may cheerfully take upon myself the sweet yoke of your gospel together with the mortification of the cross and follow you as a true disciple so that I may be united with you in heaven forever and ever. Amen.

ABOUT THE SHRINE

Six miles north of Šiauliai on the road to Meskuciai stands the Hill of Crosses, one of the most revered places of pilgrimage in Lithuania. Located just off Riga Road, the Hill of Crosses is easily accessible by car, bus, and taxi from Šiauliai. As it is a common tradition today for pilgrims to leave behind a cross and a prayer, visitors can purchase sacred objects such as crucifixes or rosaries at the various souvenir stands. Unless you are providing your own transportation, it's probably best to stay the night in Šiauliai. While there be sure to visit

• Hill of Crosses • Leave a cross and prayer at the site

SHRINE INFORMATION

There is no shrine information office at the Hill of Crosses.

TOURIST OFFICE

Tour guides, interpreters, transportation, and accommodations can be arranged through the following office:

Šiauliai Tourist Information Centre
Vilniaus Street 88
5400 Šiauliai
Tel: (1) 43.07.95
Fax: (1) 42.26.95

Šiauliai Travel Agency
Varpo 22A
5400 Šiauliai
Tel: (1) 43.39.95
Fax: (1) 43.84.61

Šiauliai Tourism Information Centre
Vilniaus st. 213
5400 Šiauliai
Tel: (1) 422-644
Fax: (1) 420-480

PLACES TO STAY

Aronija
Gumbines st. 10
5400 Šiauliai
Tel: (1) 423-672
Fax: (1) 423-672

Norna
Tilžės st. 126c
5400 Šiauliai
Tel: (1) 425-594
Fax: (1) 429-326

Saulininkas
Lukauskio st. 5A
5400 Šiauliai
Tel: (1) 436-555
Fax: (1) 421-848

Tomal
Tilžės st. 63a
5400 Šiauliai
Tel/Fax: (1) 455-541

Vaivorykšte
Gytariu st. 25
5400 Šiauliai
Tel: (1) 416-124
Fax: (1) 415-537

HOW TO ARRIVE AT THE HILL OF CROSSES

The Hill of Crosses is located six miles north of Šiauliai.

ROAD

From Šiauliai, take A12 north in the direction of Meskuciai. The Hill of Crosses is about one mile east off the road to Joniskis and Riga. Look for the sign "Kryziu Kalnas 1.5" (Hill of Crosses).

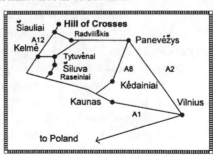

TRAIN

The Hill of Crosses is not accessible by train. The nearest train station is at Šiauliai—which has excellent connections from other Lithuanian cities.

BUS

From Šiauliai, it is a short bus ride to the Hill of Crosses. Tell the ticket office person and the bus driver you want to visit Kryziu Kalnas (Hill of Crosses).

TAXI

One of the most convenient ways to see the Hill of Crosses is to hire a taxi. For a rather minimal cost, you can pay a taxi driver to drive you there, wait while you visit the site, and then drive you back. If you decide to do this, however, be sure to clarify the price with the taxi driver *before* you depart for the Hill of Crosses.

TIPS AND HINTS

If you're traveling by public transport you may need to spend a night in Šiauliai because you have to get to Šiauliai first to catch a bus or taxi to the Hill of Crosses (and then another bus or taxi back into town to make further connections elsewhere).

One of the busiest weeks at the Hill of Crosses is Easter Week.

DID YOU KNOW?

Newlyweds often come here after their wedding ceremony to ask for God's blessing.

✠

Our Lady of Šiluva

"Why are you weeping? Who hurt you?"

Recognized as one of Lithuania's most celebrated Marian shrines, the sanctuary of Our Lady of Šiluva receives several hundred thousand pilgrims each year. Home to the site of a Church-approved Marian apparition from the seventeenth century, the shrine has recently gained widespread attention and continues to grow in popularity. In 1993 the sanctuary received its most famous pilgrim yet—Pope John Paul II.

One of the three Baltic states, Lithuania was a part of the former Soviet Union. With a turbulent history of invading neighbors, the country has long experienced troubled times. Despite its past difficulties, the citizens of Lithuania have seldom wavered in their faithfulness to the Mother of God. Over and over again, they have placed their country under the patronage and protection of the Blessed Virgin Mary.

The history of Our Lady of Šiluva shrine began in 1457 when Peter Gedgaudas, a wealthy Lithuanian nobleman, built the first church in the area. Over time, a small community grew up around the place of worship. Serving as a diplomat for Vytautas the Great, Mr. Gedgaudas often traveled abroad. Once, after making a trip to Rome, he returned with a painting of the Virgin and Child Jesus, which he placed in the sanctuary of the new church.

The sixteenth century brought troubled times for the Catholic Church in Lithuania when Lutheranism and Calvinism arrived, attracting a number of converts. Among those who switched their faiths were the nobility and intellectuals. This, unfortunately, resulted in the confiscation of many Catholic properties by Protestant authorities.

In 1570 the church at Šiluva became a target of appropriation as well. Knowing this, the parish priest, Fr. John Halubka, hid the church's documents and possessions and the treasured image of the Ma-

In the summer of 1608 the Virgin Mary appeared to a few shepherd children in Šiluva, holding the Baby Jesus in her arms as she wept sadly. After an exhaustive investigation, the Church approved the apparition, and in 1993 Pope John Paul II prayed at the site. *(Author)*

donna and Child Jesus in a chest under a large rock near the church. This later proved to be providential, as Protestants eventually seized the church.

Less than two decades later, however, a new law was passed that gave Catholics the right to repossess church properties unjustly taken from them. To reclaim control of a particular place, though, they had to present to the authorities documents clearly proving their previous ownership. This latter legality proved to be almost fatal for the church in Šiluva. No records could be found proving that Peter Giedgaudas had given the land to the Catholic Church in 1457. Hence, the church remained in the possession of Protestant rulers.

Twenty years later an extraordinary event occurred in Šiluva, changing the life of the citizens. During the summer of 1608 a beautiful lady appeared to a few children who were out shepherding their flocks. Holding a child in her arms, the lady was seen weeping bitterly as she stood on a large rock. Startled by the vision, one of the young shepherds quickly ran back to the village to inform others of the incident. Upon hearing the news, a Calvinist teacher decried the lady to be the work of the devil.

As word about the event spread throughout the town, the curious and devout began to make their way to the rock. It was not long before the lady appeared again—but this time to everyone present. All who were standing near watched as the lady's tears dropped to the large stone below her. The Calvinist teacher, who had been mocking the people for listening to the tales of children, eventually approached the lady and asked, "Why are you weeping? Who hurt you?" Sadly, the vision replied, "Formerly in this place my Son was adored and honored, but now all that the people do is seed and cultivate the land." Upon saying this, the beautiful lady and child vanished.

Almost immediately, news of the miraculous event reached the local bishop's office. The prelate subsequently dispatched his representative, Fr. John Kazakevicius, to examine and verify the reports. Part of the canon's investigation included questioning all those who witnessed the event.

As the inquiry by the Catholic Church was commencing, a second miracle occurred. A blind man, who had heard about the apparitions, remembered the oak chest that the pastor had buried years before under the large rock. When the authorities led him to the place, the blind man's sight was immediately restored (this event is documented in historical records). With the ability to see now, the man pointed out the exact location of the chest. The chest was opened, and inside was the cherished and undamaged portrait of the Virgin and Child, as well as documents proving the ownership of the church property.

After a number of court battles, the Calvinists eventually returned the land to the Catholics. Shortly afterward, a local priest built a small wooden church with his own means at the site. In 1663 the bishop replaced it with a larger chapel built over the rock of the apparition—with the altar positioned over the stone. Great numbers of pilgrims continued to venerate the miraculous portrait.

The image of the Virgin and Child became so loved and adored that, with the approval of Pope Pius VI, the bishop formally approved the devotion paid to Our Lady of Šiluva. In addition, another image at the shrine grew in popularity. In 1770 a lady had placed a statue of the Virgin Mary and the baby Jesus near the altar. So numerous were the prayers answered through Our Lady's intercession that in 1886 the statue received the name "Our Lady— Health of the Sick." So cherished was the statue that the people placed it atop the rock of the apparition.

In the ensuing years, crowds to Šiluva continued to increase. To accommodate the influx of pilgrims, larger churches had to be built in 1818 and

1924. Devotion to Our Lady of Šiluva thrived until 1940—the year the Soviet Union gained control of the independent Lithuania. With an official "state religion" of atheism, Catholic services were forbidden in the new U.S.S.R. Yet despite the risk of severe punishment, many Lithuanians continued to meet secretly for Mass and other religious services.

This lasted until 1989, the year Lithuania declared its independence from the Soviet Union. With its newfound freedom, the Catholic Church was once again able to celebrate services open. At Šiluva, that meant pilgrims could begin visiting their beloved shrine again without fear of repercussions.

Today, the shrine has regained its foothold as a major place of pilgrimage. Although the miraculous image is usually exposed only during public ceremonies, another much-beloved portrait depicting the apparition remains on display. From the testimony of thousands, Our Lady of Šiluva continues to serve as a powerful intercessor before God and a source of many blessings and healings for her people.

PRAYER TO OUR LADY OF ŠILUVA

O most Holy Virgin Mary, you who appeared to the shepherds in the fields at Šiluva, you whose tears bathed the rock where once an altar stood, you who with plaintive voice said, "You plow and seed here where formerly my Son was honored," grant that we, moved by your tears, may once, as our forefathers did, revive the spirit of adoration of your Son in our hearts, strengthen the tottering structure of the shrine that is the family, and seek forgiveness for the negligences and sins of our nation.

O Mother of God, we desire to raise up the glory of your revelation from forgotten ruins, that we may all the more honor you the patroness of our country and, with your help, obtain for our nation the spirit of a living Faith. Through Christ our Lord. Amen.

Our Lady of Šiluva, pray for us.

ABOUT THE SHRINE

The shrine of Our Lady of Šiluva is located in north-central Lithuania and is open throughout the year. Although the miraculous image is concealed behind a golden-framed painting depicting the apparition of the Blessed Mother, it is exposed during public ceremonies (however, visiting pilgrims can often request the custodians of the shrine to unveil it for them). The greatest feast day at the shrine is the Nativity of the Blessed Virgin Mary, September 8. A week of celebrations and festivities follows and continues through September 15. The chapel containing the image is decorated with beautiful frescoes and paintings. While there be sure to visit

• Our Lady of Šiluva shrine • Miraculous image of the Madonna
• Celebrations and Festivities

SHRINE INFORMATION

M. Jurgaicio a.2a
Raseiniu raj.
LT-4407 Šiluva
Tel: (28) 43.298, (28) 43.190
Fax: (28) 43.190
E-mail: lenktaitis@kaunas.omnitel.net

TOURIST OFFICE

There is no tourist office in Šiluva. However, there are other tourist offices
and travel agencies in Lithuania that can provide information on Šiluva
(see Tourist Office for *Our Lady Gate of Dawn* and *Hill of Crosses*).

PLACES TO STAY

Although there are no places to stay in Šiluva, there are a number of hotels
in nearby Šiauliai (see *Hill of Crosses*). Most pilgrims make a day-trip to
the shrine of Our Lady of Šiluva from Šiauliai.

HOW TO ARRIVE AT ŠILUVA

Šiluva is about 40 miles south of Šiauliai and 120 miles northwest of
Vilnius.

ROAD

From Šiauliai, take A216 south
to Šiluva. From Kaunas, take A1
west to Raseiniai, then continue
north to Šiluva via 148.

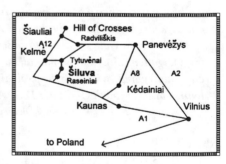

TRAIN

Šiluva is not accessible by
train. The nearest major railway
station is at Šiauliai. From
Šiauliai, there is bus and taxi service to Šiluva.

BUS

Šiluva is accessible by bus from Šiauliai, Kaunas, Vilnius, and other nearby
Lithuanian cities. However, unless you are accompanied by a local guide or
someone who speaks the local language, it is strongly recommended to hire
a taxi or some form of private transportation to Šiluva instead.

TAXI, PRIVATE TRANSPORTATION, AND/OR HIRING A LOCAL GUIDE

If you are traveling independently in Lithuania and do not speak the Lithuanian language, keep in mind that it is best to hire a taxi or some form of private transportation to Šiluva and a local guide. Šiluva is a very small town with no hotels, places to stay, or taxis.

TIPS AND HINTS

Religious celebrations and activities take place at the shrine between September 7 and 15. This church festival is referred to as "silines."

While in Lithuania and before visiting Šiluva, stop by a local tourist office or travel agency and inquire about hiring a guide or translator for your trip to Šiluva. (This is especially important if you are traveling by bus or another form of public transportation to Šiluva and do not speak the local language.)

DID YOU KNOW?

In 1959 during a restoration of the miraculous image, signs of the picture's having been folded were found. The portrait had been shown to be folded four times—thus proving its presence in the oak chest, as attested by historical testimony.

$$+\hspace{-0.3em}\|\hspace{-0.3em}+$$
$$+\hspace{-0.3em}\|\hspace{-0.3em}+$$

Our Lady Gate of Dawn

The Pride of Vilnius

Serving as one of Lithuania's most celebrated pilgrimage sites, Our Lady Gate of Dawn sanctuary attracts more than half a million visitors each year. Also known as Aušros Vartų (Lithuanian for *Gate of Dawn*), the shrine is situated in the country's capital city of Vilnius. What draws the many pilgrims each year is the miraculous portrait of the Blessed Virgin Mary that lies within its walls.

The image dates from the sixteenth century. At that period city officials had built a great stone wall, with nine gates, around the city. One of these entrances, which lies on the southeastern side of Vilnius, earned the nickname "Gate of Dawn." It was here that two religious paintings had been placed in the niches of the wall. An image on the inside of the gate depicted the Virgin Mary, while the other on the outside depicted Christ giving a blessing.

According to the historian and Carmelite priest Hilary, the local Vilnius friars were so devoted to the painting of the Blessed Virgin that they built a monastery in 1620 near the gate. A year later they commenced construction on a monastery church at the site (which they later dedicated to Saint Teresa).

In 1671 the friars continued their expansion and built a wooden chapel over the gate. After placing the portrait inside the new sanctuary, a number of miracles were reported by those who prayed there. In total, Friar Hilary recorded seventeen miracles that occurred between 1671 and 1761. Although the Church refused to pass judgment on the miracles, word about the miraculous painting and the favors received became widespread. The portrait continued to grow in notoriety when in 1688 a group of newly consecrated Vilnius bishops marched in procession to the Gate of Dawn and prayed before the image for guidance.

Dating from the sixteenth century, the cherished portrait of Our Lady Gate of Dawn, which lies above one of the old entrance gates of Vilnius, has been the source of many miracles and cures through the years. Pope John Paul II prayed before the image in 1993 during his visit to Lithuania. *(Author)*

Disaster struck in 1715 when a fire destroyed the wooden chapel housing the miraculous painting. Fortunately, a few Carmelites had just enough time to pull the image safely from the burning sanctuary. They placed the portrait in the monastery church until a new brick chapel was built in 1726 on the original site. In 1773 the picture received its first official recognition by the Church—Pope Clement XIV granted an indulgence to all who visited the shrine.

The painting had another close accident in 1795, when the Russians occupied Lithuania and destroyed the wall that encircled Vilnius. Although everything was essentially reduced to rubble, the Gate of Dawn shrine remained standing and untouched. When Friar Hilary's book on the shrine was republished in 1823, the miraculous painting became even more famous. In response, the Carmelites began producing holy cards reflecting the image of Our Lady Gate of Dawn and passed them out freely. One of the defining moments for the shrine occurred in 1927. In that year Pope Pius XI solemnly crowned the cherished image of Our Lady Gate of Dawn.

Before World War II the shrine remained a busy place. The faithful filled the chapel every morning for Mass and every evening sang Marian hymns. The greatest number of pilgrims flocked to the shrine on November 16, the Feast of Our Lady of Mercy.

Unfortunately, the Soviet occupation of Lithuania in 1944 put an end to religious services at the shrine. Convents, monasteries, and Catholic schools also felt the effects as their buildings were either confiscated or closed. It became forbidden to practice Christianity openly.

Forty-five years later, this all changed. In 1989 Lithuania declared its independence from the U.S.S.R. With the fall of Communism, religious celebrations and activities at the shrine resumed. Thousands of pilgrims began visiting the shrine again, and in 1993 Pope John Paul II prayed before the miraculous image of Our Lady Gate of Dawn.

PRAYER TO OUR LADY GATE OF DAWN

O my Mother, Queen of heaven and earth, gifted with God's marvelous graces and elevated above all his creatures, you can obtain from God everything that you desire. In this place, where I, a sinner, now kneel before your miraculous picture, you have manifested your power numerous times, and thus you give us hope that you will intercede for us again. You saved us from erroneous teaching. You performed many miracles instantaneously restoring health to the sick. You guide Lithuania on the road of divine Providence. O most merciful and most powerful Mother, look at us, sinners, now, instill an ardent love for your Son in the hearts of the children of Lithuania, and those around the world, that they may glorify your Son Jesus Christ in peace and unity and may choose you as the special caregiver of our land. O Mary, extend your care over Lithuania and the rest of the world and protect it. Amen.

Our Lady Gate of Dawn, pray for us.

ABOUT THE SHRINE

The Gate of Dawn shrine is located in the large city of Vilnius at Aušros Vartų 12. To enter the sanctuary, which is at the top of Aušros Vartų gate, go through the door on the east side of the street shortly before the gate. The door gives way to a staircase, which leads to the small chapel containing the icon of the Virgin. Pilgrims visiting the little shrine usually come and go as they please. Other sites to visit in Vilnius include the cathedral (Arkikatedra Bazilika) and the Church of the Holy Spirit (located at Dominikonu 2). Pope John Paul II visited both of these shrines during his historic 1993 trip to Lithuania. While there be sure to visit

• Gate of Dawn Shrine • Icon of Mary • Cathedral • Church of the
Holy Spirit

SHRINE INFORMATION

Aušros Vartų 12
2000 Vilnius
Tel: (2) 622-378

The Roman Catholic Church
Šventaragio 4
2000 Vilnius
Tel: (2) 62-70-98

TOURIST OFFICE

Vilnius Tourist Information Centre
Vilnius 25
2000 Vilnius
Tel: (2) 62.07.62
Fax: (2) 62.81.69

Lithuanian Tourist Board
Vilniaus 4/35
2000 Vilnius
Tel: (2) 62-26-10
Fax: (2) 22-68-19
E-mail: vtd@ktl.mii.lt or tb@tourism.lt
Website: http://neris.mii.lt/visitors/strukt.htm and http://neris.mii.lt/ (in
menu, select *Tourist Information*)

Tourism Information Centre of Vilnius Country
Gedimino 14
2000 Vilnius
Tel: (2) 616-867
Fax: (2) 226-118
E-mail: turizm.inf@vilnius.aps.lt

Tourism Information Centre
Pilies 42
2000 Vilnius
Tel/Fax: (2) 620-762

PLACES TO STAY

Contact the tourist information office for a full listing of places to stay in Vilnius, or pick up the *Vilnius in Your Pocket* book, which gives a full description of hotels to stay in the city.

HOW TO ARRIVE AT VILNIUS

Vilnius is located in southeastern Lithuania.

ROAD

From Kaunas, head east on A1 to Vilnius. From Šiauliai, head southeast to Vilnius via Panevėžys (A9 and A2) or Kaunas (A12 and A1).

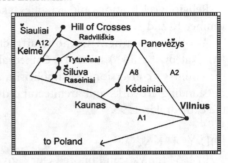

TRAIN

Vilnius is accessible by train. From cities throughout Lithuania, such as Šiauliai, there are usually only one or two daily departures to Vilnius. From Warsaw (Poland), there are also only one or two daily departures to Vilnius. Although traveling by rail from Poland to Vilnius is not recommended, train travel *within* Lithuania can be quite nice.

BUS

Vilnius is accessible by bus from many cities throughout Lithuania. From Kaunas and Šiauliai, there are several daily departures to Vilnius. (Note: in Lithuania, traveling by bus is quite popular, as trains do not serve every town and village. For distant destinations choose an express bus, but remember that overnight rides can be quite uncomfortable.)

ARRIVING IN LITHUANIA FROM POLAND

To arrive in Vilnius or other major Lithuania cities from Poland, you can choose from either the bus or train service. However, for reasons of comfort, convenience, safety, and efficiency, it is highly recommended to take the bus rather than the train to Lithuania from Poland (and vice versa). Polish cities including Warsaw, Olsztyn, and Suwałki have excellent bus service to Vilnius. From Warsaw, buses leave from the main Warszawa Zachodnia (West) station—except for one, which leaves from the Warszawa Wschodnia (East) station.

Note that it is very important to avoid taking any form of transportation (usually the train) that travels in or through Belarus—as this country is currently experiencing high levels of unrest. If you must go by train to Vilnius, the best option is to travel to Kaunas, spend the night, then continue to Vilnius in the morning. There is a direct Warsaw-Vilnius night train, but since it crosses Belarus, you are awakened in the middle of the night several times by customs officers and are required to have a Belarussian transit visa.

TIPS AND HINTS
Religious celebrations and activities take place at the shrine between November 10 and 17.

Another prominent Catholic attraction in Vilnius is its cathedral (Arkikatedra Bazilika), located at Cathedral Square. Built in 1387 to celebrate the country's conversion to Catholicism, the church features a number of outstanding artworks and architectural designs. Pope John Paul II visited the cathedral in 1993.

DID YOU KNOW?
In 1954 the Vatican honored Our Lady Gate of Dawn with a stamp that bore the likeness of the miraculous image.

Church of the Holy Spirit
Home to the First Image of Divine Mercy

Drawing pilgrims from around the world, the Church of the Holy Spirit in Vilnius houses one of Eastern Europe's most prized possessions—the original painting of Divine Mercy as revealed to Blessed Sister Faustina by Jesus. Enthroned above a side altar since 1987, the image remains the object of numerous pilgrimages.

On the first Sunday of Lent, February 22, 1931, Our Lord appeared as the Merciful Jesus in a vision to Blessed Faustina at her convent in Plock, Poland. She saw him clothed in a full white garment, his right hand raised in blessing and his other one slightly touching his chest. Underneath his left hand, two large rays were seen emanating from his heart. One was red, the other translucent.

Jesus then instructed Blessed Faustina to have an image painted according to this design. The person chosen to carry out the work was Eugeniusz Kazimirowski, an artist from Vilnius. Painting according to Blessed Faustina's instructions, he completed the first image of Divine Mercy in 1934. Three years later Faustina's spiritual confessor consecrated the image and placed it near the high altar in his church. It remained here until 1948, when St. Michael's Church had to be closed.

For the next thirty years the image experienced a pilgrimage of its own. Transferred from one place to another, the painting eventually arrived at the Church of the Holy Spirit in 1987. Six years later, in September 1993, Pope John Paul II prayed before the sacred image during his Lithuanian pastoral visit. Today, millions around the world pray before a replica of the same original image of Divine Mercy as they say, "Jesus, have mercy on us, and on the whole world."

Since 1987 the painting of the first image of Divine Mercy, as revealed to Blessed Faustina by Jesus, has been enshrined above a side altar in the Church of the Holy Spirit in Vilnius. *(Church of the Holy Spirit)*

CHAPLET OF THE DIVINE MERCY
(For recitation on ordinary rosary beads)

Begin with:
Our Father..., Hail Mary…, The Apostles' Creed.

Then, on the OUR FATHER beads, say the following words:
Eternal Father, I offer you the Body and Blood, Soul and Divinity of your dearly beloved Son, Our Lord Jesus Christ, in atonement for our sins and those of the whole world.

On the HAIL MARY beads, say the following words:
For the sake of his sorrowful Passion, have mercy on us and on the whole world.

In conclusion, recite these words three times:
Holy God, Holy Mighty One, Holy Immortal One, have mercy on us and on the whole world.

This is the prayer that Jesus dictated to Blessed Faustina in Vilnius on September 13–14, 1935. He spoke about this prayer on as many as fourteen occasions, explaining its purpose and the promises attached to it.

ABOUT THE SHRINE

Serving as the main center for the Catholic Polish-speaking community in Vilnius, the Church of the Holy Spirit is also known for another reason—it is here that the original image of the Divine Mercy is enshrined above a side altar. Administered by the Dominicans, the shrine has a splendid gold-and-white interior and is worth a visit for its art and architecture alone. Above the main altar is a remarkable crucifix that is "brought to life" by the incoming daylight. The Church of the Holy Spirit is the only sanctuary in Vilnius where Mass is said in Polish exclusively. While there be sure to visit

• Church of the Holy Spirit • Original painting of the Divine Mercy

SHRINE INFORMATION

Church of the Holy Spirit
Dominikonų St. 8
2001 Vilnius
Tel: (2) 62.95.95
Tel/Fax: (2) 22.41.81

TOURIST OFFICE

See *Our Lady Gate of Dawn* for more information about tourist offices in Vilnius.

PLACES TO STAY

Contact the tourist offices for more information about places to stay in Vilnius.

HOW TO ARRIVE AT THE CHURCH OF THE HOLY SPIRIT

The Church of the Holy Spirit is located on Dominikonų Street.
(For directions on how to arrive at Vilnius, see *Our Lady Gate of Dawn*.)

TIPS AND HINTS

To make the best of your pilgrimage trip, you can also visit the Shrine of Divine Mercy in Kraków, Poland (see *Shrine of Divine Mercy*).

The Church of the Holy Spirit can easily be visited when en route from the Gate of Dawn sanctuary to the cathedral, as it located about halfway between the two shrines.

DID YOU KNOW?

The Chaplet of Divine Mercy is traditionally said at three o'clock every day. The reason for this is that in Jesus' revelations to Blessed Faustina, he asked for a daily remembrance of his Passion at the very hour that recalls his death on the cross.

Cathedral of Vilnius

A Special Setting for Lithuania's Patron Saint

The massive structure of the Cathedral of Vilnius is recognized as a place of pilgrimage for one main reason: it is home to the Chapel of Saint Casimir and the sacred relics of this great Lithuanian patron saint. Every year the faithful come to pray at his tomb and seek his powerful intercession.

Born in 1458 as the second son of King Casimir IV and Elizabeth of Austria, Casimir came into the world as a prince and

One of the city's landmark symbols, the Cathedral of Vilnius is a massive religious structure possessing beautiful works of art and sacred objects, including the tomb of Saint Casimir—Lithuania's patron saint. *(Kathleen and Valerie Kelly)*

grew up in a world surrounded by riches and royalty. Despite his many treasures, he devoted himself at an early age to the service of the Lord. Rejecting the ordinary comforts of the palace, the saint wore the plainest of clothing, slept on the floor, and spent many nights in prayer.

When he was twenty-three, his parents wanted to arrange a marriage for him with the daughter of Emperor Frederick II, but the prince would not hear of it because he had pledged his chastity to God. Over time, the saint became known for his sense of justice, temperate character, intelligence, love for neighbor, frequent meditations on Christ's Passion, and devotion to Mary, Mother of God.

Although nothing noteworthy ever occurred in the saint's short "political" career, he became most known for his generous care of the poor. Recognized for his saintly virtues, the young prince had become very dear to the Polish people during his four-year reign in the country while his father was absent on affairs of the state in Lithuania. In 1484 the beloved Casimir died in Vilnius while on a state visit. After his death, the love and respect of the Polish and Lithuanian people for the saintly prince continued, and a number of miracles had been attributed to him through his intercession.

Only seventeen years after the prince's death, the saint's grave site had become so popular that Pope Alexander VI granted an indulgence to the chapel in which Casimir had been buried. The supreme pontiff noted that "as has been reported, his coffin is becoming renowned for the numerous miracles that have been occurring." In 1620 Pope Paul V extended the feast day of Saint Casimir to the universal Church, authorizing a Mass and a proper Divine office. In 1636 Pope Urban VIII proclaimed Saint Casimir the patron saint of Lithuania, and Pope Innocent X permitted the annual celebration of the transferring of his relics.

Today, the cathedral has returned to being a place of pilgrimage after being desecrated by the Communists. From 1956 to November 1988, the Soviet Lithuanian regime had used the cathedral as a picture gallery and had prohibited religious services. However, in front of a joyous crowd of believers and a gathering of the world press on February 5, 1989, the church was reconsecrated. Four years later the shrine received its most famous visitor— Pope John Paul II.

PRAYER TO SAINT CASIMIR

Saint Casimir, Patron Saint of Lithuania, intercede for us before the Almighty so that he will grant us the grace that our hearts be enflamed by an ardent faith and love of one another; that our youth comprehend the beauty of a chaste and virtuous life; and that the parental Providence of God may lead our entire nation down the path of devotion to his commandments toward peace and prosperity. Amen.
Saint Casimir, pray for us.

ABOUT THE SHRINE

Serving as the country's most important national symbol, the Cathedral of Vilnius is open daily and receives pilgrims throughout the year. A vast spiritual edifice, the cathedral lies near the heart of the city at Arkikatedros Square. To the right of the high altar lies the cathedral's greatest showpiece, the Chapel of St. Casimir. Inside this small sanctuary are the sacred relics and tomb of Lithuania's patron saint, whose feast is celebrated on March 4. While there be sure to visit

• Vilnius Cathedral • Chapel of St. Casimir • Cathedral gift shop

SHRINE INFORMATION

There is no shrine information office.

TOURIST OFFICE

See *Our Lady Gate of Dawn* for tourist office information.

PLACES TO STAY

See *Our Lady Gate of Dawn* for more information about places to stay in Vilnius.

HOW TO ARRIVE AT THE CATHEDRAL OF VILNIUS

The Cathedral of Vilnius is located at Arkikatedros Square.

(For directions on how to arrive at Vilnius, see *Our Lady Gate of Dawn*.)

TIPS AND HINTS

Be sure to pick up *Vilnius in Your Pocket* at one of the kiosks in front of the Vilnius train station. This small inexpensive guidebook provides every bit of information you need to get around town, and more. For more information about these guides, visit the website at www.inyourpocket.com

When visiting the cathedral's gift shop, ask for any English materials or books. Sometimes the shop has a few rare resources on the history of the Catholic faith in Eastern Europe—materials that can't be found elsewhere.

DID YOU KNOW?

In 1948 Pope Pius XII declared Saint Casimir the patron saint of all Lithuanian youth.

Poland

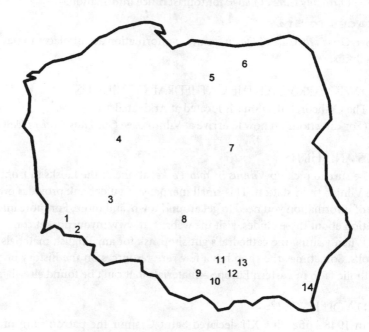

1. Our Lady of Krzeszów
2. Our Lady of Wambierzyce
3. Saint Hedwig
4. Cathedral of Gniezno & St. Adalbert
5. Our Lady of Gietrzwałd
6. Our Lady of Świętz Lipka
7. City of the Immaculate - Niepokalanów
8. Our Lady of Częstochowa
9. St. Maximilian Kolbe & Auschwitz
10. Kalwaria Zebrzydowska
11. Shrine of Divine Mercy
12. Cathedral of Kraków
13. St. Mary's Basilica
14. Kalwaria Pacławska

*awful
so sad
so gray* ✚

Saint Maximilian Kolbe and Auschwitz

"No one has greater love than this, to lay down one's life for one's friends."
JOHN 15:13

Almost everyone has heard of Auschwitz. The name alone is enough to make you shudder. It is a place where one of the worst examples of human genocide took place. However, it is also the place where one of the greatest single acts of love occurred. Here at Auschwitz, Saint Maximilian Kolbe offered his life for that of another prisoner.

His story begins in the Polish village of Zdunska-Wola where he was born on January 8, 1894, as the second child of devout parents with the name of Raymond. He was considered a mischievous child, and one day his mother asked him, "Raymond, what is to become of you?" Upon hearing these words, the saddened child retreated to his room and asked the Virgin Mary the same question. The response he received was a mystical experience whereby Our Lady appeared to him, and in her hands

One of the worst episodes of human genocide ever known occurred at Auschwitz during World War II. However, one of the greatest single acts of love also occurred here when in 1941 Saint Maximilian Kolbe offered his life for that of another prisoner and died soon after in Block #11, Cell #18. *(Author)*

she held two crowns: a white one for purity and a red one for martyrdom. The Virgin asked Raymond, "Which one do you choose?" After the young boy replied, "I want both," the Madonna smiled tenderly and disappeared.

At age sixteen Raymond entered the seminary, and on September 4, 1910, he was invested with the Franciscan habit, receiving the name of Maximilian. Exceptionally gifted intellectually, Maximilian was sent to Rome in 1912 to study theology and philosophy at the Pontifical Gregorian University. By the age of twenty-one, he earned a doctorate in philosophy; several years later, a doctorate in theology.

Maximilian wasn't only an excellent student, he was also a devout man with an extraordinary love for the Virgin Mary. During his years in the seminary, Maximilian founded the Marian organization Knights of the Immaculata. Serving as a powerful instrument for the international Marian movement, the Knights consisted of members who consecrated themselves to Jesus through Mary and worked for the salvation of all souls. A significant aspect of the Knight's apostolate was the conversion and sanctification of non-Catholics, especially those who were hostile to the faith.

For the next twenty years Father Kolbe dedicated his life to the building up of the apostolate. The extraordinary growth of his organization in the 1920s led to Maximilian's founding of Niepokalanów—a Franciscan Friary and city (see page 248). The new community promoted devotion to the Virgin Mary through the use of modern technology. By 1936 the priory grew to more than nine hundred friars publishing a monthly magazine and a daily newspaper with a circulation of more than one million.

Things took a turn for the worse in September 1939. Germany invaded Poland, and the Franciscan Priory was ransacked. Father Kolbe, along with forty other friars, was arrested and taken to a holding camp. Three months later they were released, on December 8, the Feast of the Immaculate Conception.

When Maximilian returned to Niepokalanów, he found that his friary had became a refugee camp for thousands of Poles and Jews who had escaped from Nazi persecution. Before long, Father Kolbe came under intense scrutiny by the Gestapo. Refusing German citizenship, Maximilian was labeled a "threat." He sealed his fate when he wrote in a December 1940, issue of the *Knight of Mary Immaculata*:

> No one in the world can change truth, what we can do and should do is to seek it and serve it when it is found. The real conflict is inner conflict. Beyond armies of occupation and the catacombs of concentration camps, there are two irreconcilable enemies in the depth of every soul: good and evil, sin and love And what use are the victories on the battlefield if we ourselves are defeated in our innermost personal selves?

On February 17, 1941, Kolbe was again arrested, this time on charges of aiding Jews and the Polish underground. After being stationed in a prison in Warsaw for three months, he was deported to Auschwitz. Upon entering the concentration camp, he read the mocking sign over the entrance gate: "Arbeit macht frei—Work brings freedom."

Few who passed through the gate left the camp alive. Upon entering it, prisoners were told that Jews had the right to live only two weeks, Roman Catholic priests one month. Cruelly, they were told that the only way out of the camp was through the chimneys of the crematorium.

At Auschwitz, untold millions of Jews and Roman Catholics were murdered. In his hatred for Jesus Christ, Hitler's goal was to remove all witness to the truth of the original revelation of the God of Israel (the Jewish nation), as well as all who came to believe in him in his Incarnation by the Virgin Mary (Roman Catholics).

After giving him his prisoner clothing, the guards tattooed Father Kolbe's arm with the number 16670. From there on his daily work consisted of such activities as carrying heavy blocks of stone, cutting and hauling huge tree trunks, transporting corpses, and pushing wheelbarrows full of gravel. Vicious blows and kicks from the guards accompanied each passing day.

Despite the atrocities taking place all around him, Father Kolbe became well known for his love and encouragement. In the words of one prisoner, "He was a prince among us." Still dedicated to his priestly ministry, Father Kolbe celebrated Mass with the smuggled in bread and wine.

According to camp law, if anyone attempted to escape, ten men from the same bunker would be selected for death by starvation in a windowless, underground, rat-infested, cell. Near the end of July, a prisoner from Father Kolbe's group had apparently escaped. In retaliation, the SS guards forced them all to stand all day in the blazing midday sun. In the evening, the sergeant selected ten men at random to be sentenced to death. When Francis Gajowniczek was picked, he cried out in desperation and begged the soldiers to spare his life as he was the father of a family. Suddenly, another prisoner stepped out from the ranks and offered to take his place. It was prisoner number 16670—Father Kolbe.

The head SS guard turned to the friar and asked, "Who are you?" Kolbe replied, "I am a Catholic priest." The commander then pointed and told Maximilian to go with the group of condemned men. Immediately, the guards led the ten prisoners to the death chamber of cell #18. (Horribly, the "escaped" prisoner was later found drowned in the camp toilets.)

In the following days, Father Kolbe led prayers in the death chamber as the inmates died one by one. When the soldiers came to take out a corpse, the friar would be found singing a canticle, with the inmates around him repeating the chorus. After two weeks, only four prisoners remained, one of whom was Kolbe. As the guards needed to make room for new inmates, the authorities injected carbolic acid (phenol) into the arms of the remaining prisoners. One witness, a former inmate assigned to the bunker as an undertaker, later testified to seeing Father Kolbe's face completely calm and radiant after dying. The date of his death was August 14, 1941—the eve of the Feast of the Assumption.

Thirty years after his death, Pope Paul VI beatified Maximilian, on October 17, 1971. Then, the defining moment occurred in 1982 when Pope John Paul II canonized the Franciscan. Today, he is often referred to as "the martyr of charity."

PRAYER TO SAINT MAXIMILIAN KOLBE

Crown my soul with a share in your charity and purity, Saint Maximilian. The ardent fire of your love ennobled the white purity of your life. Your red martyrdom of self-sacrifice put the finishing touch on the white martyrdom of your lifelong virtue. It was the Virgin Mary who first offered you these crowns of red and white. Implore her to obtain from God the graces that I need to walk my earthly pilgrimage in charity and purity of heart.

On the Vigil of Our Lady's Assumption, you became a living holocaust at Auschwitz fifty years ago. Now, crowned with glory in heaven, united with Mary to our Triune God, please intercede for my intentions and for all people. May this world be transformed, through charity and purity, into the Kingdom where God lives and reigns in peace forever. Amen.

Saint Maximilian Kolbe, pray for us.

ABOUT THE SHRINE

Auschwitz (Oświęcim in Polish) is a rather large town located about thirty-five miles west of Kraków. Known as one of the largest of all the Nazi death camps, today Auschwitz is a state museum—serving as a reminder to the horror of human hate. Books, pamphlets, and materials about the concentration camp in various languages are found everywhere at the site. There is also a fifteen-minute film at the visitors' center, which plays in several different languages throughout the day. Guided tours of the camps (Auschwitz and Birkenau) are also available in a number of languages, including English. Inside the Auschwitz camp is where you will find the block and cell where Saint Maximilian Kolbe was martyred. Also, in a cell (#21) near Kolbe's are the drawings of the Crucifixion and Sacred Heart, etched in by one of the prisoners. While there be sure to visit

• Auschwitz concentration camp • Saint Maximilian Kolbe's cell (Block #11, Cell #18) • Drawings of Immaculate Heart and Sacred Heart (Block #11, Cell #21) • Birkenau concentration camp • Guided tours

SHRINE INFORMATION

State Museum in Auschwitz-Birkenau
Węzniów Oświęcimia 20
32-603 Oświęcim
Tel: (033) 43-20-22, (033) 43-20-27, (033) 43-21-33
Fax: (033) 43-19-34, (033) 43-22-27

TOURIST OFFICE

Contact the State Museum for more information about Auschwitz-Birkenau.

PLACES TO STAY

Auschwitz Center of Information and Dialogue
Centrum Dialogu I Modlitwy W Oświęcimiu
Ul. Maksymiliana Kolbego 1
32-602 Oświęcim
Tel: (033) 43-10-00
Fax: (033) 43-10-01
The Catholic Church owns and runs the Auschwitz Center of Information and Dialogue (listed above). Located one block from the Auschwitz camp, the center provides comfortable and quiet accommodations, a restaurant, helpful staff who speak English, French, and Polish, as well as a library and telephone and fax services.

HOW TO ARRIVE AT OŚWIĘCIM/AUSCHWITZ

Oświęcim/Auschwitz is about twenty miles south of Katowice and thirty-eight miles west of Kraków.

ROAD

From Katowice, take 1/E75 south, turning east on 950 and following the signs to Oświęcim. From Kraków, take A4 west, then continue south following the signs to Oświęcim. Another option from Kraków is to take 952 west to Oświęcim.

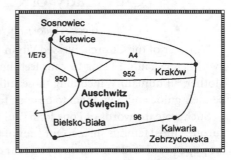

TRAIN

Oświęcim/Auschwitz is accessible by train. From Kraków and Katowice, there is frequent train service to Oświęcim. From the Oświęcim railway station, take the city bus to the Auschwitz camp (one mile). As most trains depart only in the very early morning from Kraków to Oświęcim, it is important to check the schedule the day before so you may plan accordingly. Otherwise, there are no afternoon trains until about 3 P.M.—which is often too late to leave for Oświęcim, unless you plan to spend the night.

BUS

Oświęcim/Auschwitz is easily accessible by bus from nearby cities. From Katowice and Kraków, there is frequent bus service. Upon arrival at Oświęcim, be sure not to miss your stop at the Auschwitz Museum, otherwise you will have to backtrack several miles (this is important to keep in mind as there are several different bus stops in the large city of Oświęcim). Ask the bus driver which stop is for the Auschwitz Museum.

TIPS AND HINTS

It is strongly recommended to take a guided tour of the Auschwitz and Birkenau camps as the tours are available in a number of languages (including English) and provide excellent information.

From Kraków, a trip to Auschwitz takes one very full day—so plan accordingly and be sure to get there as early as possible.

DID YOU KNOW?

Francis Gajowniczek, the prisoner for whom Father Kolbe gave his life, was present at the canonization ceremony of Saint Maximilian in 1982.

Our Lady of Częstochowa

The Black Madonna, Queen of Poland

"Mother of the Church, Blessed Virgin Help of Christians, in the humility of Peter's faith, I bring to your feet the whole Church…I bring here, O Mother, all humanity, including those still searching for the way to Christ. Be their guide and help them to be open to the God who is coming."

Such were the words of Pope John Paul II upon his recent visit to Eastern Europe's most famous shrine, Our Lady of Częstochowa. A native of Poland, the pope has visited the sanctuary on four occasions since his election to the

Chair of Peter. Today, Częstochowa remains one of the biggest pilgrimage centers in the world, attracting more than five million visitors each year.

Serving as Poland's national shrine, the sanctuary of Our Lady of Częstochowa owes its fame to a cherished icon of the Madonna. An object of veneration for centuries, the image has been the source of numerous and spectacular miracles. Although the origin of the icon is unknown, one legend says that Saint Luke the Evangelist painted the portrait on a table made by Jesus himself.

Attracting more than five million pilgrims every year, Our Lady of Częstochowa is recognized as one of the most visited places of Christian pilgrimage in the world. According to one legend, Saint Luke the Evangelist painted the world-famous image of Our Lady of Częstochowa on a table made by Jesus himself. The portrait has been the subject of numerous miracles through the centuries and today remains one of Pope John Paul II's most famous objects of devotion. *(Shrine of Our Lady of Częstochowa)*

Several centuries later, Saint Helena, the mother of Roman Emperor Constantine, is said to have discovered the image while in Jerusalem searching for the Holy Cross. Upon her return home to Constantinople, she took with her this precious painting, which her son promptly enshrined. The painting quickly became a favorite among the people for its miracles. For the next five hundred years the portrait of the Virgin remained in Constantinople.

In 803 the Byzantine emperor is said to have given the painting away as a wedding gift to a Greek princess. Marrying a Ruthenian nobleman, the young bride placed the image in the royal palace at Belz, where it remained for nearly six hundred years.

In the fourteenth century the painting came into danger as the Tartars attacked Ruthenia and occupied the city. Everything in the city was looted— except for the portrait of the Madonna. During the occupation, a mysterious cloud was said to have enveloped the chapel containing the image.

After the enemies returned to their homeland, an angel appeared in a dream to Saint Ladislaus, the prince of Belz, and ordered him to take the picture to an obscure village named Częstochowa. Fulfilling the heavenly wishes, the saint founded a monastery of Pauline monks to care for the icon. In 1386 the friars built the first church on Jasna Góra (Bright Hill).

For the next forty-five years Częstochowa experienced peace. During this time, King Jagiello had united Poland and Lithuania and built a great cathedral around the chapel containing the beloved portrait.

However, in 1430 the invading Hussites attacked Częstochowa, burning and robbing everything in sight. Among their loot was the miraculous image of the Madonna. While departing from the city, they attempted to destroy the painting. Struggling to achieve their cause, one soldier in frustration struck the painting with his sword, leaving two gashes on Our Lady's right cheek. Frightened by the incident, the soldiers fled as they abandoned the desecrated and mutilated painting.

When the monks later found the picture, it was lying in the mud, covered with dirt and blood. When the monks went to clean the portrait, they found

that all the wells had gone dry in fighting the fires from the invasion. At this time a miraculous fountain sprung up, and the monks used its water to clean the painting. The picture was later repainted in a workshop in Kraków, but the scars on the face of the Virgin Mary were left as a reminder of the sacrilege.

For the next two hundred years Poland remained in constant danger of attack from neighboring enemies. In 1655, when Częstochowa seemed to be on the verge of collapse from an invasion by Swedish troops, a handful of Polish soldiers prayed with great fervor before the holy image, begging for deliverance. Almost immediately, the enemy began to retreat. Other victories won by the Polish nation were also attributed to the miraculous help of the Madonna. In 1656, in gratitude to the Mother of God, King John Casimir declared Our Lady of Częstochowa "Queen of Poland" and designated the city as the spiritual capital of the nation.

In this century, the Polish people have again sought recourse to the Virgin. In 1919 the newly organized Soviet Russian Red Army immediately invaded the unified and newly independent country of Poland. In desperation for divine help, the priests carried the Blessed Sacrament in procession through the cities and villages, and the people prayed novenas to Our Lady of Częstochowa. On September 14, 1920, the Russians stood on the banks of the Vistula River, ready to attack Warsaw. According to the various sources, on September 15, the feast day of Our Lady of Sorrows, the Madonna appeared in the clouds above Warsaw as the citizens and soldiers prayed. This was the turning point in the war, as the enemy was routed in a series of battles later known as the "Miracle at the Vistula."

During the Nazi invasion and subsequent occupation, Hitler prohibited pilgrimages to the shrine of Częstochowa. However, this did not stop some people from secretly making the journey there during those years. In 1945, after Poland was liberated from Nazism, half a million pilgrims made the sacred journey to Częstochowa to express their gratitude to the Mother of God. On September 8, 1946, one and a half million people participated in the rededication of the entire nation to the Immaculate Heart of Mary at the shrine. In 1947 an even greater crowd gathered to implore the aid of the Holy Virgin against a new danger: Communism. Forty-two years later, that same crowd, along with the rest of the world, watched as Communism fell to defeat.

Through the years, the Holy See has repeatedly approved and sanctioned the devotion to Our Lady of Częstochowa. Pope Clement XI made papal recognition of the miraculous image in 1717. In 1925 Pope Pius XI affirmed the title of Mary as "Queen of Poland" and designated May 3 to be a feast in her honor under this name. In recent times, Pope John Paul II prayed before the Madonna during his historic visit in 1979, several months after his election to the Chair of Peter. The pope also made subsequent visits to Our Lady of Częstochowa in 1983, 1991, and 1997.

Today, the shrine continues to welcome pilgrims from around the world in record numbers. During one week in the summer of 1997, more than half a million pilgrims visited the sanctuary. With the fall of the Iron Curtain in 1989, the story of Our Lady of Częstochowa is finally reaching the far corners of the earth. As it is blessed by a rich and magnificent history, it is no wonder that the shrine ranks among the greatest in the world.

PRAYER TO OUR LADY OF CZĘSTOCHOWA

Holy Mother of Częstochowa, you are full of grace, goodness, and mercy.
I consecrate to you all my thoughts, words, and actions—my soul and
body. I ask for your blessings and especially prayers for my salvation. To-
day, I consecrate myself to you, Good Mother, totally—with my body and
soul amid joy and suffering to obtain for others and myself your blessings
on this earth and eternal life in heaven. Amen.
Our Lady of Częstochowa, pray for us.

ABOUT THE SHRINE

As one of the most famous shrines in the world, Our Lady of Częstochowa is a dynamic place to visit. Everything from being easily accessible to being rich in religious activities and events, it makes for one of the most enjoyable pilgrimage experiences. The Monastery of Jasna Góra is situated at the western end of the main thoroughfare of the city center—Al Najswietszej Marii Panny (Al NMP). Both the railway and bus stations are just south of the eastern part of Al NMP (near St. Sigismund's Church). To arrive at the monastery, take either a taxi or the twenty-minute walk. Once there, you will find the shrine's most prized possession—the miraculous icon of Our Lady with the Child Jesus—in the chapel of the basilica. Masses are celebrated daily in Latin, Polish, and other foreign languages. The shrine is open throughout the year and is especially full on feast days related to the Virgin Mary. The Information Center of Jasna Góra (at ul. O.A. Kordeckiego 2) provides excellent information concerning Mass, confession (in various languages, including English), guided tours, and room reservations. Also, be sure to make a visit to the tourist office at Al NMP 65 where maps and publications about the monastery are sold in various languages (including English). The Claromontana Shop at the shrine is an excellent place to buy religious souvenirs. While there be sure to visit

- Basilica • Chapel • Miraculous picture of Our Lady with Child Jesus • Treasury • Museum • Knights' Hall • Arsenal
- Claromontana Shop • Information Center of Jasna Góra

SHRINE INFORMATION

Jasnogórskie Centrum Informacji
(Information Center of Jasna Góra)
Ul. O.A. Kordeckiego 2
42-225 Częstochowa 25
Tel: (034) 365-38-88
Fax: (034) 365-43-43

TOURIST OFFICE

Częstochowa Tourist Information Center
Centrum Informacji Turystycznej
Al. N.M.P. 65
42-200 Częstochowa
Tel: (034) 324-13-60
Tel/Fax: (034) 324-34-12

Polish Tourist Information Center
Ul. Nowowiejskiego 3
42-200 Częstochowa-Jasna Gora
Tel: (034) 347-673
Fax: (034) 303-7686

Voivodeship Tourist Information Center
Ul. Najświętszej Marii Panny 65
42-200 Częstochowa
Tel: (034) 341-360, (034) 434-312, (034) 241-360
Fax: (034) 303-7686

PLACES TO STAY

Dom Pielgrzyma im. Jana Pałwa II (Pilgrim's House)
Ul. Kard. Wyszyńskiego 1/31
42-225 Częstochowa 25
Tel: (034) 324-70-11
Fax: (034) 365-18-70
The Pilgrims' House is a large church-operated hotel, located right behind
the monastery, offering excellent accommodations.

Diecezjalny Dom Rekolekcyjny
SS. Szarytki
Ul Sw Barbary 43
42-200 Częstochowa-Jasna Gora
Tel: (034) 324-11-77
A ten-minute walk from the monastery, this church-run hotel also provides
excellent accommodations for pilgrims.

SS. Brygidki (Sisters of St. Brigid)
Ul. Elzbiety 11
42-225 Częstochowa
Tel: (034) 365-15-76

SS. Franciszkanki (Franciscan Sisters)
Rodziny Maryi
Ul. Ks. Kard. Wyszyńskiego 77/79
42-225 Częstochowa
Tel: (034) 362-95-61

John Paul II Pilgrim's Inn
ul. Kardynała
Wyszyńskiego 1/31
Tel: (034) 343-302

Hotel Patria
ul Popieluszki 2
42-225 Częstochowa
Tel: (034) 324-70-01
Fax: (034) 324-63-32, (034) 303-72-69
Located in the monastery area, this non-church-operated hotel provides
simple and nice accommodations.

HOW TO ARRIVE AT CZĘSTOCHOWA

Częstochowa is located in south central Poland.

ROAD

From Kraków, take 4/E40 west
to Katowice, and 1/E75 north to
Częstochowa. From Warsaw, take
8/E67 and 1/E75 south to Częstochowa.

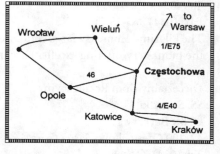

TRAIN

Częstochowa is accessible by
train. From Warsaw and Kraków,
there are about six daily fast trains. From Katowice, there are hourly departures. Częstochowa also has train service to/from Lódz (about eight trains
daily), Opole, and Wrocław. From the railway station at Częstochowa, take
the local bus or taxi service to the shrine.

BUS

The bus station is close to the railway station and operates plenty of buses
in the region. There is bus service from nearby places such as Jedrzejów,
Opole, and Kraków.

TIPS AND HINTS

The major Marian feasts at Jasna Góra are held on May 3, August 15,
August 26, September 8, and December 8, and on these days the monastery
is packed with pilgrims. On the Feast of the Assumption (August 15), pilgrims come on foot to Częstochowa from all over Poland. More than half a
million of the faithful make the journey to Jasna Góra for the feast day.

Contact the Information Center of Jasna Góra for all your pretravel plans, including booking guided tours and Mass at the monastery and reserving rooms at the Pilgrims' House (Dom Pielgrzyma).

DID YOU KNOW?

There are actually seven cuts on the Madonna's face: they are located on her neck and face and above her right eye.

$$+\!\!\parallel\!\!+$$
$$+\!\!\parallel\!\!+$$

Our Lady of Gietrzwałd

"Recite the rosary zealously...I am with you always."
OUR LADY OF GIETRZWAŁD

World-famous Marian shrines, such as Lourdes and Fátima, capture most of the headlines around the world, but there are a few other Church-approved Marian apparition sites that deserve attention. One such place is the sanctuary of Our Lady of Gietrzwałd in the beautiful countryside of northern Poland. The shrine is one of Eastern Europe's best-kept secrets.

Dating from the fourteenth century, the church first served as a major pilgrimage destination because of the

One of Eastern Europe's best-kept secrets, Our Lady of Gietrzwałd shrine is home to a Church-approved Marian apparition from the nineteenth century and a miraculous image of the Blessed Virgin that was crowned by the future Pope John Paul II on September 8, 1967. *(Kathleen and Valerie Kelly)*

precious treasure it holds within its sacred walls—a miraculous portrait of Our Lady of Gietrzwałd. Earliest historical references place the icon's existence in the area at 1568. In the seventeenth century, records indicate that special devotions and consecrations were performed under the title of Our Lady of Gietrzwałd and in conjunction with the holy image. In fact, the icon is said to have had such an impact on the local faithful that it served as inspiration for the founding of several religious communities. So beloved was the portrait at the shrine itself that the church became filled with precious gifts and souvenirs left by pilgrims who had received special healings and graces.

In the following centuries the miraculous image continued to serve as an important part of the lives of Polish Catholics. In this century, during celebrations of the ninetieth anniversary of the apparitions, the painting received a glorious honor when the primate of Poland (Cardinal Stefan Wyszynski) bestowed a golden papal crown upon Our Lady of Gietrzwałd in front of twenty thousand joy-filled pilgrims. Among the bishops who assisted the cardinal in the September 8, 1967, ceremony was Karol Wojtyła—the future Pope John Paul II.

The actual apparitions of the Virgin Mary at Gietrzwałd took place between June 27 and September 16, 1877. As in Lourdes (1858), La Salette (1846), Pontmain (1871), and Fátima (1917), Our Lady appeared to simple village children. At Gietrzwałd, one of the visionaries was thirteen-year-old Justina Szafrynska, and the other was twelve-year-old Barbara Samulowska.

Our Lady first appeared to Justina as she was preparing for her upcoming first holy Communion. After leaving the rectory, she and her mother heard the Angelus bell ringing. As they knelt down to pray, Justina suddenly saw a bright light in a nearby maple tree. Immediately, the young girl became enraptured in the vision. Completely unaware of the supernatural happenings, her mother encouraged Justina to finish her prayers so that they could continue with the rest of their daily activities. Still in a state of ecstasy, Justina responded that she could see in front of her the Virgin Mary sitting on a brilliant chair surrounded by angels. As the apparition lasted only a few minutes, Our Lady spoke little, except that she did ask the girl to return the next day.

Fulfilling the Virgin's request, Justina did return the following day—but this time with a friend, Barbara Samulowska. Together, they began reciting the rosary, when suddenly the Virgin appeared again, this time to both children. Justina described the Virgin as "a Lady of incomparable beauty, maybe sixteen to eighteen years old, surrounded by a brightness more brilliant than snow. She had gentle, shining blue eyes….and around her were long rays of light. She seemed like a living being, the only difference being the brightness." Later in the apparition, the girls watched as "the angels placed the Child Jesus on her lap."

In the fourth apparition, on June 30, the Virgin said in Polish, "I wish you to pray the rosary every day." In their ensuing sworn testimonies, the girls later reported that the Madonna's words were uttered so loudly that they thought everyone in the church had heard her.

In the fifth apparition, at the request of the priest, Justina asked the Lady for her identity. The heavenly Mother responded, "I am the Blessed Virgin Mary."

For the following two and a half months, the apparitions continued every day. With each appearance, the crowds grew larger and larger. At the request of some of the pilgrims, the girls asked Our Lady specific questions regarding imprisoned priests, alcoholics, and the fate of Poland. The Virgin's answer was always the same: "You must pray the rosary." Mary then asked that a shrine be built with a statue of the Immaculate Conception. On another occasion, Our Lady told the girls to wash at the nearby spring, which she would bless for the healing of infirmities—both physical and spiritual.

Word of the apparitions quickly spread throughout Poland, eventually reaching the rest of Europe and even North America. Vast numbers of pilgrims began making the sacred journey to the shrine. On September 8, the Feast of the Nativity, more than fifty thousand visitors came to Gietrzwałd. Thereafter, the number of pilgrims increased dramatically.

Shortly before the apparitions had ended, the Church authorized an investigation into the events. The local bishop selected both a special theological and medical committee to carry out the inquiry. On August 20 the theological committee came to Gietrzwałd and began examining the personalities and credibility of the visionaries. Separating the girls from each other immediately after each apparition, the investigators analyzed both the message and consistency of their stories. In the end, they issued a positive report, describing the girls as simple, very honest, undemanding, quiet, and uncomplicated.

The medical committee also examined the visionaries during their ecstasies. The doctors recorded the girls' pulse rates, body temperatures, and eye reactions, among other data. They ruled out any question of simulated ecstasy or pretense. In the end, they too issued a positive report.

On the one hundredth anniversary of the apparitions, the local bishop declared the authenticity of the events according to the decree of the primate and with permission from the Holy See. Today, the shrine of Our Lady of Gietrzwałd remains a prominent place of pilgrimage in Eastern Europe. With the fall of Communism, the story of the Virgin's appearance is beginning to spread openly and freely around the world for the first time in many years. And with the recent designation of the church as a "Basilica Minor" by Pope Paul VI in 1970, the fame of this holy sanctuary is expected to grow tremendously in the years to come.

PRAYER TO OUR LADY OF GIETRZWAŁD

Mother of our Lord, healer of human souls and bodies, Lady of Gietrzwałd, you who blessed this place with your presence, please turn your loving eyes toward me and ask your Son Jesus Christ for the favors I am in need of (mention requests here). *Compassionate and merciful Virgin Mother, I am forever yours. Amen.*

Our Lady of Gietrzwałd, pray for us.

ABOUT THE SHRINE

The beautiful village of Gietrzwałd lies in northern Poland, surrounded by an area of lakes, forests, and rolling green fields. The church contains many precious relics, but the most famous is the icon of Our Lady of Gietrzwałd. Offering warm hospitality to all, the Canons Regular of the Lateran are the custodians of the shrine of Our Lady of Gietrzwałd. They welcome all pilgrims to come and pray, seek healing, and ask for Our Lady's blessing. While there be sure to visit

• Shrine of the apparitions • Madonna with Child miraculous icon
• Miraculous spring

SHRINE INFORMATION

Sanktuarium Maryjne w Gietrzwałdzie
11-036 Gietrzwałd 36
Tel: (089) 512-31-02, (089) 512-31-07
Fax: (089) 512-34-06

TOURIST OFFICE

Biuro Podrózy
Star and Turist
Ul. Kosciuszki 13
10-501 Olsztyn
Tel: (089) 533-57-33; (089) 533-57-21
Fax: (089) 526-59-64

Olsztyn Tourist Office
Wysoka Brama
10-501 Olsztyn
Tel: (089) 27-27-38, (089) 27-30-90
Fax: (089) 05-26-384

PLACES TO STAY

Dom Pielgrzyma—Pilgrim's House
11-036 Gietrzwałd 36
Tel: (089) 512-34-07, (089) 512-31-07
Fax: (089) 512-34-06
The Pilgrim's House, operated by the shrine, offers excellent accommodations.

HOW TO ARRIVE AT GIETRZWAŁD

Gietrzwałd is about 120 miles north of Warsaw and 15 miles west of Olsztyn.

ROAD

From Olsztyn, take Route 16 west to Gietrzwałd.

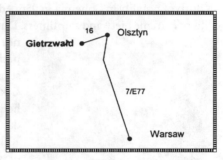

TRAIN

Gietrzwałd is not accessible by train. From Warsaw, there are frequent daily departures to Olsztyn. From Olsztyn, there is regular bus and taxi service to Gietrzwałd.

BUS

From Olsztyn, there is regular bus service to Gietrzwałd.

TIPS AND HINTS

Special indulgences are attached to visiting the shrine on certain feast days, including Sts. Peter and Paul (June 29), Our Lady of the Angels (August 2), Assumption (August 15), Pilgrimage of the Sick (first Sunday after August 15), Our Lady's Birthday (September 8), and Our Lady of the Rosary (first Sunday of October). The principal day of indulgence is the Sunday after September 8.

DID YOU KNOW?

So many miracles and healings have occurred at the shrine that the local Church officials have recorded these in a publication titled *The Book of Graces of Our Lady of Gietrzwałd*.

✠

Cathedral of Gniezno and St. Adalbert

A Millennium of Pilgrimages

Ranking among the most popular sanctuaries of Poland, the Cathedral of Gniezno receives more than one million visitors and tourists every year. A popular place of pilgrimage for the past millennium, the shrine features the elaborate tomb containing the sacred relics of Saint Adalbert, one of Poland's patron saints.

Born of nobility in Bohemia in 956, Adalbert was from his earliest years a child of extreme piety and saintliness. During his youth he spent much time

not only educating himself but also performing works of charity, such as secretly making visits to the poor and sick. Feeling a call to the religious life, he entered the seminary and was ordained a priest in 983.

In the same year, at the tender age of twenty-seven, he received episcopal ordination and was named archbishop of Prague. A tireless preacher and almsgiver, he traveled from church to church, proclaiming the mercy of God, while also spending much time visiting the poor in cottages and the prisoners in their dungeons. When asked about his grueling schedule and steadfast dedication, the prelate responded, "It is an easy thing to wear the miter and a cross; but it is a most dreadful circumstance to have to give an account of a bishopric to Christ—the Judge of the living and the dead."

Recently celebrating the one thousandth anniversary of the martyrdom of Saint Adalbert, Gniezno Cathedral has long served as one of Poland's most popular places of pilgrimage. Inside the immense shrine, near the main altar, pilgrims can be seen praying throughout the year at the spectacular reliquary containing the relics of Saint Adalbert. *(Author)*

Despite his never-ending work of spreading the gospel, much of his diocese continued to dabble in idolatry and pageantry. Finding the people fixed in their ways, Adalbert decided to renounce his position as bishop and subsequently traveled to Rome to ask the pope for release from his duties. His request was granted, and he entered a monastery.

Five years later, however, at the demands of the archbishop of Mentz, the pope ordered Adalbert to return to his bishopric. The saint agreed to go; however, the pope gave him the freedom to leave a second time. When he returned to Prague, the people received Adalbert with great joy. However, it wasn't long before he recognized the unchanging ways of the people. Exercising his license to leave freely, he left for Hungary, where he tutored the future king of Hungary—Saint Stephen.

Afterward, Adalbert and two of his companions traveled to Poland and Prussia, where they evangelized the local people and made a great number of converts. Despite their great success, they were physically beaten on several occasions, the final beating ending in their deaths. On April 23, 997, Adalbert died of stab wounds to the heart.

When Boleslas, the duke of Poland, heard about the martyrdom, he ordered the corpse brought to the abbey of Tremezno. One year later, with great pomp and ceremony, he transferred the sacred relics to Gniezno, where they were immediately enshrined in the great cathedral. In 999 Pope Sylvester canonized the martyr. Thereafter, miracles at the tomb of the celebrated saint became commonplace, and it quickly developed into one of the greatest religious sites in the country.

Today, the shrine remains a top pilgrimage destination in Poland, welcoming pilgrims and tourists from throughout Europe and abroad. One of the sanctuary's most recent extraordinary moments occurred in 1997 when Pope John Paul II made a pilgrimage to the cathedral to celebrate the 1,000th anniversary of the saint's martyrdom.

PRAYER TO SAINT ADALBERT

God our Father, you endowed Saint Adalbert with the talent of combining human wisdom with divine faith. Keep us true to his teachings, that the advance of human knowledge may deepen our knowledge and love of you. Amen.

Saint Adalbert, pray for us.

ABOUT THE SHRINE

At the heart of the medium-sized city of Gniezno lies the area's most beloved treasure—the cathedral. Home to some magnificent art and architecture, the shrine receives pilgrims and tourists throughout the year. Inside the cathedral, near the high altar, is the sanctuary's most prized possession—the elaborate silver reliquary containing Saint Adalbert's relics. Another precious treasure is its twelfth-century bronze doors in the back of the right-hand aisle, at the entrance from the porch. Depicting eighteen scenes from the life of Saint Adalbert, the doors are undeniably one of the best examples of Romanesque art in Europe. Another nearby attraction is the Archdiocesan Museum, which features a number of sacred objects from the past—including a tenth-century chalice believed to have been used by Saint Adalbert himself. His feast is celebrated on April 23. While there be sure to visit

   • Cathedral • Shrine of Saint Adalbert • Information phone • Bronze doors • Archdiocesan museum

SHRINE INFORMATION

Gniezno Cathedral
u. Kolegiaty 2
62-200 Gniezno
Tel: (061) 426-4868

TOURIST OFFICE

Gniezno Tourist Office
Franciszkanska
62-200 Gniezno
Tel: (061) 426-3701,
(061) 426-3660

PLACES TO STAY

Hotel Lech
Ul. Bł. Jolanty 5
62-200 Gniezno
Tel: (061) 426-23-85
Fax: (061) 426-12-94
Three-star hotel.

Hotel Mieszko
u. Strumykowa 2
62-200 Gniezno
Tel: (061) 426-46-25
Fax: (061) 426-46-28
Three-star hotel.

Hotel Młodziezowe
Kat. 1
u. Pocztowa 11
62-200 Gniezno
Tel/Fax: (061) 426-27-80

HOW TO ARRIVE AT GNIEZNO

Gniezno is about sixty miles west of Poznań.

ROAD

From Poznań, take 5/E261 east to Gniezno. From Bydgoszcz, take 5/E261 west to Gniezno.

TRAIN

Gniezno is accessible by train. From Poznań, there are about eight daily departures to Gniezno, and from Wrocław, about four daily departures. From Olsztyn, there are about three daily departures to Gniezno.

BUS

Gniezno is accessible by bus. Poznań, Wrocław, Toruń, and other Polish cities have regular bus service to Gniezno.

TIPS AND HINTS

Information phones are available inside the shrine, providing an excellent, but brief, description and history of the pilgrimage church in various languages (including English).

Although guided tours are usually conducted only in Polish, ask at the chapel next to the bronze doors for tours in English (or other languages).

DID YOU KNOW?

Saint Adalbert is often called the "Man of Europe" because his legacy extends to the Czech Republic, Lithuania, Germany, Poland, Slovakia, the Ukraine, Hungary, and Italy.

Kalwaria Pacławska

A Calvary in Eastern Poland

Among the many lovely shrines of Poland is the magnificent sanctuary of Kalwaria Pacławska. Surrounded by spectacular scenery, this place of pilgrimage features one large majestic church and more than forty chapels scattered throughout the nearby fields and woods. A popular destination for the Catholic faithful, the shrine lies in the far eastern corner of the country, near the Ukraine.

Upon entering the small village, you are immediately greeted by the grand twin towers of the Franciscan monastery and church. Once inside the sanctuary, you are engulfed in a sea of breathtaking art and architecture. So splendid are the decorations that the shrine ranks as one of the most beautiful in Eastern Europe. Outside the extraordinary sanctuary, you find more than three dozen chapels dedicated to Christ and his Blessed Mother.

According to legend, the shrine's history began in 1665. While hunting one day in the forest, the local administrator saw a deer with a brilliant cross between its antlers running through the trees. After seeing this incredible sight, the town official decided to place a monastery and church here. Three years later, when some Franciscans moved to the region, they fulfilled his request by constructing a wooden church at the site.

As the area resembled the Mount of Olives in the Holy Land, the monks chose to place a number of crosses on the hillsides so that people could meditate on the Passion of Christ. Over time, small chapels began replacing the crosses. Eventually, more than forty little sanctuaries filled the fields and forests on both sides of the Wiar River.

In 1775 the Franciscans consecrated a new church. Inside the sanctuary, they enshrined a miraculous image of Our Lady of Calvary above a side altar. The wonder-working picture represents the Mother of God as Queen, sitting on clouds, with a scepter in her right hand and the Child Jesus on her left arm. In 1882 the shrine received monumental honors when the miraculous picture was crowned, and Pope Clement X granted indulgences to those who would visit the shrine.

With one large majestic church and more than forty chapels scattered throughout the nearby fields and woods, the seventeenth-century shrine of Kalwaria Pacławska serves as one of southeastern Poland's most famous places of pilgrimage. *(Dom Pielgrzyma)*

Today the sanctuary remains a prominent place of pilgrimage in Poland. Among the many annual celebrations at the shrine, the most important one takes place August 11–15, with a sacred five-day solemnity in honor of the Assumption of the Virgin Mary. The ceremonies include a procession transporting the tomb of the Virgin Mary to the Burial Cottage. Along the way, the cortege stops at seven small chapels dedicated to Mary. Thousands of pilgrims participate every year in this moving celebration.

PRAYER TO OUR LADY, MOTHER OF THE UNBORN

O Mary, Mother of the Unborn, protect the gift of human life that your divine Son has allowed to be given. Give strength and joy to all parents as they await the birth of the precious child they have conceived. Give courage to those who are fearful, calm those who are anxious, and guide all of us, with your motherly care, to treasure and protect the mi-

raculous gift of human life. We ask this through your Son, Jesus Christ our Lord. Amen.

Mary, Mother of the Unborn, pray for us!

ABOUT THE SHRINE

Lying in eastern Poland near the city of Przemyśl, the Shrine of Kalwaria Pacławska is open daily and receives pilgrims throughout the year. With more than forty chapels and a guesthouse for visitors, the sanctuary offers the visitor a great place of pilgrimage. A number of processions and celebrations take place, the most important being the week of the Feast of the Assumption (August 11–15). While there be sure to visit

- Forty chapels • Miraculous image of Our Lady of Calvary
- Processions

SHRINE INFORMATION

Sanktuarium Męki Pańskiej I Matki Bożej
Kalwaria Pacławska
37-743 Nowosiółki Dydyńskie

TOURIST OFFICE

There is no tourist office in Kalwaria Pacławska.

PLACES TO STAY

Dom Pielgrzyma im. bł. Jakuba Strzemię
Kalwaria Pacławska 40
37-743 Nowosiółki Dydyńskie
Tel: (016) 678-89-44
The Pilgrim's Guest House, operated by the shrine, offers excellent accommodations.

HOW TO ARRIVE AT KALWARIA PACŁAWSKA

Kalwaria Pacławska is about fifteen miles south of Przemyśl.

ROAD

From Przemyśl, head south to Huwniki via Fedropol, then continue following the signs to Kalwaria Pacławska.

TRAIN

Kalwaria Pacławska is not accessible by train. The nearest major railway station is at Przemyśl. Warsaw has two daily departures to Przemyśl.

BUS

Kalwaria Pacławska is accessible by bus. Przemyśl has regular bus service to Pacławska via Huwniki.

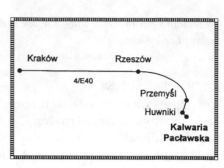

TIPS AND HINTS

With a nice guesthouse and beautiful retreat grounds, this is an excellent place to consider spending a few extra days in retreat.

DID YOU KNOW?

Kalwaria Pacławska is one of several major places of pilgrimage in Poland that feature a "Jerusalem-like setting," with dozens of chapels depicting scenes from the life of Christ and his Mother. The other two are Kalwaria Zebrzydowska and Our Lady of Wambieryce.

✠

Kalwaria Zebrzydowska

"She reigns, she heals, she consoles."
INSCRIPTION ABOVE CHAPEL ENTRANCE

In 2000, the tour didn't make it here

Consisting of more than forty chapels and one spectacular basilica, the grandiose shrine of Kalwaria Zebrzydowska is one of Poland's most beautiful and oldest places of pilgrimage. Situated between two mountain ranges, the picturesque sanctuary welcomes more than one million visitors every year from around the world. Often referred to as a "Polish Jerusalem" because of its many small chapels depicting the life of Christ and his Mother, Kalwaria Zebrzydowska serves as one of Eastern Europe's most significant places of pilgrimage.

The shrine dates from 1600, when a squire from Kraków named Mikolaj Zebrzydowski, built a small sanctuary on the Zarek Hill to represent the crucifixion scene. Modeled after a church in Jerusalem, the popular chapel was consecrated one year later in the presence of numerous clergy and local nobility. Soon afterward, the local prelate entrusted the little shrine to the Franciscans (known as the Bernardines in Poland). So popular did the small sanctuary become in the following years that Zebrzydowski decided to build more chapels on the hill, each following the model of a specific church in the Holy Land.

When the friars arrived, the squire promised to build their monastery. On December 1, 1600, Zebrzydowski put forward the plans for the new monastery (and the enlarging of the original church), and in 1604 he broke ground. The new complex was designed in plex was designed in the same fashion as a Renaissance castle—with the church and

A dynamic place of pilgrimage, Kalwaria Zebrzydowska has not only many beautiful chapels to visit throughout its hillsides but also a full program of celebrations, processions, and daily activities throughout the year. Often referred to as the "Polish Jerusalem," the sanctuary is the country's second-most famous pilgrimage destination and remains the favorite boyhood shrine of Pope John Paul II. *(Fr. Albert Mocarski, O.F.M.)*

living quarters of the monks not being separated. On October 4, 1609, the Franciscans consecrated their new home and church.

In the ensuing years a number of chapels were built throughout the hillside. By 1617 sanctuaries on the Via Dolorosa pathway were completed. Among these new chapels were Pilate's Palace, the Tomb of Christ, the Garden of Gethsemane, the Chapel of Our Lord's Arrest in the Garden, the Last Supper, Our Lord Receiving His Cross, the Second Fall of Jesus under the Cross, Saint Mary Magdalene, the Heart of Our Blessed Lady, and Our Lady's Tomb. As symbolism played a large part in the construction of each devotional sanctuary, the chapels were each built with a shape to fit their meaning. For example, some were designed in the form of a cross, a heart, or a triangle. After Zebrzydowski's death in 1620, his son, and later his grandson, took over the duties and continued the expansion.

By the end of the eighteenth century, thanks to the generosity of pious pilgrims and many benefactors, new sanctuaries were built and old ones renovated. At the beginning of the twentieth century the expansion continued as a new bridge, the Angel's Bridge, was constructed to connect the various sanctuaries.

Since the beginning, celebrations and processions have been the hallmark of Kalwaria. As early as 1611, a prayer book was published for those who came to pray and take part in various religious services. By 1617 special services known as the "Co-suffering of Our Lady" had developed: in these services, pilgrims would walk from the Tomb of Christ to the Loreto House chapel, singing songs and saying designated prayers.

During the first forty years of the sanctuary's history, pilgrims venerated a statue of Our Lady given by the founder himself, which had been brought from Loreto, Italy. In 1641 the Franciscans erected a special shrine inside the main church to house the holy image. In 1887 the cardinal of Kraków crowned the miraculous statue before an enthusiastic and festive crowd.

The shrine is probably best known, however, for its annual Passion plays, which began in the seventeenth century. The performance begins on Palm Sunday and continues on Wednesday, Maundy Thursday, and Good Friday. Local townspeople and monks perform the blend of religious ceremony and local theater, reenacting the most crucial days of Christ's life as they take on the parts of Jesus, the apostles, Roman legionaries, and other important historical figures.

Of all the visitors to Kalwaria Zebrzydowska in this century, the one who is probably most attached to it is Pope John Paul II. As a boy living in nearby Wadowice, he would often come and spend time in prayer at the various chapels. In fact, the shrine had such an impact on his life that he wrote in his book *Gift and Mystery*,

> Even as a child, and still more as a priest and Bishop, it [devotion to Mary] would lead me to make frequent Marian pilgrimages to Kalwaria Zebrzydowska....I would go there often, walking along its paths in solitude and present to the Lord in prayer the various problems of the Church, especially in the difficult times during the struggle against communism.

Today, the Holy Father continues to return to Kalwaria, the place where his father once served as a tour guide. On June 7, 1979, shortly after being elected pope, His Holiness visited the shrine and bestowed the title of "Basilica" on the main church. In 1987, while praying before the miraculous image of Our Lady, the pope offered the Virgin of Kalwaria a golden papal rose as a "sign of gratitude for what she had been, and is, in his life." Again, in the 1990s, John Paul II has returned several times to his favorite boyhood shrine. Previous to being pope, he would often visit the shrine as an archbishop, and later as a cardinal. Many times he came unannounced and walked the paths by himself in solitude.

The pilgrim visiting Kalwaria Zebryzdowska will always remember the beauty of the place and its unforgettable atmosphere of prayer and meditation. Whether you walk around the hillside of chapels or participate in the spectacular Passion play or processions in honor of Our Lady, you can't help sinking deeply into the mystery of the suffering and death of Christ and the life of his mother. Summing it up best, Pope John Paul II once said, "That is why we come here over and over again."

SONG TO OUR LADY OF KALWARIA ZEBRZYDOWSKA

O beautiful and splendid Star, Our Lady of Calvary, in you we take refuge, O Holy Mary. We have heard a lovely voice; the Holy Virgin is calling us, "Come to me, my children, come, this is just the right time." The song of birds exalt her name; it's a voice of nightingales. This is why we should be here, bowing down with hearty prayer. Our Lady of Calvary, pray for us, O Holy Mary, that we may be truly worthy to take part in future glory.

Our Lady of Kalwaria Zebrzydowska, pray for us.

ABOUT THE SHRINE

Situated amidst the hills of southern Poland, the small town of Kalwaria Zebrzydowska is located about eighteen miles southwest of Kraków. A dynamic place of pilgrimage, the sanctuary has not only many beautiful chapels to visit but also a full program of celebrations, processions, and daily activities throughout the year. Among the most prominent sites is the Zebrzydowski Chapel with the miraculous painting of Our Lady of Kalwaria with Child Jesus. What draws hundreds of thousands of pilgrims during Holy Week are the Passion plays. The procession begins on Maundy Thursday (Holy Thursday) in the early afternoon and ends about dusk, visiting about half the chapels. It resumes the next morning at about 6 A.M. and continues until about 2 P.M. Other big days of pilgrimage at the shrine include Marian feast days. The Feast of the Assumption, and the two days prior to it, include processions around the chapels. While there be sure to visit

• Basilica • Zebrzydowski Chapel • Miraculous painting of Our Lady of Kalwaria • All forty chapels

SHRINE INFORMATION

Klasztor OO. Bernardynów (The Bernardines Monastery)
Ul. Bernardyńska 46
34-130 Kalwaria Zebrzydowska
Tel: (33) 76-63-04, (33) 76-54-99
Fax: (33) 76-66-41

TOURIST OFFICE
There is no tourist office in Kalwaria Zebrzydowska.

PLACES TO STAY
Dom Pilegrzyma (Pilgrim's House)
Ul. Bernardyńska 6
34-130 Kalwaria Zebrzydowska
Tel/Fax: (33) 76-55-39, (33) 76-63-04, (33) 76-54-99
Fax: (33) 76-66-41
The Pilgrim's House is operated by the monastery.

HOW TO ARRIVE AT KALWARIA ZEBRZYDOWSKA
Kalwaria is about twenty miles southwest of Kraków in the Beskidy Mountains.

ROAD
From Kraków, take 7/E77 south, then head east on 96 and continue to Kalwaria Zebrzydowska (the trip takes about thirty minutes by car).

TRAIN
Kalwaria Zebrzydowska is accessible by train. The Kraków Płaszów and Głowny railway stations have regular train service to Kalwaria Zebrzydowska. The trip takes about one hour by train.

BUS
Kalwaria Zebrzydowska is accessible by bus. From Kraków, there are several daily buses. The main bus station in Kraków is located next to the Głowny Railway Station. The buses depart every hour in the direction of Cieszyn, Bielsko-Biała, Żywiec, and Wadowice. The trip takes about forty-five minutes by bus to Kalwaria Zebrzydowska.

HOW TO GET TO THE SHRINE AFTER ARRIVING IN KALWARIA ZEBRZYDOWSKA
The best way of getting to the shrine after arriving at the bus or railway station in Kalwaria Zebrzydowska is to simply follow one of the roads that lead up the hill to the basilica. For specific directions from the bus stop, walk along Krakowska Street toward Rynek Square, turning left onto "3-go Maja"

Street. Follow this road until you reach the smaller street of Bernardyńska—which will lead you up the hill to where the shrine is located.

From the train station, walk along Al. Jana Pawła II Street toward Rynek Square, turning left onto "3-go Maja" Street. Follow this road until you reach the smaller street of Bernardyńska—which will lead you up the hill to where the shrine is located.

TIPS AND HINTS

In the nearby town of Wadowice (8.5 miles) lies the birthplace and boyhood home of Pope John Paul II. Today it is a museum, welcoming visitors and pilgrims throughout the year. It is located just off the Rynek.

DID YOU KNOW?

The Passion play that is performed along the hillside often becomes such a realistic spectacle that some of the pilgrims have been known to rush in to rescue Jesus from the hands of his oppressors.

Shrine of Divine Mercy

Jesus, I Trust in You!

In the past twenty years, devotion to the Divine Mercy in the form proposed by Blessed Faustina has since rocketed to the top of pious Catholic practices. Now, pilgrims are flocking to the shrine in Poland to pray before the miraculous image of the Merciful Jesus and the young visionary's relics. Few other places of pilgrimage in the world are growing as fast in popularity and number of visitors as the Shrine of Divine Mercy.

Blessed Faustina, the favored visionary of the revelations, came from a very poor Polish family and was the third of ten children. Since her childhood she distinguished herself by love of prayer, hard work, obedience, and a great sensitivity toward human poverty. At the age of twenty, after having only three years of education and working briefly as a domestic servant, she entered the Congregation of the Sisters of Our Lady of Mercy.

As a religious, she performed the humblest of tasks in the convent, usually those of cook, gardener, and doorkeeper. Throughout her religious life she was endowed with numerous extraordinary graces such as apparitions, visions, concealed stigmata, participation in Christ's Passion, bilocation, prophecy, and the ability to read human souls. Though so enriched by supernatural gifts, she showed a simple, universal, and deeply evangelical model of Christian perfection, which consists in the attitude of trust in God and mercy toward one's neighbor.

To this simple and uneducated nun, Jesus chose to be his apostle of Mercy. The mission he entrusted her had a threefold purpose:

1. To remind the world of the merciful love of God for every human being.
2. To convey new forms of devotion to the Divine Mercy.
3. To inspire an apostolic movement that would renew Christian life according to the spirit of trust and mercy.

Between 1931 and 1938 Our Lord appeared to Blessed Faustina, a Sister of Mercy in Poland, entrusting her with the mission of spreading devotion to the Divine Mercy. Here, Pope John Paul II is praying before the image of the Merciful Jesus at the shrine on June 7, 1997. *(Congregation of the Sisters of Our Lady of Mercy)*

On the first Sunday of Lent, February 22, 1931, Our Lord Jesus Christ appeared to the simple nun at her convent in Plock, Poland. Bearing a wonderful message of mercy for all humankind, he appeared wearing an ankle-length white garment, with his right hand raised in blessing and his left arm touching the clothing at the breast. From this area of the heart, two large rays were coming forth, one red and the other translucent.

As Blessed Faustina gazed intently at the vision, her soul became overwhelmed with deep reverence and great joy. After a while Jesus spoke to her: "Paint an image according to the pattern you see, with the inscription: 'Jesus, I trust in You!'" Then he went on to say that he desired that this image be venerated first in her convent chapel and then throughout the world. For those who would venerate the image with complete trust in God and charity for their neighbor, he promised great progress on the road to Christian perfection, the grace of eternal salvation, and many other blessings.

Upon the request of her spiritual director, Blessed Faustina asked whether the words *Christ, the King of Mercy* could be the inscription on the image.

Jesus replied that he is the King of Mercy and that he desired the image to be displayed in public on the First Sunday after Easter (Feast of Mercy).

When her spiritual director asked about the meaning of the rays, she received this explanation from the Lord:

> The two rays denote Blood and Water—the pale ray stands for the Water that makes souls righteous; the red ray stands for the Blood which is the life of souls. These two rays issued forth from the depths of my most tender Mercy when my agonizing heart was opened by a lance on the cross....Happy is the one who will dwell in their shelter, for the just hand of God shall not lay hold of them.

When Blessed Faustina saw for the first time the artist's depiction of her vision, she broke down in tears. Expressing her disappointment to the Lord, she asked, "Who will paint you as beautiful as you are?" Upon asking this question she heard the response, "The greatness of this image lies not in the beauty of the color or the brush, but in my grace."

On one occasion in speaking about the painting, Jesus stated that his gaze from the image is like the gaze from the cross. Another time he said, "I am offering people a vessel with which they are to keep coming for graces to the fountain of Mercy. That vessel is this image with the inscription: Jesus, I trust in You!"

As a further sign of his forgiving love, Jesus called for a Feast of the Divine Mercy to be celebrated in the whole Church. He then lovingly spoke to Blessed Faustina:

> I want this image to be solemnly blessed on the first Sunday after Easter; that Sunday is to be the Feast of Mercy. On that day, the depths of my Mercy will be open to all. Whoever will go to confession and Holy Communion on that day will receive complete forgiveness of sin and punishment. Humankind will not enjoy peace until it turns with confidence to my Mercy.

Jesus further asked that this Feast of the Divine Mercy be preceded by a novena to the Divine Mercy, which would begin on Good Friday. He gave her an intention to pray for on each day of the novena, saving for the last day the most difficult intention of all, the lukewarm and indifferent, of whom he said:

These souls cause me more suffering than others; it was from such souls that my soul felt the most revulsion in the Garden of Olives. It was on their account that I said, "My Father, if it is possible, let this cup pass me by." The last hope of salvation for them is to flee to my Mercy.

Along with being the recipient of these apparitions, Blessed Faustina also received the extraordinary grace of the invisible stigmata in 1936. Two years earlier, she had begun to write about her experiences in her diary—which later totaled approximately six hundred pages and has become a world-renowned book under the title *Divine Mercy in My Soul: The Diary of Sister Faustina M. Kowalska.* On October 5, 1938, the servant of God died in the odor of sanctity in the convent at Kraków-Lagiewniki.

After her death, the devotion to the Divine Mercy as revealed in her diary began to spread quickly. Despite the tragic war years of 1939–1945, the devotion especially grew in strength throughout Poland and Lithuania as people turned to the merciful Savior for comfort and hope. However, on March 6, 1959, the Holy See, acting on erroneous information, prohibited the spreading of Divine Mercy Devotion in the form proposed by Blessed Faustina's writings.

As a result, there followed almost twenty years of total silence. Then, on April 15, 1978, the Holy See, after a thorough examination of original documents unavailable to it in 1959, completely reversed its decision and again permitted the devotion. The person primarily responsible for this reversal of decision was Karol Cardinal Wojtyla—the future Pope John Paul II. On April 18, 1993, it was this pope who beatified Sister Faustina at St. Peter's Square in Rome before an excited and enthusiastic crowd. Then on June 7, 1997, Pope John Paul II returned to Kraków to pray before the miraculous image of the Merciful Jesus and Blessed Faustina's relics.

Today, the Shrine of Divine Mercy in Poland receives pilgrims from throughout the world, including the Philippines, Australia, and America. The greatest crowds arrive on the first Sunday after Easter, which is the Feast of Divine Mercy. Along with Our Lady of Częstochowa, it remains the most famous and popular shrine in Eastern Europe.

PRAYER TO OBTAIN GRACES THROUGH THE INTERCESSION OF BLESSED FAUSTINA

O Jesus, who filled Blessed Faustina with profound veneration for your boundless Mercy, deign, if it be your holy will, to grant me, through her intercession, the grace for which I fervently pray....

My sins render me unworthy of your mercy, but be mindful of Sister Faustina's spirit of sacrifice and self-denial, and reward her virtue by granting the petition that, with childlike trust, I present to you through her intercession.

ABOUT THE SHRINE

The Shrine of the Divine Mercy is located in Kraków, in the southern district of Łagiewniki. The convent is located on the street Siostry Faustyny, just off Zakopianska/E77. The shrine welcomes pilgrims throughout the year—with the greatest crowds arriving on the first Sunday after Easter, which is the Feast of the Divine Mercy. Mass is celebrated at the shrine daily at 6:30 A.M. and 3:20 P.M. On Sundays and feast days Mass is at 8:00 A.M., 11:00 A.M., 3:20 P.M., and 7:00 P.M. There is adoration of the Blessed Sacrament exposed at the Divine Mercy altar each day from noon until 3:20 P.M. While there be sure to visit

- Shrine of Divine Mercy • Miraculous image of the Merciful Jesus
- Blessed Faustina's tomb • Religious services and adoration

SHRINE INFORMATION

Sanktuarium Bożego Miłosierdzia—Shrine of Divine Mercy
Ul. Siostry Faustyny 3
30-420 Kraków-Łagiewniki
Tel: (012) 266-58-59
Tel/Fax: (012) 267-61-01 or (012) 266-23-68

TOURIST OFFICE

American Information Center "Usis Kraków"
Ul. Słolarska 9
Kraków
Tel: (012) 421-67-67

Centrum Informacji Turystycznej PAPT
Ul Pawia 6
Kraków
Tel: (012) 422-60-91
Tel/Fax: (012) 422-04-71

Dexter Tourist Office
Rynkek Główny
Kraków
Tel: (012) 21-77-06
Fax: (012) 21-30-36

Jordan Tourist Office
Ul Floriańska 37
Kraków
Tel: (012) 22-77-64

[handwritten: Bożena / Boż zhen ah our tour guide in Krakow & just to war]

PLACES TO STAY

[handwritten: oct.17?]

Sanktuarium Bożego Miłosierdzia—Shrine of Divine Mercy
Ul. Siostry Faustyny 3
30-420 Kraków-Łagiewniki
Tel: (012) 266-58-59
Fax: (012) 267-61-01
Tel/Fax: (012) 266-23-68

[handwritten: (WIELICZKA) salt mine 17-10-00 salt mine?]

Strawberry Youth Hostel
Ul. Racławicka 9
Kraków
Tel: (012) 636-15-00
The youth hostel offers good, inexpensive accommodations for young adults visiting Kraków.

HOW TO ARRIVE AT THE SHRINE OF DIVINE MERCY

The shrine and convent are located south of Old Town Kraków.

ROAD

From southern Poland, take E77 north into Kraków, turning right on Siostry Faustyny. The shrine will be on your right about one hundred yards up the street. (The shrine is located in the Łagiewniki section of Kraków.)

TRAM

From the main train station in Kraków, take tram #19, and exit at the Borek Falecki tram stop. However, if it is your first time in Kraków, it is best to take a taxi to the shrine—as it can be quite difficult to recognize the Borek Falecki stop on the tram without knowing the area.

TIPS AND HINTS

If possible, try to make reservations in advance for accommodations at the convent's guesthouse. It is a beautiful experience to be able to stay overnight on the grounds of the Divine Mercy Shrine.

To learn more about devotion to the Divine Mercy and Jesus' appearances to Blessed Faustina, consult the book *Divine Mercy in My Soul: The Diary of Sister Faustina M. Kowalska.*

DID YOU KNOW?

Approximately twenty years after Blessed Faustina's death, more than twenty-five million pieces of Divine Mercy literature had been distributed around the world.

╬

Cathedral of Kraków

Beautiful

Poland's Spiritual Capital

Recognized as one of the most popular tourist destinations in Poland, Wawel Hill comprises both the Kraków cathedral and castle. Serving as the nation's spiritual capital, the cathedral has witnessed most of the royal coronations and funerals of the last millennium. For more than five hundred years the castle of Wawel Hill served as the seat of the Polish kings.

Although the present-day cathedral dates from the fourteenth century, the original church was erected at the spot around 1020 by the first Polish king. Among the most impressive sights at today's cathedral are the St. Stanislaus Shrine, Sigismund Chapel, Holy Cross Chapel, Cathedral Treasury, and the Royal Crypts.

Without a doubt, the church's greatest possession is the highly elaborate shrine of Saint Stanislaus, which features the silver coffin of Poland's beloved patron saint. Canonized in 1253, Saint Stanislaus served as the bishop of Kraków from 1072 to 1079.

Other highlights include the Cathedral Treasury, which features a number of precious objects, including the thousand-year-old spear of Saint Maurice. Near the back of the church are the Royal Crypts, containing the tombs of many of the Polish kings and their families.

ABOUT THE SHRINE

Located near the center of the city, Wawel Hill is comprised of both the cathedral and castle. Guided tours of the complex are available in a number of languages, including English. The guides' office is located at the entrance to the hill, opposite the equestrian statue of Tadeusz Kosciuszko. A guided tour can take several hours. Among the main highlights of a visit to the cathedral are the Shrine of Saint Stanislaus and the Cathedral Treasury. While there be sure to visit

- Wawel Cathedral • Wawel Castle • Shrine of Saint Stanislaus • Cathedral Treasury • Cathedral Museum • Sigismund Tower • Royal Crypts

SHRINE INFORMATION

Zarząd Bazyliki Metropolitalnej na Wawelu
Wawel 3
31-001 Kraków
Tel: (012) 42-22-643

TOURIST OFFICE

See *Shrine of Divine Mercy* for more information about tourist offices in Kraków.

PLACES TO STAY

See *Shrine of Divine Mercy* for more information about places to stay in Kraków.

HOW TO ARRIVE AT KRAKÓW

Kraków is located in south-central Poland. Wawel Cathedral lies in the southern part of Old Town Kraków.

ROAD

Two of the major highways connecting with Kraków are E40/4 E77/7.

TRAIN

Kraków is accessible by train from all cities in Poland and many international cities. The main train station is Kraków

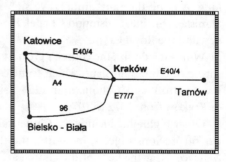

Głowny, located on the northeastern outskirts of the Old Town. All international trains arrive here, as do many of the domestic ones as well. The Kraków Płaszów receives only domestic trains.

BUS

Kraków's central bus station is located next to the Głowny train station. The bus service is often an excellent option to nearby cities such as Auschwitz, Częstochowa, and Zakopane.

WALKING TO WAWEL CATHEDRAL

From Kraków's Main Market Square *Rynek Główny,* head south on Grodzka street to the Wawel Cathedral and Castle.

TIPS AND HINTS

Near the entrance of the cathedral is the Irsa book shop, which has a few small publications and guidebooks of the shrine in English.

For a nice view of the center, head to the top of the cathedral's Sigismund Tower.

DID YOU KNOW?

In the year 1000 the Kraków diocese was established.

✠

St. Mary's Basilica

A Classic Example of Gothic Architecture

St. Mary's Basilica, also referred to as the Mariacki Church, is a magnificent example of Gothic architecture in Poland. Situated in the main Market Square of Kraków, the shrine welcomes thousands of pilgrims every day.

Built over time with the addition of a new feature each year, the present-day church dates from the fourteenth century. One of the most famous features of the basilica is its left front steeple that is topped with a gilded crown of royalty. What makes this tower so special is the legend that surrounds it. According to the story, the watchman sitting atop the church's steeple attempted with a trumpet call to alert the citizens of Kraków to the invading Tartars. However, the musical alarm was broken in mid-phrase as the enemy pierced the watchman's throat. Today, to commemorate the event, the same trumpet call (*hejnal*) is played from the tower

Welcoming tourists and visitors from all over the world, the fourteenth-century St. Mary's Basilica, which lies at the heart of Old Town Kraków, features a world-famous altar and serves as a splendid example of Gothic architecture. *(Author)*

every hour. The simple melody, which served in medieval times as a warning call, continues the tradition of breaking off in midtune.

Inside the shrine, the church's most prominent attractions are its massive altar and the two chapels of Our Lady of Częstochowa and Saint Anthony. The main altar, the largest of its kind in Europe, is the masterpiece of Wit Stwosz. The base of the altar presents a magnificent carved reproduction of the genealogical tree of Jesus and Mary. Although the Nazis stole the sacred altar during World War II, it was later recovered and restored to the church in 1957.

Among the shrine's two most visited chapels is that of Our Lady of Częstochowa. In this small sanctuary is a cherished replica painting of Our Lady of Częstochowa that dates from 1638. The other famous chapel is the one dedicated to Saint Anthony. Also called the Chapel of the Villains, it was in this sanctuary that criminals sentenced to death would spend their last moments before being led to the scaffold.

ABOUT THE SHRINE

St. Mary's Basilica lies in the center of Old Town Kraków, overlooking the main square. Of great significance is the world-famous altar of the Virgin Mary (Wit Stwosz Altar). Grace-filled with incredibly beautiful chapels, altars, and paintings, the basilica is a "must-see" for anyone visiting Kraków. While there be sure to visit

- St. Mary's Basilica • Altar of the Virgin Mary • Chapel of Our Lady of Częstochowa • Chapel of St. Anthony • Altar of Our Lady of Loreto • St. Stanislaus's Altar

SHRINE INFORMATION

Parafia Bazyliki Najswietszej Maryi Panny
Pl. Mariacki 5
31-042 Kraków
Tel: (012) 422.05.21
Fax: (012) 421.07.85

TOURIST OFFICE

See *Shrine of Divine Mercy* for more information about tourist offices in Kraków.

PLACES TO STAY

See *Shrine of Divine Mercy* for more information about places to stay in Kraków.

HOW TO ARRIVE AT THE BASILICA OF THE HOLY VIRGIN MARY

The basilica is located in the center of Kraków's Main Market Square Rynek Główny. The tourist information office is located across from it. For more information about how to arrive in Kraków, see *Wawel Cathedral.*

TRAIN AND BUS

The main railway station (Główny) and bus station are conveniently located in the northeastern section of Old Town Kraków. It is about a ten-minute walk to the basilica and Krakow's Main Market Square.

TIPS AND HINTS

The church is open throughout the year, and the hours of visiting are noon to 6 P.M. Monday through Saturday, and 2 P.M. to 6 P.M. on Sunday. Guidebooks are available in various languages, including English, at the ticket stand.

Consider spending a full afternoon or longer at St. Mary's Basilica and Kraków's Market Square as there are a number of other sites to visit—and it's a great place to have lunch and shop for gifts.

DID YOU KNOW?

Since 1928 the trumpet call of the *hejnal* is broadcast every day at noon by the Polish Radio.

$$+\|+$$
$$+\|+$$

Church of the Assumption

A Place of Abundant Blessings

Throughout the history of the Catholic faith, Marian shrines have served as important places of pilgrimage. Such is the case with the Church of the Assumption in the small village of Krzeszów in southwestern Poland, near the Czech border.

Since 1735 pilgrims have been making their way here to pray before a miraculous portrait of the Mother of God. So popular has the image become over the centuries that on June 2, 1997, Pope John Paul II made a sacred journey here to crown the cherished image of the Virgin and Child. More than one million pilgrims came to partake in the ceremonies and celebrations.

The massive shrine that houses the miraculous picture dates from the eighteenth century. Rich in detail, the beautiful twin-towered church fea-

On June 2, 1997, Pope John Paul II crowned the miraculous image of Our Lady of Krzeszów before a jubilant and enthusiastic crowd of one million pilgrims. *(Fr. Augustine Wegrzyn)*

tures an interior filled with elaborate paintings, frescoes, sculptures, and carvings. Above the high altar rests the cherished image of the Madonna. Behind this is a mausoleum of the Holy Piasts.

While some come to present their petitions to the Mother of God, others have come to give thanks for favors received. Despite the reasons for their visits, all are deeply affected by the graces they receive. Today, thousands are still taking advantage of the opportunity to make the sacred trip to Krzeszów.

PRAYER TO OUR LADY OF KRESZÓW

Our Lady of Kreszów, I commend to your care and mercy my body and soul, both now and at the hour of my death. I also entrust to you all my hopes and desires, all my worries and oppressions, and I pray that with your grace my deeds may be performed and governed according to your Son's will. Amen.

Our Lady of Kreszów, pray for us.

ABOUT THE SHRINE

Krzeszów is a small town located near the city of Kamienna Góra in south-central Poland. Along with praying before the miraculous image, pilgrims can spend time at the numerous chapels scattered throughout the surrounding countryside. Also the faithful can visit the outdoor Way of the Cross, dating from the early eighteenth century. While there be sure to visit

- Church of the Assumption • Miraculous image • Mausoleum
- Chapels • Way of the Cross

SHRINE INFORMATION

Sanktuarium w Krzeszówie
58-405 Krzeszów Kamiennogórski, 287
Tel: (075) 74-123-80

TOURIST OFFICE

There is no tourist office in Krzeszów.

PLACES TO STAY

Pani Lucyna Zielonka
Krzeszów Kamiennogorski 280
58-405 Krzeszów
Tel: (075) 74-123-24

Siostry Elzbietanki
Krzeszów Kamiennogorski 29
58-405 Krzeszów
Tel: (075) 74-123-35

HOW TO ARRIVE AT KRZESZÓW

Krzeszów is about four miles from Kamienna Góra and twenty-five miles from Jelenia Góra.

ROAD

From Jelenia Góra, head south on highway 367, following the signs to Kamienna Góra. Once in Kamienna Góra, follow the signs and head south to Krzeszów.

TRAIN

Krzeszów is not accessible by train. The nearest train station is at Kamienna Góra, and the nearest major train station is at Jelenia Góra.

BUS

Krzeszów is accessible by bus. Kamienna Góra has hourly bus service to Krzeszów on weekdays and less frequent service on weekends. From Jelenia Góra, there is frequent bus service to Kamienna Góra.

Note: In this region of Poland, buses are a much better means of transportation for local travel than the trains. However, trains still remain the better option for long-distance travel (i.e., Jelenia Góra to Kraków or vice versa).

TIPS AND HINTS

Another nearby "Catholic attraction" is St. Joseph's Church. Built between 1690 and 1696, the small shrine features a number of beautiful paintings and artworks.

DID YOU KNOW?
The Church of the Assumption and St. Joseph's Church are considered among the finest Baroque churches in Poland.

City of the Immaculata—Niepokalanów

A Homegrown Franciscan Town

Although many people around the world have heard of Saint Maximilian Kolbe and his incredible sacrifice for a fellow prisoner at Auschwitz, not so many are familiar with the Marian-centered Franciscan friary and town he established in Poland: Niepokalanów. As a devout son of the Blessed Mother, Saint Maximilian founded this priory to help in his life's mission of spreading devotion to the Virgin Mary and defending the Catholic faith through the modern media.

The story of how Saint Maximilian embarked on his apostolate dates from his early seminary years in Rome. At the time, the Catholic Church had become the target of many brazen and blasphemous outrages by the Communists and Masons. Increasingly saddened by the events, Saint Maximilian witnessed as demonstrators carried banners such as "Satan must reign in the Vatican. The pope will be his slave" past the Vatican windows.

Niepokalanów, the City of the Immaculata, is home to the Franciscan friary founded by Saint Maximilian Kolbe in the late 1920s. Offering a virtual treasure chest of activities and sites related to the life of the saint, the shrine is open throughout the year and welcomes thousands of pilgrims from around the world. *(Author)*

Fired by a warrior-like spirit, Saint Maximilian became determined to "fight back" by organizing a spiritual army that would capture souls for the Immaculate Queen. His inspiration came to him in 1917 on the anniversary of the Virgin Mary's apparition to Alphonse Ratisbonne, a longtime anti-Catholic and agnostic who was later converted to the faith through the Miraculous Medal. On October 16, 1917, in the basement of the seminary, Saint Maximilian and his six companions quietly met and enrolled themselves as Knights of the Immaculata—a new organization that the saint had founded. Spearheading a powerful Marian movement, the knights would consist of members who would consecrate themselves to Jesus through Mary and work for the salvation of all souls. A significant aspect of the knights' apostolate would be the conversion and sanctification of non-Catholics, especially those who were hostile to the faith.

After being ordained to the priesthood in 1918, Saint Maximilian began the monthly magazine *The Knight of the Immaculata*. Promoting devotion to the Immaculate Virgin and serving as a source of Catholic apologetics, the publication instantly met with success. In a short period, circulation increased from five thousand to more than fifty thousand.

The phenomenal growth of the apostolate in the late 1920s led to the founding of Niepokalanów, a town and Franciscan friary. In Polish, the name means "City of the Immaculata." The Franciscan community's mission was to combine prayer with cheerfulness and poverty with modern technology and to promote, via the mass media, devotion to the Virgin Mary.

Soon the friary became one of the largest in the world, both in size and in its activities. So self-sufficient was Niepokalanów that the town came to include 760 inhabitants, with doctors, dentists, farmers, mechanics, tailors, builders, printers, gardeners, shoemakers, and cooks. In fact, Father Maximilian later acquired a fire brigade and turned some of his monks into firemen as well.

The friary itself continued to grow and came to include a seminary, a mission house, a printing establishment, and a radio station. With each passing year, *The Knight of the Immaculata* experienced such astonishing success that Father Maximilian was forced to install ultramodern machinery in his printing department. By 1935 the friary added a daily Catholic newspaper, which within a few short years became one of Poland's leading newspapers. Not content with using just the print media, Father Maximilian established a radio station, which also proved to be a success.

With an intense missionary spirit, Saint Maximilian set out for Japan in 1930 and founded another "City of the Immaculata" in Nagasaki. So exceptionally gifted was Father Kolbe that exactly one month after his arrival he had acquired a printing press and was distributing a magazine. After establishing the priory at Japan, he then sailed to Malabar, India, where he founded a third monastery. Saint Maximilian Kolbe also had a dream to establish a "City of the Immaculate" in Russia, but this was never realized.

In 1936 Saint Maximilian returned to Poland to serve as the spiritual father and superior of Niepokalanów and to head what was now one of the largest Catholic publishing houses in the world. Shortly before World War II the priory had included more than nine hundred friars publishing a monthly magazine and a daily newspaper with a circulation of more than one million.

Things took a turn for the worse in September 1939. Germany invaded Poland, and the Franciscan priory was ransacked. Father Kolbe, along with forty other friars, was arrested and taken to a holding camp. Three months later the friars were released—on December 8, the Feast of the Immaculate Conception.

When Maximilian returned to Niepokalanów, he found that his friary had become a refugee camp for thousands of Poles and Jews who had escaped from Nazi persecution. Before long, Father Kolbe came under intense scrutiny by the Gestapo as he allowed his printing press to continue publishing papers that took a patriotic, independent line, critical of the Third Reich. After refusing German citizenship, Maximilian was labeled a "threat" by the Nazis. He sealed his fate when he wrote in a December 1940, issue of *The Knight of the Immaculata*:

> No one in the world can change truth, what we can do and should do is to seek it and serve it when it is found. The real conflict is inner conflict. Beyond armies of occupation and the catacombs of concentration camps, there are two irreconcilable enemies in the depth of every soul: good and evil, sin and love. And what use are the victories on the battle-field if we ourselves are defeated in our innermost personal selves?

On February 17, 1941, Saint Maximilian was again arrested, this time on charges of aiding Jews and the Polish underground. Twenty brothers offered to go to prison in Kolbe's place but were refused. After being stationed in a prison in Warsaw for three months, Saint Maximilian was deported to Auschwitz, where he later gave his life for that of a fellow prisoner.

After suffering setbacks during the atrocities of World War II and the Nazi invasion, Niepokalanów has since regrouped, and today it remains a fully functioning monastery and community. On any day of the year, pilgrims can be seen visiting or praying at such sites as the saint's chapel, bedroom, and museum. The faithful come in droves to witness the place where the mission and spirit of the beloved Saint Maximilian Kolbe lives on.

Prayer to Saint Maximilian Kolbe

O Lord Jesus Christ, who said, "Greater love than this no man has that a man lay down his life for his friends," through the intercession of

Saint Maximilian Kolbe, whose life illustrated such love, we beseech you to grant us our petitions…(here mention requests you have).

Through the Knights of the Immaculata movement, which Maximilian founded, he spread a fervent devotion to Our Lady throughout the world. He gave up his life for a total stranger and loved his persecutors, giving us an example of unselfish love for all—a love that was inspired by true devotion to Mary.

Grant, O Lord Jesus, that we too may give ourselves entirely without reserve to the love and service of our Heavenly Queen in order to better love and serve our neighbors, in imitation of your humble servant Maximilian. Amen.

Saint Maximilian Kolbe, pray for us.

ABOUT THE SHRINE

Home to the Franciscan friary begun by Saint Maximilian Kolbe, the small town of Niepokalanów offers the visiting pilgrim a virtual treasure chest of activities and sites related to the saint and his legacy. The shrine is open throughout the year, and the Franciscan brothers are always willing to lend a helping hand to the visitors. Mass is celebrated daily for pilgrims at 11:00 A.M. While there be sure to visit

- Franciscan Minor Basilica • Statue of the Immaculata (the first object placed on the soil in 1927) • Saint Maximilian's first room (the exhibition dedicated to the saint) • Panorama of Poland's Millennium (a puppet show for pilgrims, presenting the history of Christianity in Poland) • Mystery Play presenting the Passion of Christ • Statue of Saint Maximilian Kolbe • Place on which John Paul II celebrated Mass in 1983 • Franciscan cemetery • Center giving information about religious life • Souvenir shop

SHRINE INFORMATION

Klasztor Ojców Franciszkanów
Niepokalanów
96-515 Teresin k. Sochaczewa
Tel: (046) 861-37-62, (046) 861-37-23
Fax: (046) 861-34-90

TOURIST OFFICE

There is no tourist office in Niepokalanów.

PLACES TO STAY

Pilgrim's House
Klasztor Ojców Franciszkanów
Niepokalanów
96-515 Teresin k. Sochaczewa
Tel: (046) 861-37-62, (046) 861-37-23, (046) 861-34-90
Fax: (046) 861-34-90

The Pilgrim's House, operated by the Franciscan friary, provides accommodations for about 180 people in two houses.

HOW TO ARRIVE AT NIEPOKALANÓW

Niepokalanów is about twenty-three miles west of Warsaw.

ROAD

From Warsaw, take 2/E30 east (in the direction of Sochaczew), turning south at the sign indicating Niepokalanów-Teresin-Szymanów.

TRAIN

Niepokalanów is accessible by train. From the Warsaw Śród-mieście railway station (located about two hundred yards from Warsaw's main train station: Warsawa Centralna), there is almost hourly train service to Niepokalanów, as well as from Sochaczew.

BUS

Niepokalanów is accessible by bus. Warsaw, Sochaczew, and other nearby cities have regular bus service to Niepokalanów. However, the train service is much more convenient and efficient.

TIPS AND HINTS

To join the Militia Immaculata, which was began by Saint Maximilian Kolbe, contact the U.S.A. National Center at

Marytown
1600 W. Park Avenue
Libertyville, IL 60048-2593
Tel: (847) 367-7800
Fax: (847) 367-7831
E-mail: marytwn@TheRamp.net
Website: http://www.marytown.org

DID YOU KNOW?

As the friars at Niepokalanów used the most modern technology and equipment, they invented several devices themselves. In fact, one of their patents won first prize at two different trade fairs.

✠

Our Lady of Święta Lipka

A Blossoming Shrine in Northern Poland

Lying between two beautiful lakes in the deeply forested area of northern Poland is the renowned sanctuary of Święta Lipka. Home to world-famous art and an illustrious statue-moving organ, the shrine remains one of the country's most prominent places of pilgrimage.

The legendary history of the shrine dates from several centuries ago. According to the story, a falsely accused prisoner from the nearby village of Kętrzyn had been sentenced to death. With little hope left, the inmate began praying fervently for a miracle that would prove his innocence to the executioners. Suddenly, the Virgin Mary appeared to him and presented the prisoner with a tree trunk out of which to carve her image.

The next day, as the

Attracting visitors from around the world for its artworks, architecture, and history, Święta Lipka remains one of Poland's most famous places of pilgrimage. Among the shrine's most prized possessions is its famous five thousand-pipe organ, which features moving statues of angels. (Author)

guards presented the incarcerated man before the judges, the inmate showed them his resulting sculpture. The officials were so awestruck by the image that they took it to be a sign from heaven and gave the condemned man his freedom. On his way home, the newly liberated man placed the miraculous statue on the first lime tree he encountered, as requested by the Virgin Mary. The result—the first wayside shrine in Święta Lipka.

Immediately, villagers who stopped by the tree and prayed before the image began reporting miracles. In the early part of the fourteenth century the first chapel was erected at the site. As the little sanctuary's fame grew, the need for shrine custodians became much greater. In response, Jesuits came in 1631 and took over the responsibilities of caring for the pilgrims.

Between 1687 and 1693 a large shrine replaced the chapel. The complex soon consisted of a huge church attached to the religious order's cloister. The best artists from the area were hired, and the result was a fantastic interior of frescoes and paintings—many of which included trompe l'oeil images. At the center of the church was placed a stone sculpture of the Holy Lime Tree with a statue of the Virgin Mary above it. The sculpture is said to rest on the spot where the legendary tree once stood. In time, the shrine's most famous possession—its five thousand-pipe organ, which features moving statues—was also assembled.

Today, Święta Lipka continues to attract visitors from around the world for its art, architecture, and tradition. In this century the shrine received one of its most glorious honors when on August 11, 1968, the future Pope John Paul II, with Cardinal Wyszynski, ceremoniously crowned the image of Our Lady of Święta Lipka inside the sanctuary.

PRAYER TO OUR LADY OF ŚWIĘTA LIPKA

O Blessed Lady, with Jesus always before you, you watch over all your children. You resist war and persecution, and so we come before you with confidence to implore your motherly intercession. We beseech you to help end all division, violence, and persecution. We look for your protection in our trials. Remove all that separates us from one another, and lead us into unity with Jesus. Hear our prayer, O Blessed Lady, and draw us closer to one another. Amen.

Our Lady of Święta Lipka, pray for us.

ABOUT THE SHRINE

The tiny hamlet of Święta Lipka lies between two lakes in the beautifully forested area of northern Poland. Inside the spectacular basilica, near the central niche, is the stone sculpture of the Holy Lime Tree. The prize possession of Święta Lipka, however, is its organ—a lavishly ornate instrument equipped with statues of saints and angels that move while the organ is being played. Short organ presentations are held every day at the shrine throughout the year. There are usually a few priests at the shrine who speak English and can provide a tour. Ask at the religious souvenir stand, located just inside the cloister entrance to your right. While there be sure to visit

• Basilica • Holy Lime Tree • Organ concerts • Guided tours

SHRINE INFORMATION

Sanktuarium Świętolipskie
11-407 Święta Lipka 29
Woj. Olsztyńskie
Tel: (089) 755-14-81
Fax: (089) 755-14-60

TOURIST OFFICE

There is no tourist office in Święta Lipka.

PLACES TO STAY

Dom Pielgrzyma
11-407 Święta Lipka 29
Woj. Olsztyńskie
Tel: (089) 755-14-81
Fax: (089) 755-14-60

The Pilgrim's House, operated by the shrine, provides very simple and basic accommodations.

HOW TO ARRIVE AT ŚWIĘTA LIPKA

Święta Lipka is about forty miles northeast of Olsztyn and eight miles west of Kętrzyn.

ROAD

From Olsztyn, take 16 east to Mrągowo, then continue north to Święta Lipka via Pilec.

TRAIN

Święta Lipka is not accessible by train. The nearest railway stations are at Giżycko and Olsztyn.

BUS

Święta Lipka is accessible by bus. From Kętrzyn, Giżycko, Olsztyn, Mrągowo, and other nearby towns, there is regular bus service to Święta Lipka.

TIPS AND HINTS

While in Święta Lipka, take some time to rent a canoe or walk around one of the lakes. It's a very beautiful place to spend some extra time.

If you are hoping to make a pilgrimage to Lithuania from Poland, Święta Lipka is an excellent place to make the transition. If using public transportation, from Święta Lipka, head east to Suwałki, then take the bus into Lithuania from here. Suwałki has a nice, modern bus station and provides daily service to Lithuanian cities such as Kaunas and Vilnius (and vice versa).

Did You Know?

After the prisoner had placed the miraculous image in the tree, the sheep were said to kneel down before the statue.

Saint Hedwig

A Polish Heroine

Among the many Polish heroes and heroines through the centuries, Saint Hedwig remains one of the most cherished, for she was loved by the people

The Basilica of St. Hedwig, a popular place of pilgrimage, lies in the small Polish town of Trzebnica near Wrocław. The beautiful and ornate church features the elaborate tomb of Saint Hedwig. *(Dom Zakonny Salwatorianów)*

for her great kindness and generosity. The saint's tomb in southwestern Poland remains a favorite pilgrimage destination for the faithful.

Born in 1174, Saint Hedwig came from a family that always bore a relationship with the royalty and ruling classes. Two of her sisters married kings, her husband and two sons became dukes, and her father served as a count and prince. Despite the privileges of being part of the upper class, Saint Hedwig always sought to serve God first, using her inherited luxuries only for fulfilling God's will.

From cradle to childhood, Saint Hedwig was always seen as a pious and virtuous girl. One of her great desires in life was to help the poor and disadvantaged. At the age of twelve, her parents arranged for her marriage to Henry, duke of Silesia. Together, they had six children. Once Henry succeeded to his father's dukedom in 1202, Hedwig successfully petitioned him to build a great monastery for Cistercian nuns at Trzebnica. After the founding of this abbey, the duke and duchess established more monasteries throughout the region. They also expanded into other areas, founding two hospitals, one of which was for female lepers. After their last child was born, Henry and Hedwig agreed to a mutual vow of perpetual continence, which they made in the presence of the bishop.

Although their children brought them great joy, they also caused much pain. Two of the sons created their own factions and fought against each other in battle over their father's estates. This, of course, laid a great burden upon the saintly Hedwig, who was bitterly torn by the selfishness exhibited by her two children, Henry and Conrad.

After 1209 Hedwig made the new monastery at Trzebnica her principal residence. Joining the nuns in their daily activities and practices of penance, the saint slept in the dormitory, wore a hair shift underneath her cloak, fasted regularly, and walked everywhere barefoot. She also devoted much of her time to works of charity and mercy.

When her husband died in 1238, Hedwig put on the religious habit at Trzebnica but did not take the corresponding vows. Instead, she made the decision to remain free so that she could administer her own property for the relief of the suffering. At the same time, Hedwig's daughter, Gertrude, had become the abbess of the monastery at Trzebnica.

In the last years of her life, Hedwig received the gifts of infused knowledge, prophecy, and miracles. The first was demonstrated when she learned of her son's death three days prior to receiving the news, and the second when she accurately predicted the day of her own death. The gift of miracles was demonstrated on several occasions, one of which included the recovery of a nun's sight when Hedwig blessed her with the sign of the cross.

The saint continued in her ways of holiness until her death on October 15, 1243. Hedwig was canonized in 1266 by Clement IV, and her relics were enshrined the following year in the cathedral at Trzebnica. In 1706 the saint received an extraordinary honor when her feast day was added to the general Western calendar.

PRAYER TO SAINT HEDWIG

All-powerful God, may the prayers of Saint Hedwig bring us your help, and may her life of remarkable humility and incredible generosity be an example to us all. Lord, I ask for your light, wisdom, and strength in making good choices every day, and I pray that my life may become a song sung to your glory. Amen.

Saint Hedwig, pray for us.

ABOUT THE SHRINE

Situated in a valley and on the slopes of the Trzebnica Hills in the vicinity of Wrocław, the small town of Trzebnica is home to fifteen thousand inhabitants. A lively cultural town, Trzebnica has numerous festivals and celebrations throughout the year, including the annual Week of Christian Culture. Guided tours of the Basilica of Saint Hedwig and other holy sites in Trzebnica are conducted by the Fathers of the Savior and by the Saint Charles Borromeo Sisters. For more information on requesting tour guides, contact the shrine information office below. While there be sure to visit

- Basilica of St. Hedwig • St. Hedwig's Chapel • St. Hedwig's Museum • Convent • St. Peter's Church • The Fourteen Saint Succorers' Church • Rotunda of Five Tables

SHRINE INFORMATION

St. Hedwig of Silesia Pilgrim's House
Dom Zakonny Salwatorianów
Ul. Jana Pawła II 3
55-100 Trzebnica
Tel: (071) 312-11-18; (071) 312-14-15
Fax: (071) 387-07-13

TOURIST OFFICE

Osir
Ul. Kościelna 9
55-100 Trzebnica
Tel: (071) 312-11-71

PLACES TO STAY

St. Hedwig of Silesia Pilgrim's House
Ul. Jana Pawła II 3
55-100 Trzebnica
Tel: (071) 312-11-18; (071) 312-14-15
Fax: (071) 387-07-13

Osir
Ul. Lesna 2
55-100 Trzebnica
Tel: (071) 312-07-47
A complex of chalets: 130 beds, with 2, 3, or 4 beds in each room.

Zajazd Lesny
Ul. Lesna 2
55-100 Trzebnica
Tel: (0-71) 12.07.47
Has ten beds in double rooms.

Domagala Maria
Ul. Obornicka 14
55-100 Trzebnica
Tel: (0-71) 12.16.87
Has eleven beds in single, double, and triple bedrooms.

Pod Platanami Hotel
Ul. Kilinskiego 2
55-100 Trzebnica
Tel: (0-71) 12.09.80
Has nineteen beds in single, double, triple, and quadruple bedrooms.

HOW TO ARRIVE AT TRZEBNICA

Trzebnica is about twenty miles north of Wrocław.

ROAD

From Wrocław, take 5/E261 north to Trzebnica. From Poznań take 5/E261 south to Wrocław.

TRAIN

Trzebnica is not accessible by train. The nearest major railway station is at Wrocław.

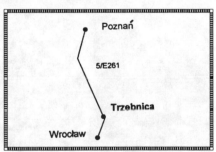

BUS

Trzebnica is accessible by bus. Wrocław has regular bus service to Trzebnica, and you are let off near the church (three to five minutes walking). In Wrocław, the bus station is located next to the railway station.

TIPS AND HINTS

If possible, try to stay overnight at the St. Hedwig of Silesia Pilgrim's House. The accommodations are excellent, and it is within a minute's walk from the basilica.

DID YOU KNOW?
Saint Hedwig was a vegetarian for forty years.

+╫+
+╫+

Our Lady of Wambierzyce

*Jesus said to him, "What do you want me to do for you?" The blind man
said to him, "My teacher, let me see again." Jesus said to him,
"Go; your faith has made you well." Immediately he regained his sight
and followed him on the way.*

MARK 10:51–52

In the southwestern corner of Poland, near the Table Mountains, lies one
of the country's oldest places of Christian pilgrimage. Here, thousands of
pilgrims come every year to walk the shrine grounds of Wambierzyce and
pray at the numerous chapels, gates, and grottos covering the surrounding
hills.

The shrine dates from its legendary beginnings in 1218. According to the
story, a blind man from the local village had miraculously recovered his sight

after praying before a
statue of the Virgin
Mary, which had been
placed in a hollow lime-
tree trunk on the side of
a road. In honor of the
extraordinary event,
the townspeople built a
small wooden chapel at
the site of the miracle.

As word about the
numerous favors re-
ceived at the little sanctuary spread, a bigger
church had to be built.

One of the oldest Polish places of Christian pilgrimage, Our Lady of
Wambierzyce features a Jerusalem-like setting: the surrounding
countryside is dotted with more than eighty stations depicting
important events in the life of Jesus and Mary. *(Bazylika w
Wambierzcach)*

However, this still did not prove adequate, as the shrine's fame continued to
grow. Hence, the local church officials commenced construction on a two-
towered basilica in 1695. Although it took sixteen years to complete, in just a
few years the new church collapsed in its entirety—except for its facade. Despite this major setback, plans for another giant sanctuary were immediately

put into place. Using the surviving Renaissance facade, the townspeople built the new church, which has survived ever since.

Today, the shrine features a number of unique features and sacred objects. In front of the main church is a monumental staircase of thirty-three steps leading to the facade of the grandiose church. Running around the church is the square cloister, which is lined with chapels and Stations of the Cross and adorned with paintings and votive offerings.

Enshrined in a special chapel inside the basilica is the shrine's prized possession—the miraculous (miniature) statue of Our Lady of Wambierzyce. The small sanctuary is engulfed in ex-votos and other gifts of thanksgiving. The shrine's real claim to fame, however, rests with its Jerusalem-like setting in the surrounding countryside, which features more than eighty stations depicting important events in the life of Jesus and Mary.

PRAYER TO OUR LADY OF WAMBIERZYCE

O generous and merciful Mother of God and all people, you have been adored for ages in Wambierzyce shrine! Trustfully looking at your image known for numerous graces, we beseech you to lovingly protect the pope and the entire Church with your maternal care. Protect the world from wars, bless our nation and defend it from disasters, and kindle faith and love in our families. Obtain the grace of conversion for sinners, health for the sick, and joy for the sad. Show the right path to the young, and pray for the grace of numerous vocations to the priesthood and consecrated life. Child of God, carried at the hands of the most holy Mother Mary, have mercy on us and bless us. Amen.

Our Lady of Wambierzyce, pray for us.

ABOUT THE SHRINE

Located near the Table Mountain foothills, the shrine of Our Lady of Wambierzyce is open throughout the year and welcomes pilgrims on a daily basis. Along with praying before the miniature miraculous image of the Virgin Mary, the faithful spend their time visiting and touring the various chapels, grottos, gates, and sculptures that are scattered throughout the surrounding hillsides. With two guesthouses in its care, the shrine is well equipped for receiving large numbers of pilgrims. While there be sure to visit

- Wambierzyce Sanctuary • Miraculous image of the Virgin Mary
- Chapels • Grottos • Sculptures • Stations of the Cross

SHRINE INFORMATION

Sanktuarium Matki Bożej Wambierzyckiej Królowej Rodzin
Pl. NMP 11
57-411 Wambierzyce
Tel: (074) 87-12-170

TOURIST OFFICE

Turystyczny
Dom Wycieczkowy
Pl. NMP 1
57-411 Wambierzyce
Tel: (074) 871-21-86

PLACES TO STAY

Dom Pielgrzyma "Nazaret"
57-411 Wambierzyce

Dom Pielgrzyma "Betlejem"
57-411 Wambierzyce

Note: Both hotels listed above are guesthouses for pilgrims. To make
reservations, contact the shrine information office.

HOW TO ARRIVE AT WAMBIERZYCE

Wambierzyce is about ten miles from Kłodzko and sixty miles from
Wrocław.

ROAD

From Wrocław, take 8/E67
south to Kłodzko, then continue
to Wambierzyce via Scinawka
Średnia or Szalejów Grn.

TRAIN

Wambierzyce is not accessible
by train. The nearest major railway station is at Kłodzko.

BUS

Wambierzyce is accessible by bus. Klodzko, Nowa Ruda, and Polanica-
Zdrój, and other nearby towns have regular bus service to Wambierzyce.

TIPS AND HINTS

The largest pilgrimages to Wambierzyce take place on July 8, August 15, and September 8.

East of the church, on ul Objazdowa Street, is the Szopka. Here, visitors can view a set of tiny mechanized figures (all carved of limewood) depicting scenes from Jesus' life. Included in the scenes are the Nativity, Crucifixion, and Last Supper. In the main Nativity scene, representing Jesus' birth in Bethlehem, are more than eight hundred figures, three hundred are mobile.

DID YOU KNOW?

The architects placed thirty-three steps in front of the shrine in remembrance of Christ's being crucified at that age.

Romania

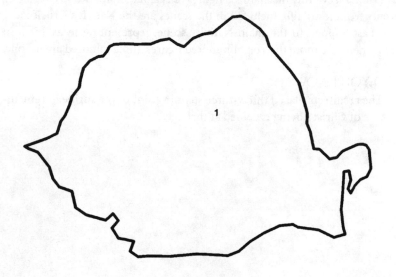

1. Our Lady of Csíksomlyó

ROMANIA

✠

Our Lady of Csíksomlyó

A Shrine of Elegance and Beauty

In the Transylvania area of Romania lies the most famous place of pilgrimage in the country—Our Lady of Csíksomlyó Sanctuary. Here, enshrined above the high altar, is the church's most venerated object, a miraculous image of the Blessed Virgin Mary. Drawing pilgrims from all over the country and

beyond, the shrine features a sanctuary that is adorned with a spectacular array of bright and elegant colors—a sight unmatched in almost any other church in the world.

The shrine dates from the fourteenth century, when the Franciscans settled in the area and founded a church. At the time, most of the residents

Enshrined above the high altar is the church's most venerated object, a miraculous image of the Blessed Virgin Mary. Since the sixteenth century the Franciscan shrine of Our Lady of Csíksomlyó has served as Romania's most famous place of pilgrimage. *(Ferences Kolossor, Csíksomlyó)*

consisted of the Hungarian Seklers. So close did the relationship between the Franciscans and the local townsfolk become that the people often referred to the friars as their "dear friends."

As the people had experienced a number of misfortunes in their lives, they came often to the church to pray before the miraculous statue of Our Lady of Csíksomlyó. Although the origin of the carved wooden sculpture is unknown, there are a number of theories about it. One source states that it was the work of the Sekler townspeople, while another asserts that it is the original carving of Veit Stoss, a great German sculptor of the sixteenth century who traveled through Transylvania. Still another tradition says that the Franciscans, driven out by the Turks from the Romanian plains, brought it along and that it is thus distinctly Romanian. Whether or not one of these stories is correct, the image has since become an object of great devotion for people of all nations.

Since the sixteenth century miracles have been associated with the image, as testified by historical records. During times of tremendous upheavals, the faithful have found refuge in Our Lady of Csíksomlyó. As at other Marian shrines such as Guadalupe, Częstochowa, and Altötting, the local townspeople often resort to the Virgin of their area for guidance and protection.

As a sign of their great love and gratitude for Our Lady of Csíksomlyó, the Sekler folk built a splendid and majestic church in her honor and embellished the inside of the sanctuary with brilliant and intensely vivid colors. Byzantine features were also added to the sumptuous church. Upon its consecration in the fifteenth century, the sanctuary became an even more popular place of pilgrimage.

In the ensuing years, the monastery and shrine encountered various difficulties as the complex was attacked many times. While the surrounding buildings were burnt down to the ground six times, the statue remained untouched. On one occasion an enemy soldier unsuccessfully attempted to pierce the miraculous statue with his lance. With each invasion, the people ran to the shrine to pray before the holy image and beg for the Virgin's protection.

Despite the periods of unrest, the faithful have always been able to experience peace when praying at the shrine of Our Lady of Csíksomlyó. Through the years it has continued to serve as a haven of tranquillity and calm, just like the surrounding mountains and green plains. Although relatively unknown by the Western world, the shrine continues to serve as a beacon of hope for Romanians and all who search for freedom.

PRAYER TO OUR LADY OF CSÍKSOMLYÓ

Mother, I commend and entrust to you all that goes to make up earthly progress, asking that it should not be one-sided but that it should create conditions for the full spiritual advancement of individuals, families, communities, and nations.

I commend to you the poor, the suffering, the sick, and the handicapped, the aging and the dying. I ask you to reconcile those in sin, to heal those in pain, and to uplift those who have lost their hope and joy. Show to those who struggle in doubt the light of Christ your Son. Amen.

Our Lady of Csíksomlyó, pray for us.

ABOUT THE SHRINE

The shrine of Our Lady of Csíksomlyó is located about a mile from Miercurea-Ciuc, in the beautiful green countryside of Romania. Both a church and a Franciscan monastery comprise the place of pilgrimage. Inside the splendid church, above the high altar, rests the precious statue of Our Lady. Filled with brilliant colors, the sanctuary rivals all churches for its beauty and elegance. Pilgrims visit the shrine throughout the year. While there be sure to visit

• Shrine of Our Lady of Csíksomlyó • Statue of Our Lady • Franciscan monastery

SHRINE INFORMATION

Mănăstirea Franciscanilor din Şumuleu—Ciuc
Str. Szek, Nr. 148. Jud. Harhita
4100 Miercurea–Ciuc.
Tel: (066) 112-449
Tel/Fax: (066) 171-449

TOURIST OFFICE

Biroul de turizm şi tranzacţii S.A.
Turisztikai hivatal şs Utazasi iroda
4100 Miercurea–Ciuc.
Tel: (066) 112-951
Tel/Fax: (066) 172-096

PLACES TO STAY

Hotel Harghita
4100 Miercurea–Ciuc.
Tel: (066) 116-119
Fax: (066) 172-181

Centrul de Studiu Dr. Jakab Antal
Dr. Jakab Antal tanulmányi Ház
4100 Miercurea—Ciuc.
Tel: (066) 113-452
Tel/Fax: (066) 172-145

HOW TO ARRIVE AT MIERCUREA CIUC/CSÍKSOMLYÓ

Miercurea Ciuc/Csíksomlyó is about forty-five miles north of Braşov.

ROAD

From Braşov, take highway 12 north to Miercurea-Ciuc. From Bucharest, take highway 1 north and continue to Miercurea-Ciuc via Braşov.

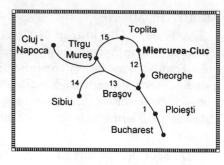

TRAIN

Miercurea-Ciuc/Csíksomlyó is accessible by train. The nearest major train station, however, is at Braşov, which is one of Romania's most important rail junctions. From Braşov, there are daily train departures to Miercurea-Ciuc/Csíksomlyó.

BUS

Miercurea-Ciuc/Csíksomlyó is accessible by bus from nearby cities. From Braşov, there are daily bus departures. (The bus departs Braşov from *autogara* 1, near the train station.)

TIPS AND HINTS

The main pilgrimage to the shrine takes place on Trinity Sunday (the Sunday after Pentecost). For more information about the shrine and city, visit the website: http://clmc.topnet.ro/somlyo/asomlyo.htm

DID YOU KNOW?

The statue of Our Lady of Csíksomlyó resembles a peasant Madonna. With characteristics of the Southeastern European racial mixture, the Madonna features a rather darker complexion and black hair.

Slovakia

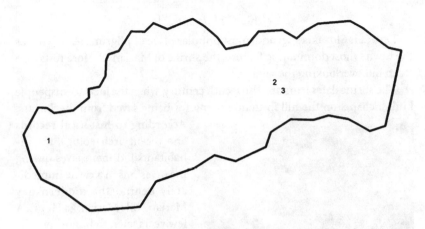

✛

Our Lady of Levoča and the Marian Hill

Celebrating Life at the Top

Levoča is Slovakia's second-most popular place of pilgrimage. Serving as the town's most dominating feature, the shrine of Mariánska Hora rests on a steep hill overlooking the village.

The shrine dates from the thirteenth century, when the local townspeople built a chapel on the hill in thanksgiving for being saved from the Tartars. According to historical records and recent archaeology, the inhabitants hid themselves during the invasions in a castle immediately behind the modern-day Marian Hill (Mariánska Hora). A few years later, to honor the Virgin Mary for her protection during the raids, the local faithful made a thanksgiving pilgrimage to the hilltop sanctuary. With each passing year they continued this tradition, and it has since developed into Slovakia's most cherished singular pilgrimage.

In the fourteenth century the Franciscan friars established a monastery in Levoča and contributed to the spread of Marian devotion at the hilltop—and the popularity of its annual pilgrimage.

Every year thousands of pilgrims make the sacred journey up to the hilltop sanctuary of Mariánska Hora. The greatest celebrations and festivities occur annually on the first weekend of July, when more than a quarter of a million pilgrims join in the annual Marian pilgrimage to the shrine. *(Author)*

However, despite their involvement, both the chapel and pilgrimage area remained under the control of the local diocese. In 1322 the Levoča rector ordered the restoration of the Marian chapel. Then in 1470 the local Church officials rebuilt and enlarged the chapel so that it could accommodate the increasing numbers of pilgrims. At this time they also enshrined above the high altar a beloved Madonna sculpture.

In the following years the pilgrimages continued uninterrupted, despite the difficult times of the Reformation. During the eighteenth and nineteenth centuries the chapel was again expanded. In 1906 construction commenced on an entirely new church. In 1914 the new shrine was completed, and eight years later the local bishop consecrated a newly built, giant Gothic altar.

In recent years the shrine received its most precious honor when the church was designated a "Basilica Minor." Today, thousands make the sacred journey to the hilltop sanctuary every year. The most impressive time of the year occurs on the first weekend of July, when a Marian pilgrimage takes place at the shrine and up to a quarter of a million pilgrims converge on the place. Along with hourly Masses throughout the day, there are a number of celebrations and festivities.

PRAYER TO THE MOTHER OF GOD
(Eastern Rite Prayer)

O Mary, Mother of God, as you are above all creatures in heaven and on earth, more glorious than the cherubim, more noble than any here below, Christ has given you to his people, firm bulwark and protectress, to shield and save sinners who fly to you. Therefore, O Lady, all-embracing refuge, we solemnly recall your sweet protection and beg the Christ forever for his mercy. Amen.

ABOUT THE SHRINE

The pilgrimage church on Mariánska Hora (Mary's Hill) sits above the town of Levoča, with a lovely view of the surrounding countryside. The best way of reaching the shrine is by taxi or private transportation. Upon arriving at the church, you can spend time praying inside or walking around the beautiful landscape. The high point of the shrine's year is the first weekend in July, when the most popular religious pilgrimage in Slovakia takes place. More than 250,000 pilgrims come to Mariánska Hora for the festivities and celebrations.

SHRINE INFORMATION

Contact the tourist office for more information about the shrine and pilgrimage to Mariánska Hora.

TOURIST OFFICE

Kultúrno informačné centrum
Nám. Majstra Pavla 58
05401 Levoča
Tel: (0966) 513-763

Fax: (0966) 510-418
E-mail: lips@levonet.sk
Website: www.levoca.sk

Levoča turistickoinformačné centrum
Košická
05401 Levoča
Tel: (0966) 513-880

PLACES TO STAY

Arkada Hotel
Námestie Majstra Pavla 26
05401 Levoča
Tel: (0966) 512-372
Fax: (0966) 512-255
Three-star hotel.

Barbakan
Košická 15
05401 Levoča
Tel: (0966) 514-310, (0966) 513-608
Fax: (0966) 513-609
Three-star hotel.

Satel
Námestie Majstra Pavla 55
05401 Levoča
Tel: (0966) 512-943
Three-star hotel.

Faix
Probstnerova cesta 22
05401 Levoča
Tel: (0966) 512-335

HOW TO ARRIVE AT LEVOČA

Levoča is about thirty miles northwest of Košice.

ROAD

From Košice, head north on 68/E50 to Prešov, then head west on 18/E50 to Levoča .

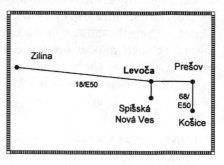

TRAIN

From Prague or Košice, there is daily train service to Spišská Nová Ves (the nearest major railway station to Levoča). From Spišská Nová Ves, take the train to Levoča for the final part of your journey (twenty minutes).

BUS

There is regular bus service to Levoča from surrounding cities and towns; however, the train service to Levoča is often much more efficient.

Tips and Hints

After arriving in Levoča, stop by the local tourist office as the people there are of great assistance in providing information about the shrine and will help you get there.

Did You Know?

In 1995 Pope John Paul II made a pilgrimage to the top of Mariánksa Hora.

Church of St. Jacob

Home to the World's Largest Wooden Altar

One of Slovakia's greatest cultural monuments and religious structures, the Church of St. Jacob is home to the world's largest wooden altar. Situated at the heart of the old town center of Levoča, the splendid Gothic church is essentially an incredible museum of medieval religious art.

Built around the fourteenth century, the shrine features more than a dozen side altars. One aspect that makes the church fascinating and unique is the amount of wood used in decoration and embellishment. Another great attraction is the sanctuary's organ, which is believed to be the largest in the country.

The renowned main altar, created by the master artist Paul, is an architectural wonder, with elaborate statues and reliefs of religious figures and events. Recognized as one of the masterpieces of European art, the immense altar reaches almost sixty feet high. It is popularly regarded as having perfect composition and color harmony.

Today, the Church of St. Jacob remains a popular site for pilgrims making the sacred journey to the church on the Marian Hill. With these two shrines in one town, Levoča remains one of Slovakia's top pilgrimage destinations.

Our Lady of Sorrows

A Slovakian Tradition

Devotion to Our Lady of Sorrows has long been a part of Slovakian tradition. Over the centuries Slovaks have experienced a number of tragedies as they have been the object of many ruthless invasions. Each intrusion always brought with it severe sufferings and heartache. Despite it all, Slovaks have persevered and borne their afflictions with great courage. Much of their strength has been derived from their intense devotion to Our Lady of Sorrows.

At the center of this devotion is the basilica dedicated to Mary under this title. Located in the town of Šaštin, the basilica was built between 1733 and

1744 on the spot where a miraculous state of the Blessed Virgin has been venerated for centuries. Serving as one of the most celebrated pilgrimage centers in the greater part of Central Europe, Our Lady of Sorrows attracts more than two hundred thousand visitors each year.

The shrine dates from 1564. While riding in their coach, Imrich Czobor II, the Lord of Šaštin, got into a heated debate with his wife, Angelika. After quarreling for some time, the husband finally shoved his wife out of the coach in frustration. Heartbroken and in tears, the wife, who had often been mistreated by Imrich, made a vow to have a statue made of Our Lady of Sorrows if her husband would change for the better.

Shortly after making the promise, Angelika did begin noticing a change in Imrich. He began to become much more gentle, kind, and loving. He also began asking forgiveness for all his past actions and inconsiderate deeds.

Located in the western Slovakian town of Šaštin, the national shrine of Our Lady of Sorrows dates from the eighteenth century, when a miraculous statue of the Virgin Mary was enshrined within its sacred walls. Today, the shrine receives more than two hundred thousand pilgrims each year. *(Author)*

In fulfillment of her vow and in thanksgiving for receiving help in difficult family problems, Angelika arranged for a statue of Our Lady of Sorrows to be made and placed on a triangular column at the place where her husband had previously thrown her from the coach. In time, the site became so popular that locals erected a chapel at the spot and placed the statue inside for public veneration. Word began to spread about the pilgrimage site, and before long pilgrims from Slovakia and neighboring countries flocked to the shrine in droves.

The history of the shrine is a long and glorious one, though filled with a number of tribulations as well. In 1654, due to the outbreak of the Turkish wars, the statue had to be temporarily transferred to the Czobor home. In 1732 an ecclesiastical commission declared the statue "miraculous," after an extensive investigation by ecclesiastical authorities. In honor of the declaration, twenty thousand pilgrims joined the archbishop in transferring the statue in solemn procession back to the chapel.

In 1733, when the Order of Saint Paul arrived at Šaštin, the Paulines accepted the role of caring for the statue. Almost immediately, they began building a shrine and monastery. Forty years later the Paulines transferred the miraculous statue to the newly completed church.

Unfortunately, in 1786 Emperor Joseph II banished the Order of Saint Paul from the area. In their place, the diocesan priests took control of the shrine. The monastery subsequently became the property of the emperor.

One of the biggest years for the shrine took place in 1864. In honor of the three hundredth anniversary of the miraculous statue, the archbishop of Esztergom crowned the statue on September 8 with two jewels blessed by Pope Pius IX. More than 120,000 pilgrims and 300 priests attended the extraordinary celebrations.

In 1924 the shrine experienced another change of ownership. The local apostolic administrator entrusted the shrine and monastery to the care of the Salesians. Three years later the sanctuary received another extraordinary honor. Pope Pius XI declared Our Lady of Sorrows the patroness of Slovakia, by the papal decree *Celebre apud Slovaccham gentem.*

One of the darkest moments for the shrine occurred on April 14, 1950. On this date the Communist militia marched into town, captured the Salesians, and sent them to the concentration camp in Podolinec.

In contrast, 1964 brought Šaštin a year of celebrations and festivities. In honor of the 400th anniversary of the miracle, Pope Pius VI declared the shrine a "Basilica Minor," on November 11. In 1987 the Marian Year sparked a new flow of pilgrims to Šaštin and the beginning of general repairs to the basilica. Three years later the Salesians returned and began restoring the monastery.

On April 22, 1987, although Pope John Paul II did not have an opportunity to visit the shrine, he did circle the basilica in his helicopter and promised to return as a pilgrim. In 1995, the Holy Father fulfilled his promise as he returned to Šaštin and celebrated Mass with a crowd of three hundred thousand people. Today, churches across Slovakia are dedicated to Our Lady of Sorrows, demonstrating the country's constant devotion to the sufferings of Mary.

PRAYER TO OUR LADY OF SORROWS

Father, as your Son was raised on the cross, his Mother Mary stood by him, sharing his suffering. May she, who is also our spiritual Mother and patroness in heaven, help us to find renewed strength at the cross of Christ and so come to share in his rising to new life, where he lives and reigns with you and the Holy Spirit, one God forever and ever. Amen.

ABOUT THE SHRINE

Located at the center of town, the shrine receives thousands of pilgrims from throughout Europe and other parts of the world. Mass is celebrated daily, and the shrine is especially full on special feast days. The highlight for pilgrimages each year occurs on September 15 and 16, the feast days of Our Lady of Sorrows. Today, the Salesians of Don Bosco still serve as custodians of the basilica. While there be sure to visit

• Basilica of Our Lady of Seven Sorrows • Miraculous Statue of Our Lady

SHRINE INFORMATION

Bazilika Sedembolestnej
90841 Šaštín-Stráze
Tel: (0802) 592-714, (0802) 592-715, (0802) 592-716
Fax: (0802) 592-718

TOURIST OFFICE

There is no tourist office in Šaštín-Stráze.

PLACES TO STAY

As Šaštín-Stráže has no hotels or other places to stay, most pilgrims make day-trips from Bratislava and Vienna (Austria).
See the *Cathedral of St. Stephen* for places to stay in Vienna.

HOW TO ARRIVE AT ŠAŠTIN

Šaštín-Stráze is about forty-five miles north of Bratislava.

ROAD

From Bratislava, head north on E65, exit at Kúty, and follow the signs east to Šaštin.

TRAIN

Šaštin is accessible by train. From Vienna (Austria), there is regular service to Šaštin, with at

least one change in Kuty. From Bratislava, there is regular service to Šaštin; however, you must also change trains in Kúty. From Trnava, there is a direct train to Šaštin. From the railway station in Šaštin, it takes about ten or fifteen minutes to walk to the shrine (the basilica is visible from the train station).

There is also another railway station called Šaštin-Stráze, which is about fifteen to twenty minutes from the shrine by bus. It is important to note that this railway station is different from the Šaštin train station (which is very close to the shrine). Many long-distance trains arrive at the Šaštin-Stráze station. If you arrive at this station, you can take the local bus or train to Šaštin.

BUS

There is bus service to Šaštin from nearby cities, including Bratislava and Trnava. From the Šaštin-Stráze train station, there is bus service to Šaštin (fifteen to twenty minutes). Be sure to let the bus driver know you are going to the basilica (Bazilika Sedembolestnej) so that he/she can drop you off near there. Otherwise, the normal bus stop in Šaštin is almost a mile from the shrine.

TIPS AND HINTS

The most popular days of pilgrimage to the shrine are May 24 (Our Lady Help of Christians), Pentecost Sunday, and September 15 (Our Lady of Sorrows). Also Fátima devotions take place on the first Saturday of each month.

When contacting or visiting the shrine, ask for Father A. Silhar—he is currently the only English-speaking priest at the shrine.

DID YOU KNOW?

The *Seven Sorrows of Mary* consist of the following:

First Sorrow: Mary hears the prophecy of Simeon at the presentation of her Son in the Temple, forty days after his birth. He prophecies that a sword of sorrow will pierce her heart during the lifetime of the child (Luke 2:35).

Second Sorrow: Mary and Joseph flee into Egypt with the child. King Herod has put out an order to kill all baby boys two years of age and younger, born in Bethlehem (Matthew 2:13).

Third Sorrow: The parents search for the lost child in Jerusalem. At that time, Jesus is twelve years old. He stays in the Temple and is found three days later by his parents, then returns with them to Nazareth (Luke 2:48).

Fourth Sorrow: During his Passion, Mary meets Jesus on the way to the cross (John 19:17).

Fifth Sorrow: Mary stands at the foot of the cross as Jesus is dying (John 19:25).

Sixth Sorrow: Mary holds her deceased Son.

Seventh Sorrow: Mary assists at the burial of Jesus (Luke 23:55).

Turkey

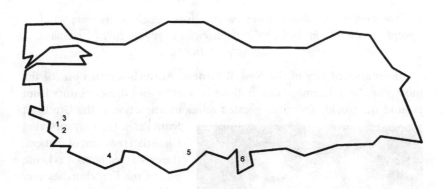

1. House of the Virgin Mary
2. Church of the Virgin Mary & Council of Ephesus
3. Saint John the Evangelist
4. Saint Nicholas of Bari
5. Saint Thecla
6. Grotto of Saint Peter

✠

Grotto of Saint Peter

"For a whole year they met with the church and taught a large number of people, and it was in Antioch that the disciples were first called Christians."
ACTS 11:26

As an ancient city of the New Testament, Antioch remains one of the most popular pilgrimage destinations in Turkey and draws visitors from around the world. The city's greatest religious attraction is the Grotto of

Drawing visitors from around the world, Saint Peter's Grotto once served as a first-century worship and meeting place for early Christians figures such as Saint Peter, Saint Paul, Saint Barnabus, Saint Mark, Saint Luke, and the first bishops of the town. The cave is located in the south-central Turkish city of Antakya, former Antioch in biblical times. *(Katolik Kilisesi)*

Saint Peter. The only surviving Christian remnant of that era, the cave is recognized as being one of the first churches ever built and used by Jesus' disciples.

Although the origin of the grotto is unknown, it is believed to have once been the property of Saint Luke the Evangelist, who was from Antioch. After the arrival of the apostles in the area, the saint is said to have donated it to the new, flourishing Christian community. In time, the cave came to be used for worship and as a meeting place of the first Christians, including figures such as Saint Peter, Saint Paul, Saint Barnabus, Saint Mark, Saint Luke, and the first bishops of the town.

Antioch, which is modern-day Antakya, has a special place in Christian history for several reasons. First, after the destruction of Jerusalem in A.D. 70, Antioch became the new hotbed of Christianity. Second, Saint Matthew is said to have written his gospel here, and third, it is the site where Christianity began to confront the issue of inculturation. Fourth, it is the city where many of the apostles and early disciples settled after their exodus from Jerusalem. For example, Scripture recounts that after the martyrdom of Stephen,

Christians from Cyprus and Cyrene "on coming to Antioch, spoke to the Hellenists also, proclaiming the Lord Jesus" (Acts 11:20).

Antioch also became an important mission base for the spreading of the gospel to the Gentiles, and it served as the departure point for several of Saint Paul's apostolic journeys. The ancient city also served as Saint Peter's residence for several years and was the hometown of Saint John Chrysostom, the great Christian preacher whose writings later became world renowned.

As for the Grotto of Saint Peter in Antioch, it is essentially a cave built into the side of a wall. Although it has retained its original look from the early days of Christianity, there have been a few cosmetic changes over the years. In front of the cave are arches, a nave, and two aisles, which were built by the Crusaders. Above the small esplanade, covering the site of an ancient Christian cemetery, is an Oriental-style facade built in the last century. Three doors open into the cave, where traces of the ancient mosaic floor can still be seen. Some of the frescoes covering the walls remain visible, and at the back of the grotto is a tunnel that used to be an escape route. To the right is a small spring that flows from the rock, and water is collected in a little basin—which doubles as a font.

The grotto remained in the hands of the Catholic Church from the apostolic era until the thirteenth century, when the Arabs invaded the area and took over Antioch. For the next three centuries the Muslims were in possession of the sanctuary, until they in turn handed it over to the Orthodox Church in the sixteenth century. Then in 1856 the grotto was returned to the Catholic Church, and the Capuchin friars were subsequently given the responsibility of administering the shrine. Today, they remain the custodians of the sanctuary and warmly welcome all who come to pray at this early Christian site.

PRAYER FOR THE CHURCH

We pray to you, almighty and eternal God, who through your Son Jesus Christ have revealed your glory to all nations! We pray that through your Church we may continue to spread your works of mercy and charity and your message of salvation to the whole world, with an unchanging faith in the confession of your name. Amen.

ABOUT THE SHRINE

The grotto Church of Saint Peter (Senpiyer Kilisesi) is located just outside the large city of Antakya, to the northeast, two miles from the city center. The shrine is open every day (except Monday) from 8 A.M. to noon and 1:30 to 6 P.M. Mass is celebrated at the grotto every Sunday beginning at 3

P.M. (The Orthodox liturgy is performed every Sunday at 8 A.M. in the summer and 8:30 A.M. in the winter.) Priests who wish can celebrate Mass in the grotto with their pilgrims.

SHRINE INFORMATION

Katolik Kilisesi
Kurtuluş Cad. Kutlu Sokak No. 6
P.K. 107
31002 Antakya
Tel: (0326) 215-67-03
Fax: (0326) 214-18-51

TOURIST OFFICE

Hatay Turizm Derneği
Atatürk Cad.
Vali Ürgen Alani, No. 47
31002 Antakya
Tel: (0326) 216-06-10
Fax: (0326) 213-57-40

PLACES TO STAY

Contact the tourist office for more information about places to stay.

HOW TO ARRIVE AT ANTAKYA

Antakya is located in south-central Turkey, just north of the Syrian border.

ROAD

From Iskenderun, head south on 825 to Antakya. From Syria, head north on 825 to Antakya.

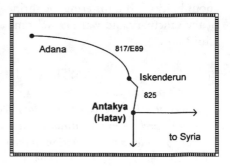

TRAIN

Antakya is not accessible by train. Bus service is the most common form of public transportation in this part of Turkey.

BUS

Antakya is accessible by bus. There is frequent bus service to Antakya from many Turkish cities, including Adana, Ankara, Antalya, Istanbul, Izmir, Kayseri, and Konya. Antakya also has bus service to and from major cities in neighboring countries, including Syria and Israel. (However, be sure to have the necessary documents and visas in advance if you plan to travel to or from these countries.)

How to Arrive at Saint Peter's Grotto

There is no bus to the grotto; however, you can take a taxi or walk there. A taxi ride is about $4 round-trip from downtown Antakya. To reach the shrine on foot (if it's not too hot), head northeast along Istiklal Caddesi and Kurtulus Caddesi. After about a mile, there will be a signpost indicating a right turn for the church (Sen Piyer Kilisesi). Follow the dirt track toward the mountains, and after about ten minutes you will come upon the church, set into the hillside just above the track. The entire trip to the shrine takes about half an hour on foot.

TIPS AND HINTS

When you buy souvenirs from the vendor (inside the gate), your proceeds go to the upkeep of the church.

DID YOU KNOW?

The coffee drink "cappuccino" is named after the Capuchin Order of Friars.

✠

Saint Nicholas of Bari

The "Real" Santa Claus

Throughout the world the mythical person of Santa Claus is celebrated as a jolly old man who brings gifts to people at Christmastime, and his magnetic personality, cheerfulness, affection, and warmth are seen to embody the spirit of Christmas. What few people realize, however, is that this modern-day fictitious character is actually derived from a real-life person from the fourth century—Saint Nicholas.

Father Christmas, also better known as Saint Nicholas, was born in modern-day Turkey about A.D. 300 in the town of Patara. A devout and religious child, he later entered the religious life to become a monk. Not long afterward, the archbishop elected the talented and benevolent Nicholas as the abbot of the monastery. Here, the saint fulfilled his daily duties with extraordinary piety and zeal. One of the most famous stories of his charity involves his giving of anonymous gifts to three daughters of a poor man who were left without a dowry. On successive nights, Nicholas dropped off bags of coins at their house through a window. This "gift from heaven" allowed them to marry.

As the saint had become famous for his great acts of charity and defense of the faith, he was soon chosen to serve as the archbishop of the huge metropolitan archiepiscopal see of Myra. According to ancient writers, the saint became renowned for his charity, his severe asceticism, and his fight against paganism. During the rule of Diocletian he suffered persecution and imprisonment. After the triumph of Constantine he became free and later attended the Council of Nicaea in 325, at which he condemned Arianism. On December 6, in the year 342 or 345, he died in Myra and was buried in his own cathedral. After his death the fame of Saint Nicholas immediately spread throughout the whole Christian world, and he became the most universally honored of all the saints with the exception of the apostles.

Immediately, the church containing his relics became a great place of pilgrimage. Many of the faithful who prayed at his tomb began to experience a number of miracles. In fact, a scented oil termed "the Manna of Saint Nicholas" flowed from the tomb and was known to cure the sick.

Miracles also continued through his intercession, especially for those at sea. By the late ninth century in the Greek Church, Nicholas was esteemed as one of the greatest saints. During the troubled times of the tenth century, many of the faithful immigrated to southern Italy from Turkey. Wanting their saint to "come with them," a group of merchants and sailors from Bari in southern Italy decided to "take" Saint Nicholas with them. They followed through on their plans and on May 9, 1087, the relics of Saint Nicholas reached Bari by ship. The local faithful immediately enshrined them in the new Church of Saint Nicholas. With the translation of his sacred relics to southern Italy, Father Christmas became known as Saint Nicholas of Myra and Saint Nicholas of Bari.

The new sanctuary instantly became a major source of pilgrimages as well, just like the Church of Saint Nicholas in Demre-Kale (Myra), Turkey. The secretion of healing oil from the relics was repeated in Bari, as at Myra. In the ensuing years, the miracles attributed to Saint Nicholas's intercession continued to multiply.

Today, the Church of Saint Nicholas in Demre-Kale remains one of the most popular Christian pilgrimage destinations in southern Turkey. Neither vast nor brilliant like many shrines, the church is most appealing for the charming legends and stories that surround its hometown saint. For this reason, thousands are taking the time each year to make the sacred journey to the *real* home of "Santa Claus."

PRAYER TO SAINT NICHOLAS OF BARI

God, Our Father, we pray that through the intercession of Saint Nicholas you will protect our children. Keep them safe from harm, and help them grow and become worthy of your sight.

Give them strength to keep their faith in you and to keep alive their joy in your creation. Through Jesus Christ our Lord. Amen.

Saint Nicholas, pray for us.

ABOUT THE SHRINE

Amidst the fertile lands of inland Turkey, in the southwestern part of the country, lies the village of Demre. To reach the shrine from the main square, head west for a short distance on the street Müze Caddesi. There are signs pointing to Noel Baba, the Church of Saint Nicholas. Admission to the church is $3 (half price for students). The grave of Saint Nicholas, broken by the Italian sailors, is in one of the side chapels of the church. Although most of the relics of Saint Nicholas lie at the shrine in Bari, Italy, there are a few on display in the Antalya Museum. While there be sure to visit

• Church of Saint Nicholas • Saint Nicholas Altar (with a
reliquary in the shape of a hand raised in benediction, typical
of artistic depictions of the saint)

SHRINE INFORMATION

Noel Baba Kilisesi
Demre-Kale (Antalya)
Tel: (0242) 871.2311

TOURIST OFFICE

Kaş Kaymakamligi
Turizm Danisma Mudurlugu
Cumhuriyet Meydani No. 5
07580 Kaş (Antalya)
Tel/Fax: (0242) 836-1238
Fax: (0242) 836-1695

PLACES TO STAY

Hotel Andriake
Finike Caddesi
P.K. 62 Demre (Antalya)
Tel: (0242) 871-46-40, (0242) 871-22-49
Fax: (0242) 871-54-40
Three-star hotel, with a restaurant offering international cuisine.

Hotel Kiyak
Gökyazi mah.
Demre (Antalya)
Tel: (0242) 871-45-09, (0242) 871-20-92
Fax: (0242) 871-20-93
The Church of Saint Nicholas is about a half mile away from Hotel Kiyak.

Hotel Topçu
Şehir Merkezi Girişi
07570 Demre (Antalya)
Tel: (0242) 871-45-06, (0242) 871-2200
Fax: (0242) 871-54-40, (0242) 871-2201
The Church of Saint Nicholas is about a half mile away from Hotel Topçu.

Grand Kekova Hotel
Zümrüt Kaya Köyü
Kaş-Demre (Antalya)
Tel: (0242) 871-34-62
Fax: (0242) 871-53-66

HOW TO ARRIVE AT DEMRE–KALE (MYRA)

Demre is about one mile from Myra and twenty-five miles east of Kaş. Note also that Demre is officially called, and signposted as, Kale.

ROAD

From Antalya, head west on Route 400 to Demre-Kale-Myra. From Kas, head east on Route 400 for the short trip to Demre-Kale-Myra.

TRAIN

Demre is not accessible by train. There are no nearby train stations.

BUS

Demre-Kale is accessible by bus. From Antalya, the bus trip is about three hours to Demre-Kale-Myra; from Fethiye, about two and a half hours; and from Kaş, about one hour.

TIPS AND HINTS

Some of Saint Nicholas's relics are on display in the Antalya Museum.

DID YOU KNOW?

Saint Nicholas is the patron saint of children, virgins, merchants, sailors, scholars, and pawnbrokers.

House of the Virgin Mary

*When Jesus saw his mother and the disciple whom he loved
standing beside her, he said to his mother, "Woman, here is your son."
Then he said to the disciple, "Here is your mother." And from that hour
the disciple took her into his own home.*

JOHN 19:26–27

On the western coast of Turkey, in the city of Ephesus, lies one of the greatest treasures of the Christian and Muslim faiths. Here, at the end of a long and narrow path, is the house believed to have been the home of the Blessed Virgin Mary during her last days on earth. More than one million pilgrims from every walk of life make the journey to this holy place each year. Recently, the little building has received considerable attention because of the

According to tradition, the house where the Blessed Virgin Mary spent her last days on earth lies near Ephesus, Turkey. Each year, more than one million pilgrims, both Christians and Muslims, make the sacred journey to the holy site. *(Author)*

latest research and excavations that support the long-held beliefs about those who once lived there.

According to tradition, the apostle John took Mary into his care and later brought her to Ephesus to avoid the persecutions of Christians in Jerusalem. Scripture affirms that Jesus spoke from the cross to entrust his mother to Saint John.

After the deaths of both Mary and John the house they occupied apparently fell into ruin, but the foundation remained intact. Although the belief that the Virgin Mary resided in Ephesus was widespread through the centuries, the discovery of her home did not take place until 1881 and then again in 1891. The house of the Virgin was first discovered in 1881 by a French priest through the study of the revelations of Venerable Anne Catherine Emmerich (1774–1824), a German Augustinian nun who was favored with numerous visions of the life of Our Lady. His findings, however, went unpublished and were generally discounted.

Ten years later, inspired by the detail of Emmerich's writings, a group of explorers under the leadership of Father Jung of the Order of Lazarists again followed her descriptions to relocate the Virgin Mary's home. After combing the hills and talking to local peasants and authorities, they came upon the site and ruins of the Virgin Mary's house as described by Emmerich. After excavating the area, the explorers were amazed to find that their discoveries conformed very closely to the descriptions provided by Emmerich. For example, Catherine had revealed that the Virgin Mary prepared her meals at a fireplace located in the center of the room and that spring water was present. Excavations confirmed the presence of ashes and spring water.

After they presented their discoveries to the archbishop of Smyrna in 1896, a formal declaration of the discovery was published. In subsequent years the Vatican allowed religious ceremonies to be celebrated at the site. Before and after the discovery of the house, many of the popes had offered their implicit recognition of the site as being the home of the Blessed Virgin Mary. Pope Benedict XIV (1740–58) in his treatise on the Feast of the Assumption once wrote:

> John amply fulfilled Christ's order; in every way he forever cared for Mary with a sense of duty; he had her live with him while he remained in Palestine, and he took her with him when he departed for Ephesus, where the Blessed Mother at length proceeded from this life into heaven.

Pope Saint Pius X (1903–1914) granted plenary indulgences for pilgrimages to the shrine and sent his apostolic blessing to all those involved in the restoration of the house. In 1951 Pope Pius XII (1938–1958) declared Mary's home an official sanctuary for pilgrims and confirmed the plenary indulgences for those who made the journey to the shrine. Before being elected to the Chair of Peter, Pope John XXIII had visited Ephesus. In 1961 he reaffirmed the plenary indulgences for pilgrims visiting the home. Six years later Pope Paul VI (1963–1978) made a pilgrimage to the holy shrine. After being elected pope in 1979, John Paul II also visited the Virgin Mary's home and again confirmed the significance of the house as a place of worship. So popular has the shrine become since then that approximately ten thousand people of all faiths visit the shrine each week. As Muslims recognize Mary as the Mother of Jesus, the house remains especially sacred to them also.

As many pilgrims can attest, a visit to the holy house is truly an unforgettable and inspiring experience. In the words of one pilgrim: "The experience of being in the home where Jesus' mother lived was truly spiritual. I did not take pictures. It seemed impossible to capture on paper the feeling of peace, awe, and shared community." Others who visit the holy site have felt Mary's presence and walk away with this same feeling that this indeed is a holy place.

PRAYER OF MARY'S HOUSE

Little House of Our Lady,
Restored and standing anew
From centuries' devastation,
On a mountainside she knew.

She came to you for haven
From a land beset with strife,
Far from the stress and tumult
That threatened her holy life.

You sheltered her in her sorrow,
Quietly soothing her fears,
Filling the lonely hours
Throughout her declining years.

Warmth from your hearthstone fire,
Its light on the walls aglow,
Brought to her peace and comfort
That only she could know.

Little house, she still remembers
Your gracious and tender care,
And comes on light rays from heaven
To the dim-lit chapel there.

Eyes have beheld her beauty,
Minds have been freed from all fear,
Hearts rejoice in the message
Of Our Lady standing near.

ABOUT THE SHRINE

The site upon which the Virgin Mary's house stands is now a Selçuk municipal park—better known as Meryemana. Since there is no *dolmus* (bus) service to the shrine, you must take a taxi or other private transportation or be on a tour from Selçuk. The Holy House is about 4 miles from Ephesus' Lower (northern) Gate, 3.5 miles from the Upper (southern) Gate, and 5.5 miles from Selçuk. Along the roads to the shrine are beautiful views of the surrounding countryside. Entry into the park costs about $2 (this goes for upkeep of the park). Pilgrims visit the house throughout the year, but it is particularly busy on feast days associated with the Blessed Virgin Mary. On August 15 each year the archbishops of Ankara, Istanbul, and Izmir celebrate Mass for the pilgrims at the shrine. At the entrance of the park is a small restaurant and snack stand. Many souvenir stands abound, and near the spring visitors can purchase small plastic bottles for their holy water. Mass is celebrated (in French) at 10:00 A.M. every Sunday and at 7:15 A.M. on weekdays. While there be sure to visit

• House of the Virgin Mary (Meryemana Kultur Parki) • Religious ceremonies

SHRINE INFORMATION

Father Superior
Capuchin Friary
Meryem Ana Evi
35922 Selçuk (Ephesus)
Tel/Fax: (0232) 892-60-08
Note: It is best to fax the shrine office between 7:30 P.M. and midnight Western Turkey time (Western Turkey is seven hours ahead of Eastern Standard Time in the U.S.A.).

TOURIST OFFICE

Selçuk Tourist Information Office
Atatürk mah.
Efes Müzesi karsisi No. 23
35922 Selçuk (Ephesus)
Tel: (0232) 892-1328
Fax: (0232) 892-1945

Müze karsisi
Agora çarsisi No. 35
35920 Selçuk (Ephesus)
Tel: (0232) 892-6328

PLACES TO STAY

Hotel Sezgin
Kahramanlar cad. Zafer Sokak No: 15
Kuşadasi
Tel: (0256) 614-4225, 614-6489, 614-4225
Fax: (0256) 614-6489, 614-6489, 614-4225
Website: www.travelturkey.com
Hotel Sezgin offers excellent accommodations and provides tours to Ephesus. Receive a 10 percent discount at the hotel by showing them this book *Catholic Shrines of Central and Eastern Europe*.

HOW TO ARRIVE AT EPHESUS–MERYEMANA

Ephesus is about five miles from Selçuk on the western coast of Turkey, and Meryemana is about four miles from Ephesus.

ROAD

From Izmir, take E87/550 south to Selçuk, then follow the signs to Ephesus-Meryemana.

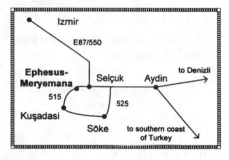

TRAIN

Although Ephesus and Meryemana are not accessible by train, the closest rail station is in nearby Selçuk. From Izmir and Denizli there are several train departures to Selçuk. Keep in mind that during the summer trains in western Turkey can often be hot, crowded, and late.

BUS

Bus service to Selçuk is frequent from many Turkish cities. Selçuk is a stopping place for many buses traveling between Izmir and Denizli, Antalya, and other southwestern points. There is also frequent *dolmus* (bus) service to Selçuk/Ephesus from Kuşadasi. Selçuk's bus station is across from the Tourism Information Office. Once in Selçuk, take the local bus to Ephesus and/or Meryemana (five miles; frequent service in summer).

TAXI AND PRIVATE TRANSPORTATION

There are a number of hotels and local tour organizations that provide transportation to the sites of Ephesus and Meryemana. Taxi service to Ephesus and Meryemana is also an option.

AIR

A modern international airport is located between the port city of Izmir and Ephesus. Adnan Menderes airport, beyond Izmir's southern limit, is only slightly more than a half-hour's ride from Selçuk.

CRUISE SHIP

If you arrive by cruise ship, local transportation is available at the dock, and it is recommended that the services of a taxi be used, as many of the shore trips by the cruise groups do not include Meryemana. This can be determined ahead of time from the cruise director.

WALKING

Ephesus is a pleasant thirty or forty-five minutes' walk from Selçuk. To arrive there, walk along the shady lane at the side of the highway—many visitors enjoy this exercise when it's not too hot.

TIPS AND HINTS

For further information on the Holy House of Our Lady, contact the following U.S. organization:

The American Society of Ephesus, Inc.
327 North Elizabeth Street
Lima, Ohio 45801
U.S.A.
Tel: (419) 225-2261
Fax: (419) 227-8835
Booklets and pamphlets related to the shrines of Ephesus are available from this office.

DID YOU KNOW?

In the early days of the Church, only places of worship were dedicated to persons who had lived or died in the area. Hence, the presence in Ephesus of the first basilica in the world dedicated to the Virgin Mary is evidence that she resided here at one time.

Saint John the Evangelist

As he (Jesus) went from there, he saw two other brothers,
James son of Zebedee and his brother John in the boat with their
father Zebedee, mending their nets, and he called them.
Immediately they left the boat and their father, and followed him.

MATTHEW 4:21–22

Amidst the ruins of Selçuk, near Ephesus, visitors find the tomb of one of the greatest apostles ever—Saint John the Evangelist. Every year thousands of pilgrims arrive at the site to pray at his grave and to see the area where the early Christian Church once carried out its missionary activities.

At the top of Ayasoluk Hill in Selçuk, amidst the ruins of St. John's Basilica, thousands of pilgrims and tourists each year visit the grave of Saint John the Evangelist. Currently, restoration is under way to rebuild the sacred shrine that once housed his tomb. *(Author)*

Over the centuries, Saint John has often been referred to by different titles, such as "the Beloved Disciple," "the Theologian," "the Divine," and "the Evangelist." Born under Roman rule in Palestine, Saint John was the son of Zebedee, a wealthy fisherman who lived near the sea. Growing up, both he and his brother James helped their father in the trade of fishing.

One day, while John was busy mending their nets on the sea, Jesus called him and his brother to be his apostles (Matthew 4:21–22). After they accepted the invitation, Christ gave them the nickname of Boanerges, or "Sons of Thunder." In the ensuing years, John figured greatly in the life of his Lord. Among the most memorable moments are the saint presence at Christ's Transfiguration, the agony in the garden, and the Last Supper. In this last event, the Evangelist rested his head on Christ's chest and asked who it was that would betray him. Several days later, it was John who stood at the foot of the cross with the Blessed Virgin Mary as Jesus entrusted the care of his Mother to him. Scripture recounts this: "When Jesus saw his mother and the disciple whom he loved standing beside her, he said to his mother, 'Woman, here is your son.' Then he said to the disciple, 'Here is your mother.' And from that hour the disciple took her into his own home" (John 19:26–27).

When Mary Magdalene brought word to the apostles of the empty tomb, it was John and Peter who ran to the site. On the day of the Ascension, the Beloved Disciple was among those who bade Christ farewell on the Mount of Olives. At Pentecost, John gathered with the Virgin Mary and the other apostles for the coming of the Holy Spirit. In the following years the saint undertook a number of missionary journeys, either with Peter or alone, to various provinces of Palestine to spread the Christian faith and resolve problems of the newly established Church.

In A.D. 44 his brother James was beheaded by order of Herod Agrippa I, grandson of Herod the Great. Eight years later, John attended the Council of Jerusalem in A.D. 52, at which the apostles officially rejected the view that Gentile converts were obliged to observe the Mosaic Law completely. After the Roman Emperor Titus destroyed Jerusalem in A.D. 70, the saint left Israel and headed north into Asia Minor (modern-day Turkey) and settled in Ephesus. Here, he continued spreading the faith through his writings and preaching. Shortly before A.D. 95, however, Domitian banished John to the Greek island of Patmos. While here, he took up residence in a cave and wrote the famous last book of the New Testament—*Revelation* (see *Cave of the Apocalypse*).

After the death of Domitian in A.D. 96, John returned to Ephesus, and it is believed he then wrote his gospel and three other epistles. Throughout his life in Ephesus, the saint strove to spread the Christian faith among the Jews and people of Asia Minor. While helping the apostle Timothy (bishop of Ephesus) in his missionary work, John did everything from ordaining clergy to appointing teachers for the region's spiritual needs to combating the heretical Gnostics. Around the year A.D. 100 the Beloved Disciple died in peace in Ephesus at the age of about ninety-four. Soon afterward, his tomb became the site of many miracles, as attested by a number of the early Church Fathers.

Today, all that remains atop Ayasoluk Hill is his grave. The glorious basilica that once enclosed the saint's sacred relics fell into ruins several centuries ago. Currently, efforts are under way to rebuild the church so that the relics of the great apostle may once again be venerated within a sacred sanctuary.

PRAYER TO SAINT JOHN THE EVANGELIST

God our Father, you have revealed the mysteries of your Word through John the apostle. By prayer and reflection may we come to understand

the wisdom he taught. Grant this through Our Lord Jesus Christ, who
lives and reigns with you and the Holy Spirit, forever and ever. Amen.
Saint John the Evangelist, pray for us.

ABOUT THE SHRINE

The grave of Saint John the Evangelist lies amid the ruins of St. John's Basilica on Ayasoluk Hill in Selçuk. To arrive by road, as you exit Selçuk (heading for Ephesus), look for the sign "St. Jean." The entrance to the ruins is located on St. Jean Sok street, right off Atatürk Caddesi. The church site is open every day, and there is a small entrance fee. While there be sure to visit

• Ruins • St. John's Basilica • Saint John's grave

SHRINE INFORMATION

There is no shrine information office.

TOURIST OFFICE

See *House of the Virgin Mary* for tourist office information.

PLACES TO STAY

See *House of the Virgin Mary* for places to stay.

HOW TO ARRIVE AT EPHESUS

For directions on how to arrive at Selçuk, see *House of the Virgin Mary.*

TIPS AND HINTS

In Selçuk, the Ephesus Museum features a collection of Turkish statuary, mosaics, and artifacts spanning the past 1,500 years. The museum is located next to the Selçuk tourist office on Kuşadasi Caddesi.

DID YOU KNOW?

Saint John is said to be the only apostle who did not die a martyr.

$$+\!\!+\!\!+$$
$$+\!\!+$$

Church of the Virgin Mary and Council of Ephesus

Theotokos—the Mother of God

The Church of the Virgin, also known as the Double Church, is a place of pilgrimage recognized not for its current activities but for its history. Although it lies in ruins today in modern-day Ephesus, it is a sanctuary that will forever remain immortalized in Christian history for the events that took place within its walls about fifteen centuries ago.

What brought this church into the spotlight was the fact that it is regarded as the first basilica in the world dedicated to the Blessed Virgin Mary, and that it was the site of the Third Ecumenical Council (A.D. 431). Here, it was confirmed that the Virgin is the mother of Christ's human and divine natures, and she was thus declared *Theotokos*—the Mother of God. At the

same time, the council defined the hypostatic union of the two natures in the one Person of Christ.

In the seventh or early eighth century the basilica was destroyed during the Arab invasions. In the following years a smaller brick church replaced it, but this too fell into disrepair by

Although the Church of the Virgin lies in ruins today, it remains one of Turkey's most famous Christian places of pilgrimage, for it was here that the Council of Ephesus took place and where Mary was declared *Theotokos*—the Mother of God. *(Author)*

the thirteenth century. Thereafter, the local people turned the site into a cemetery.

Today, however, the place has regained its fame as it now serves as part of Ephesus's world-renowned ruins. For Catholics, the site will always remain chiseled in history, for it was here that the Church, through the inspiration of the Holy Spirit, declared Mary the Mother of God.

PRAYER TO OUR LADY OF EPHESUS

Most holy and Immaculate Virgin Mary, who followed the Beloved Disciple into Asia and who was proclaimed Mother of God at Ephesus, protect the Church of Smyrna, sole survivor of the Seven Churches of the Apocalypse, heir to all their traditions and Mother of all the Churches.

Bestow, we beseech you, your maternal and benevolent protection on the entire Church, both in the West and in the East, the cradle of our faith.

Our Lady of Ephesus, Queen assumed into heaven, you who are Mother to all humankind, guard and protect us from all perils, both spiritual and

physical. Intercede with your divine Son for us who, following the example of our fathers, place in you all our trust and all our love. Amen.
Our Lady of Ephesus, pray for us.

ABOUT THE SHRINE

A major tourist destination, Ephesus is one of the largest and best-preserved ancient cities around the Mediterranean. Inside the Ephesus ruins lies the Church of the Virgin Mary, also called the Double Church. It was here that the third Ecumenical Council (A.D. 431) took place. As you enter the gates to the ruins, turn to your right and follow the path until you reach the church (the site is well marked by a sign). Be sure to have a map of the area in hand before embarking on your walk. There is a small entrance fee for the archaeological site. While there be sure to visit

• Ephesus ruins • Church of the Virgin Mary • Great Theater

SHRINE INFORMATION

There is no shrine information office.

TOURIST OFFICE

See *House of the Virgin Mary* for tourist office information.

PLACES TO STAY

See *House of the Virgin Mary* for places to stay.

HOW TO ARRIVE AT EPHESUS

For directions on how to arrive at Ephesus, see *House of the Virgin Mary.*

TIPS AND HINTS

At the entrance of the Ephesus ruins are several shops that sell excellent English guidebooks about the area.

If visiting during the summer, try to arrive at the ruins early in the morning, before the extremely hot weather of midday sets in.

DID YOU KNOW?

Amid the ruins of Ephesus is the Great Theater where Saint Paul preached "that gods made with hands are not gods" (Acts 19:24–40).

✚

Saint Thecla

A Protomartyr among Women

Although the story of Saint Thecla is one that has been shrouded in much legend and fanciful narratives, we do have a fairly good picture of this woman who handed her life over to Christ in the first century. Serving as one of the most famous names from the apostolic era, Saint Thecla is recognized as being the first Christian woman convert of Saint Paul.

From the writings of the early Church Fathers, we get a sense of who she was and how she lived. Saint Methodius, in his *Banquet of the Ten Virgins*, relates that the saint was well versed in the areas of philosophy and literature and that she spoke with great eloquence, ease, strength, sweetness, and modesty.

According to Saint Augustine, Saint Epiphanius, Saint Ambrose, and other early writers, Saint Paul converted her to the Christian faith at Iconium about A.D. 45, and his discourses are said to have kindled in her a great love of virginity. Saint Gregory of Nyssa states that she renounced all desires of the flesh and practiced great austerities so that nothing remained in her but spirit and reason.

After her conversion, in her desire to serve nobody but Christ, the saint broke off her engagement to the rich, young nobleman Thamyris. In revenge, her ex-fiancé delivered her over to the civil authorities and urged that she be condemned and thrown to the wild beasts.

When his plea was accepted, the soldiers brought the young virgin to the amphitheater for her execution. However, a number of miracles are said to have occurred, protecting her from death. One account says that the lions walked gently up to the saint, licked her feet like kisses, then meekly backtracked like lambs. After a few more unsuccessful attempts by the government to execute Saint Thecla, she eventually escaped and retired to a cave outside present-day Silifike. She remained there for the rest of her life, where she spent each passing day in prayer and good works, particularly healing the sick.

In A.D. 480 the Byzantines built a church over the cave in her honor. Before long, numerous miracles began to be attributed through the saint's intercession, and veneration of Saint Thecla spread throughout Christendom.

Today, the great cathedral in Milan, Italy, is dedicated to God in her honor and is said to possess some of her precious relics.

PRAYER TO SAINT THECLA

Holy Father,

We glorify you because in your holiness, you have crowned Saint Thecla with the gifts of your Spirit, and now in heaven you have glorified her, so she may be a model of Christian virtue and intercede for us, being so close to your mercy. We ask you, therefore, by her intercession, to strengthen our faith, fortify our hope, and ignite our love.

Grant us, Lord,

Comfort in moments of tribulation, protection while in danger, serenity while afflicted, peace and harmony between nations, peace within the family, security in employment, and strength and health to fulfill our duty. Accept our humble petition (state request) which today, confiding in the intercession of Saint Thecla, we present to you with a filial heart. Amen.

Saint Thecla, pray for us.

ABOUT THE SHRINE

The site of Saint Thecla, called Meryemlik in Turkish, lies about one mile south of Silifke. You can reach the site via two different routes. The shorter, but steeper, road, half a mile long, begins from the highway to Konya. After passing through a small gorge, it leads directly to the site of Meryemlik (Saint Thecla's site). The second route, three miles long, is the road leading in the direction of Antalya. From the crossroad in Silifke, drive about 2.5 miles, then turn right at the sign for Ayatekla. After a five-minute drive you will arrive at the site of Saint Thecla. The ruins of the basilica and a nearby cistern will be evident, but not the entrance to the cave. But as soon as you arrive, a guardian will appear, who will sell you a ticket and unlock the iron gate to the cave for you. While there be sure to visit

• Basilica of Saint Thecla (the ruins) • Cupola church • North church • Ancient dwelling • Necropolis • Cisterns

SHRINE INFORMATION

There is no shrine office at the Cave of St. Thecla.

TOURIST OFFICE

Silifke Turizm Danisma Bürosu
Gazi Mah., Veli Bozbey Caddesi No.6
33960 Silifke/İÇEL

Tel: (0324) 714-11-51
Fax: (0324) 714-53-28

PLACES TO STAY

Most of the area's housing lies at Tasucu, six miles west of Silifke. Although there are no special religious accommodations in Silifke, there are a few hotels. Contact the tourist office for more information on possible accommodations. One option in Silifke is the following hotel:

Çadir Oteli
Gazi Mah. Atatürk Cad. No: 16
33940 Silifke
Tel: (0324) 714-24-49, (0324) 714-12-44, (0324) 714-45-95,
(0324) 712-27-32
Fax: (0324) 714-12-44

HOW TO ARRIVE AT SILIFKE

Silifke is about ninety miles southwest of Adana.

ROAD

Silifke lies on the major coast-line Route 400 connecting Antalya with Adana.

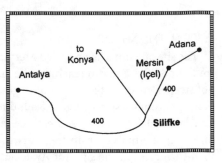

TRAIN

Silifke is not accessible by train. Mersin is the nearest city with a railway station. The trains from here connect with most major Turkish cities.

BUS

Silifke is accessible by bus. Located at the junction of the coastal highway, Silifke serves as an important transportation point. Buses connect frequently with cities such as Adana, Alanya, Ankara, Antalya, Konya, Mersin, and many other Turkish cities.

TIPS AND HINTS

The easiest way to arrive at the cave of Saint Thecla is to hire a taxi.

DID YOU KNOW?

Saint Thecla is commemorated in the Roman liturgy and is named in the canon of the Ambrosian Mass.

Part 3

Appendixes

MEDJUGORJE

+‖+
+‖+

A World-Renowned Pilgrimage Destination

Serving as one of the most famous pilgrimage destinations in the world today, Medjugorje was once a virtually unknown village to the outside world. However, that all changed in 1981 when the Virgin Mary reportedly began

appearing to six small children there. Since then, more than twenty million pilgrims have visited the site of the alleged apparitions.

The story begins on June 24, 1981, when six teenagers reported that they had encountered the Blessed Virgin Mary on a hillside near the village. The

In the past two decades, more than twenty million pilgrims have made a journey to Medjugorje–the site where the Virgin Mary has reportedly been appearing to six children since 1981. *(Patti Fersch)*

children described the lady as being very young and indescribably beautiful, possessing dark hair and blue eyes. Dressed in gray and white, she wore a white veil with an arc of stars appearing above her head. On the third day of the apparitions, the teenagers asked who she was, and the lady replied, "I am the Blessed Virgin Mary."

In the ensuing years, the lady continued to appear daily to the children, each time giving them a message. In one of her first messages, the lady said, "I have come to tell the world that God exists. He is the fullness of life, and to enjoy this fullness and peace, you must return to God." Members of the group, either individually or collectively, experienced ecstasies for as long as forty-five minutes when meeting with the beautiful woman. After each apparition, the children would repeat the message they had received to the people present. The core themes of the lady's directives have remained constant through the years: pray, fast, confess, read the Bible, and center your life around the Eucharist.

Today, four of the six now-grown children continue to have daily apparitions, while the other two experience them less frequently. The visitations take place, on a regular schedule and virtually every evening, in the Apparition Room of the parish rectory near the village Church of St. James. After each appearance, one of the visionaries relays the message on to the attending crowds.

Since 1981, Medjugorje has captured worldwide attention. Television crews and mass-media outlets from around the globe have continued to descend on this small Bosnian village to cover the incredible story and events. The fanfare has even captured the attention of the medical community. Over the years, numerous pilgrims have experienced miraculous healings while visiting Medjugorje. At present, almost four hundred healings have been reported (a large number of which are accompanied by extensive documentation detailing the person's injury or illness, and their recovery). Scientists and doctors of many different faiths have also spent time rigorously examining the six seers—both during and outside the time of the apparitions. Their conclusions have always remained constant and uniform: the visionaries are of sound mind and body.

To date, the Vatican has not recognized the authenticity of the visions. In April of 1991, at the former Yugoslavia bishops' conference in Zadar, the prelates made the following declaration:

> The bishops, from the very beginning, have been following the events of Medjugorje through the Bishop of the diocese (Mostar), the Bishop's Commission and the Commission of the Bishops Conference of Yugoslavia on Medjugorje. On the basis of the investigations so far it cannot be affirmed that one is dealing with supernatural apparitions and revelations. However the numerous gatherings of the faithful from different parts of the world, who come to Medjugorje, prompted both by motives of belief and various other motives, require attention and pastoral care in the first place of the diocesan bishop and with him of the other bishops also, so that in Medjugorje and in everything connected with it a healthy devotion to the Blessed Virgin Mary may be promoted in accordance with the teaching of the Church.

On August 15, 1993, the committee of bishops added a further declaration on Medjugorje:

> We bishops, after a three-year-long commission study accept Medjugorje as a holy place, as a shrine. This means that we have nothing against it if someone venerates the Mother of God in a

manner also in agreement with the teaching and belief of the Church…Therefore, we are leaving that to further study. The Church does not hurry.

Only time will tell if and when the Church will approve the authenticity of the apparitions of the Blessed Virgin Mary at Medjugorje. In the meantime, the village is sure to continue to rank as one of the world's most popular pilgrimage destinations as we enter the third millennium.

ABOUT THE SHRINE

Medjugorje is situated in the beautiful countryside of southwestern Bosnia-Hercegovina. The twin-towered Church of St. James, built since the apparitions began, is the focus of the village. Lining the town are rows of shops selling religious souvenirs. Along with St. James, the two most popular sites to visit are Mt. Podbrdo (Apparition Hill) and Mt. Krizevac (Cross Hill). Mt. Podbrdo is the site where the visionaries reportedly first saw Our Lady. Many pilgrims gather here to pray the rosary–both day and night. It takes a minimum of ten to fifteen minutes to climb up Apparition Hill. Mt. Krizevac is the hill above Medjugorje, where in 1934 the local villagers erected a large concrete cross on the hill in commemoration of the 1900th anniversary of Jesus' death. Today, wooden crosses and bronze images line the path up the hill, representing the Stations of the Cross. Climbing Mt. Krizevac (Cross Mountain) takes a minimum of thirty to forty minutes. While there be sure to visit

• St. James Church • Apparition Hill • Cross Mountain

SHRINE INFORMATION

St. James Parish
88266 Medjugorje
Information Office: Tel: (088) 651-988; Fax: (088) 651-444
Parish Office: Tel: (088) 650-206, (088) 650-310, (088) 651-333;
Fax: (088) 651-444
Note: The country code for Bosnia-Hercegovina is 387.
For the most comprehensive and up-to-date information regarding Medjugorje, visit the website:
http://www.medjugorje.org/index.html

TOURIST OFFICE

Tourist Association of Medjugorje-Bijakovici
Mala Livada B.B.
88266 Medjugorje

Tel/Fax: (088) 651-011

E-mail: tzm-medjugorje@int.tel.hr

Website: http://www.tel.hr/tzm-medjugorje/ulazaken.html

PLACES TO STAY

The three main types of accommodations available in Medjugorje are private lodging, hotels, and boardinghousing. Private lodging is the most plentiful, with more than 80 percent of the total accommodation arrangements being in private homes (these amount to approximately eight thousand beds). There are also several hotels with approximately four hundred rooms. Finally, boardinghouses account for about one thousand beds. For more information about accommodations, contact the Medjugorje Tourist Office or visit the website (see previous page).

HOW TO ARRIVE AT MEDJUGORJE

Medjugorje is about 130 miles southeast of Split (Croatia), 120 miles northwest of Dubrovnik (Croatia), and 20 miles south of Mostar (Bosnia-Hercegovina).

ROAD

From Split, head southeast on E65/M2, then turn and head east to Medjugorje.

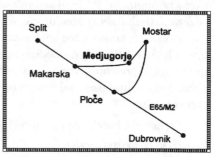

TRAIN

Medjugorje is not accessible by train. One of the nearest major railway stations is in Split. From Split, there is daily bus service to Medjugorje.

BUS

Medjugorje is accessible by bus. Many Croatian cities provide daily bus service to Medjugorje, including Split, Dubrovnik, Zagreb, and Rijeka. There is also frequent daily bus service from Mostar to Medjugorje.

AIRPORT

The two nearest airports are in Split and Dubrovnik. There is also an airport in Mostar, but it is temporarily out of use.

TRAVELING TO MEDJUGORJE

As Medjugorje is situated within Bosnia-Hercegovina, a country that has experienced war throughout much of the 1990s, most travelers (groups and independent) begin their journeys in Croatia—with Split and Dubrovnik being the two most common starting points. Traveling from Croatia to Medjugorje is regarded as safe; however, if you wish to go farther into central Bosnia, you do so at your own risk. Before traveling to Medjugorje, it is advisable to check on the current political and safety conditions by contacting the St. James' Information office at telephone (088) 651-988, fax (088) 651-444.

TIPS AND HINTS

1. Bring along a sturdy pair of shoes that provide excellent support for your ankles and feet, especially if you plan to climb either Apparition Hill or Cross Mountain. Both sites have rocky terrain and are slippery in rainy weather. Also, bring a flashlight with you, as this can be very useful when night climbing–a common activity at the pilgrimage site.

2. Pack a waterproof jacket or cape, especially if traveling to Medjugorje between November and March. During the summer, sunglasses or brimmed hats are important accessories to bring to protect your eyes from the harsh sunshine.

3. Before making a pilgrimage to Medjugorje, be sure to contact the St. James' Information office about your intended arrival dates (especially if you are the organizer of a pilgrim group).

4. The daily evening program in the church includes the rosary and Mass.

5. Medjugorje receives its largest number of pilgrims on Marian feast days and major Church holidays. Other important days of celebration at Medjugorje include:

   First Saturday in June: Soldiers' Day
   June 24: International Peace March
   June 25: Anniversary celebrations
   July 20–28: International Music Festival
   July 25: Feast of St. James, Parish Patron Saint
   July 31–August 6: International Youth Prayer Meeting
   First Sunday after September 8: Exaltation of the Cross
   October 3: Vigil of St. Francis
   December 31: Prayer Vigil

6. Mass is celebrated daily in Croatian, English, German, Italian, French, and in an Eastern-European language.

DID YOU KNOW?

The name *Medjugorje* is of Slavic origin and means "area between two mountains."

TRAVEL RESOURCES AND THE INTERNET

CATHOLIC WEBSITES
Provides information about Kevin J. Wright's book *Catholic Shrines of Western Europe: A Pilgrim's Travel Guide.*
http://www.catholicshrines.com

CATHOLIC TRAVEL PRODUCTS AND RESOURCES
Provides an array of products and resources for all your travel needs.
http://www.pilgrimageshop.com

CURRENCY CONVERTER
http://www.oanda.com/cgi-bin/travel

E-MAIL
If you plan to use the Internet while traveling abroad, it is important to obtain an e-mail account that can be accessed anywhere in the world, such as one of the following:
* Hotmail is a worldwide web-based free e-mail:
  http://www.hotmail.com
* NetAddress is a worldwide web-based free e-mail:
  http://www.netaddress.usa.net

EUROPEAN NATIONAL TOURIST OFFICES
Austria: http://www.anto.com
Czech Republic: http://www.czech.cz/new_york
Germany: http://www.germany-tourism.de
Greece: http://www.compulink.gr/tourism
Hungary: http://www.hungarytourism.hu
Lithuania: http://neris.mii.lt/visitors/strukt.htm
Poland: http://www.polandtour.org
Turkey: http://www.turkey.org/turkey

EUROPEAN TRAVEL COMMISSION
http://www.visiteurope.com

HEALTH AND TRAVEL INFORMATION
Provides health information, country descriptions, entry requirements, and embassy and consulate locations: http://www.tripprep.com

HOTELS

Provides a listing of more than fifty thousand hotels: http://www.hotelguide.ch

Provides an index of more than ten thousand hotel sites around the world, organized geographically: http://www.all-hotels.com/

Provides a listing of hostels: http://www.hostels.com

Lodging Guide Worldwide: http://www.lgww.com

INTERNET CAFÉ LISTINGS

Internet cafés are coffee-shops with computers that provide travelers access to the Internet. The cost is typically about $5 per half hour. Internet cafés provide one of the most useful and exciting ways to keep in touch with family and friends while traveling abroad. These "modern-day" coffee-shops are found in most major European cities including Kraków (Poland), Budapest (Hungary), Vienna (Austria), Athens (Greece), and Prague (Czech Republic). For a full listing of these cafés, visit these sites:

- http://www.cyberiacafe.net/cyberia/guide/ccafe.htm
- http://www.netcafeguide.com

SEARCHING THE INTERNET FOR CATHOLIC SHRINE AND PILGRIMAGE INFORMATION

When searching the Internet to obtain information about Catholic shrines and pilgrimage organizations, here are a few important keywords to try: "Catholic Shrines," "Catholic Shrines of Europe," "Catholic Pilgrimage," "Catholic Travel," "Catholic Tourism," "Marian Shrines," "Pilgrim's Travel Guide," "Catholic Tours," and "pilgrimage shop."

TOURISM BUREAUS AND EMBASSIES

Provides addresses and phone numbers for tourism offices around the globe: http://www.mbnet.mb.ca/lucas/travel or http://www.towd.com

Provides embassy information and links: http://www.embpage.org

TRAVEL ACCESSORIES AND RAILPASSES

Provides travel accessories, guidebooks, railpasses, and information: http://www.ricksteves.com

TRAIN INFORMATION

Provides information and sales of European passes: http://www.ricksteves.com/rail

Provides information and sales of Eurail passes: http://www.railpass.com
Provides fares and timetables for the 1,500 most traveled routes in Europe: http://www.raileurope.com

TRAVEL INFORMATION ABROAD

U.S. Department of State's Travel Warnings and Consular Information Sheets: http://travel.state.gov/travel_warnings.html or http://travel.state.gov
Visa Requirements: http://travel.state.gov/foreignentryreqs.html

TRAVEL INFORMATION AND NOTES

http://www.travelnotes.org

TRAVEL SEARCH ENGINES

http://www.yahoo.com/Recreation/Travel
http://www.infoseek.com/Travel

TRAVEL WEBSITES AND LINKS (FURTHER LISTINGS)

http://www.ricksteves.com/tips/links.htm

WORLDWIDE WEATHER AND FORECASTS

http://weather.yahoo.com or http://www.weather.com

BIBLIOGRAPHY

Aradi, Zsolt. *Shrines to Our Lady Around the World*. New York: Farrar, Straus and Young, 1954.

Avizienis, Rasa, and William J. Hough. *Guide to Lithuania*. Old Saybrook, Conn.: The Globe Pequot Press, 1995.

Ball, Ann. *A Handbook of Catholic Sacramentals*. Huntington, Ind.: Our Sunday Visitor, 1991.

Broschart, Charles B. *Call Her Blessed*. Staten Island, N.Y.: Alba House, 1961.

Buturac, Dr. Josip. *Marija Bistrica*. Zagreb, Croatia: Katalogizacija u publickaciji, 1996.

Cimok, Fatih. *A Guide to the Seven Churches*. Istanbul, Turkey: A Turizm Yayinlari, 1998.

Cruz, Joan Carroll. *Eucharistic Miracles and Eucharistic Phenomena in the Lives of the Saints*. Rockford, Ill.: Tan Books and Publishers, 1987.

———. *The Incorruptibles*. Rockford, Ill.: Tan Books and Publishers, 1977.

———. *Miraculous Images of Our Lady*. Rockford, Ill.: Tan Books and Publishers, 1993.

———. *Miraculous Images of Our Lord*. Rockford, Ill.: Tan Books and Publishers, 1995.

———. *Relics*. Huntington, Ind.: Our Sunday Visitor, 1984.

Derbent, Sumer. *Virgin Mary*. Istanbul, Turkey: Hitit Color, 1997.

Dailide, Ricardas. *The Mount of Crosses*. Vilnius, Lithuania: Zurnalas "Veidas," 1993.

Dorcy, Sister Mary Jean, O.P. *Shrines of Our Lady*. New York: Sheed & Ward, 1956.

Dydynski, Krzysztof, and others. *Eastern Europe on a Shoestring–Fourth Edition*. Oakland, Cal.: Lonely Planet Publications, 1997.

Ellegast, Abbot Burkhard. *Stift Melk*. Melk, Austria: Ing. H. Gradwohl, 1986.

Edmonds, Anna G. *Turkey's Religious Sites*. Istanbul, Turkey: Damko Publications, 1997.

Faber, Erica Papp. *Catholic Near East: Hungary's Weeping Icon of Máriapócs*. November–December 1997.

Forbelsky, Josef, Jan Royt, and Mojmír Horyna. *The Holy Infant of Prague*. Prague, Czech Republic: Aventinum, 1992.

Foskolos, Ev. A. *The Panhellenic Holy Shrine of Our Lady of the Annunciation of Tenos: History–Miracles–Activity*. 1991.

Frossard, Andre. *Forget Not Love, The Passion of Maximilian Kolbe*. San Francisco, Cal.: Ignatius Press, 1987.

Hartwagner, Dr. Siegfried. *Pfarr-und Wallfahrtskirche, Heiligenblut*. Innsbruck, Austria: Verlag Hofstetter, 1987.

Hatchwell, Emily, and Simon Calder. *Travellers Survival Kit–Eastern Europe*. Oxford, England: Vacation Work, 1994.

Hlobil, Ivo. *The Cathedral of St. Vitus*. Ljubljana, Slovenia: Opus Publishing, 1997.

Holy Linden. Warsaw, Poland: Ornament Publishing (no publishing date given).

Kavaliauskas, Juozas. *Siluva in the Old Days and Now*. Kaunas, Lithuania: Spausdino UAB "Judex," 1997.

Kirchmeir, Msgr. Georg, and Margaret Hasenmüller. *Wies Church Pilgrimage Guide*. Lechbruck, Germany: Edition Wilhelm Kienberger Gmbh, 1995.

Laurentin, René. *Pilgrimages, Sanctuaries, Icons, Apparitions: An Historical and Biblical Account*. Milford, Ohio: The Riehle Foundation, 1994.

Lambert, Anthony J. *On the Rails Around Eastern Europe–A Comprehensive Guide to Travel by Train*. Chicago, Ill.: Passport Books, 1996.

Lierde, Bishop Peter Canisius Johannes Van. *Prayers and Devotions, 365 Daily Meditations, Pope John Paul II*. New York: Viking, 1984.

Lord, Bob, and Penny Lord. *This Is My body, This Is My blood, Miracles of the Eucharist*. Slidell, La.: Journeys of Faith, 1986.

Monastery of Klosterneuburg. Vienna, Austria: Kellner (no publishing date given).

Monks of Heiligenkreuz. *The Cistercian Monastery Heiligenkreuz*. Mödling, Austria: Heiligenkreuzer Verlag, 1985.

Passionsspiele Oberammergau 1634-1984. Eigenverlag, Germany: Gemeinde Oberammergau, 1984.

Pechloff, Ursula. *Stift Zwettl.* Zwettl, Austria: Cistercian Monastery of Zwettl, 1995.

Picucci, Egidio. *Meryem Ana Evi.* Izmir, Turkey: Hz. Meryem Ana Evi Dernegi, 1997.

Posch, Waldemar P. *Gurk Cathedral.* Carinthia, Austria: Gurk Cathedral Custodians, 1985.

Quatman, Joseph B. *House of Our Lady.* Lima, Ohio: The American Society of Ephesus, 1991.

Rozlozníková, Virgínia, and Stefan Péchy. *Levoca–Guide through the Town and its Environs.* Presov, Slovakia: Bambow, 1997.

Sanktuarium Maryjne. Olstyn, Poland: Pracownia Poligraficzna (no publishing date given).

Shapiro, Michael. *Net Travel: How Travelers Use the Internet.* Sebastopol, Cal.: Songline Studios, 1997.

Soldo, Fra Josip Ante. *Zlato Na Grudima Majke.* Sinj, Croatia, Svetiste Gospe Sinjske, 1987.

St. Stephen's Cathedral. Vienna, Austria: Kellner (no publishing date given).

Swat, Tadeusz. *Basilica of Holy Virgin Mary.* Kraków, Poland: Wydawnictwo Ornament (no publishing date given).

Tamás, Fr. Nagy László, O.F.M. *Máriabesnyo.* Vác, Hungary: Kucsák Könyvkötészet és Nyomda, 1998.

The Sacred Cave of the Apocalypse on Patmos. Thessaloniki, Greece: Vasiliki Tsoulkanaki, 1995.

Todd, Oliver. *The Lourdes Pilgrim, A Prayerbook and Guide.* Essex, England: Matthew James Publishing, 1997.

Várszegi, Archabbot Asztrik. *Pannonhalma.* Veszprém, Hungary: Prospektus Printing House, 1997.

Weichselbaum, Msgr. Dr. Josef. *Maria Taferl.* München, Germany: Verlag Schnell & Steiner, 1992.

Wright, Kevin J. *Catholic Shrines of Western Europe: A Pilgrim's Travel Guide.* Liguori, Mo.: Liguori Publications, 1997.

INDEX

ABOUT THE AUTHOR

Kevin J. Wright is a graduate of Washington State University, where he received a B.S. in Business Administration.  Among many activities at WSU, he played two years of intercollegiate baseball and served as president of two organizations, including the Catholic Newman Center. After graduating from college with a number of honors, Kevin embarked on a major pilgrimage trip to Europe that led to the writing of his award-winning book *Catholic Shrines of Western Europe: A Pilgrim's Travel Guide.* With a great interest in pilgrimages, he has since backpacked through eighteen European countries, researching and visiting the major shrines and sanctuaries. Currently, while working for a premier tour company that specializes in escorted trips around the world, Kevin also leads guided tours through Europe and the Holy Land, provides seminars and talks throughout North America on Catholic travel, and serves as a contributing writer to several national publications. To contact him personally, you can e-mail him at kevinjwright@hotmail.com or visit his website at http://www.catholicshrines.com

MORE GREAT TRAVEL BOOKS FROM LIGUORI...

Liguori Pilgrim Travel Guidebook Series

These books are more than just travel guides. They're spiritual references that inspire and inform—whether you're a traveler or wish to enjoy a special pilgrimage without ever leaving home. A cornucopia of fascinating details, each books provides brief histories and descriptions of the places profiled, as well as addresses, telephone numbers, helpful travel tips, and dozens of eye-catching photographs.

If you're a Catholic traveler or pilgrim, a summer vacationer, a retired Catholic, a college student, an armchair traveler, a Catholic trivia and history buff, or are someone merely interested in places Catholic, the *Liguori Pilgrim Travel Guidebook Series* enables you to seek out the places that continue to inspire, refresh, and renew the Catholic spirit.

THE LIGUORI GUIDE TO CATHOLIC USA
A Treasury of Churches, Schools, Monuments, Shrines, and Monasteries

Jay Copp

A tapestry of Catholic life in the United States, this guidebook takes you to more than 500 churches, shrines, monuments, schools, and monasteries across the country.

#33012 • 336 pages; paperback • $15.95

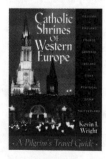

CPA Award Winner!

CATHOLIC SHRINES OF WESTERN EUROPE
A Pilgrim's Travel Guide

Kevin J. Wright

Catholic Shrines of Western Europe covers more than 70 of Catholicism's most celebrated shrines and sanctuaries in nine Western countries.

#33010 • 256 pages; paperback • $13.95

MARIAN SHRINES OF THE UNITED STATES
A Pilgrim's Travel Guide

Theresa Santa Czarnopys & Thomas M. Santa, C.Ss.R.

Packed full of practical and essential information, this book takes you on a pilgrimage to more than 50 popular and lesser-known U.S. shrines and sanctuaries.

#52260 • 240 pages; paperback • $13.95

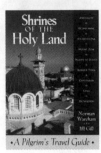

SHRINES OF THE HOLY LAND
A Pilgrim's Travel Guide

Norman Wareham & Jill Gill;
Foreword by Allan Weinert, C.Ss.R.

Shrines of the Holy Land invites you to go on pilgrimage to more than 80 of the Holy Land's most celebrated shrines and sanctuaries.

#62830 • 256 pages; paperback • $13.95

Order from your local bookstore or write to

Liguori Publications
Box 060
Liguori, MO 63057-9999

Please add 15 percent of your total ($3.50 minimum,
$15 maximum) for shipping and handling.